PELICAN BOOKS

A Future for All

Malcolm Wicks is the Director of the Family Policy Studies Centre and was previously Research Director and Secretary of the Study Commission on the Family. After graduating from the London School of Economics in 1968, he carried out research at the University of York and then at the Centre for Environmental Studies. He was a lecturer in social administration at Brunel University and, from 1974 to 1977, was Social Policy Analyst in the Home Office Urban Deprivation Unit. He then became a lecturer in social policy at the Civil Service College.

He is the author of *Old and Cold: hypothermia and social policy* (1978) and co-author of *Government and Urban Poverty: inside the policy-making process* (1983). He was also the co-author of the Fabian pamphlet *Deserting the Middle Ground: Tory social policy* (1978); *Crisis or Challenge? family care, elderly people and social policy* (1982) and was editor of *Families in the Future: a policy agenda for the '80s* (1983).

He has contributed to a number of books including *Labour and Equality* (1980); *Families in Britain* (1982); *Community Care* (1982); *The Future of the Welfare State* (1983) and *Energy and Social Policy* (1983). His most recent publications, which he co-authored, are *The Forgotten Army: family care and elderly people* (1984) and *Benefit or Burden? the objectives and impact of child support* (1986). Malcolm Wicks has been a member of the Labour Party since 1966 and is the Prospective Parliamentary Candidate for Croydon North-West. He also chairs the Croydon Labour Parties' Local Government Committee and is a School Governor and a member of his local Community Health Council. He is married and has three children.

Malcolm Wicks

A Future for All

Do We Need the Welfare State?

Penguin Books

Penguin Books Ltd, Harmondsworth, Middlesex, England
Viking Penguin Inc., 40 West 23rd Street, New York, New York 10010, U.S.A.
Penguin Books Australia Ltd, Ringwood, Victoria, Australia
Penguin Books Canada Limited, 2801 John Street, Markham, Ontario, Canada L3R 1B4
Penguin Books (N.Z.) Ltd, 182–190 Wairau Road, Auckland 10, New Zealand

First published 1987

Made and printed in Great Britain by
Richard Clay Ltd, Bungay, Suffolk
Filmset in Monophoto Ehrhardt

Contents

Acknowledgements

My general debt is to the very many friends, colleagues, teachers and students who, over the years, have helped me to understand better the nature of social policy and politics.

With this book, several people have been particularly helpful. At an early stage, my then research assistant, Chris Rossiter, gave much support. Lynne Feetham, Rachel Hoare, Sue Haylock and Julia Mathias helped prepare the manuscript for publication. David Piachaud made useful comments on Chapter 10. In the final stages, Melanie Henwood provided invaluable assistance and helped in numerous ways to bring the project to a conclusion. Margaret Wicks prepared the index.

Thanks too to those at Penguin Books for their understanding and patience.

March 1986

1 Introduction

... a vital new debate is beginning, or perhaps an old debate is being renewed, about the proper role of government, the welfare state and the attitudes on which it rests.

Margaret Thatcher[1]

If general elections are about a democracy deciding on its future – as they should be – then the elections of 1979 and 1983 will determine the destiny of Britain's Welfare State for much of a decade. And, in turn, this is shaping substantially the nature and character of British society, its values, and the aspirations and attitudes of its citizens.

Over forty years after Beveridge's famous wartime report on social security, social policy is moving steadily and swiftly away from the road it followed since the reforms of the 1940s. The consensus on the responsibility of the State for human welfare is over. Yet while there is much concern about specific cuts to social services and anxiety about the level of benefits, there is less awareness of how these pieces of policy fit together and of the picture that is emerging – the move towards a residual Welfare State, characterized by increasing inequalities, deepening poverty, greater reliance on the means test, a growing role for the private market and, consequently, social division and conflict.

The Government's Reviews of Social Security,[2] and subsequent legislation, have raised the political temperature, however. The Welfare State and its future is set to become a crucial – and possibly decisive – issue at the next general election.

Current controversy is rooted in postwar developments. Throughout the 1970s there had been increasing uncertainty, from both left and right, about the performance of the Welfare State, and much of this concern focused on the alleged 'burdens' of public expenditure and taxation. The writing on the wall appeared with the election of Margaret Thatcher to the leadership of the Conservative Party: economic factors and political eagerness came together to pose a major threat to social policy. In 1975, she had told an American audience that a vital new debate was beginning in Britain. The debate, she said, centred on 'the progressive consensus' – that is, the doctrine that the State should be active on many fronts in promoting equality, in the provision of social welfare and in the redistribution of wealth and income. She made it very clear that she was not part of this consensus.[3]

The hijack of the Conservative Party by the New Right occurred at a time of changing public attitudes towards the Welfare State. There was greater interest in the balance between public expenditure on services and the level of income taxation. Other anxieties about the performance of social welfare institutions – their complexity, bureaucracy and failure to tackle basic problems – also came to the surface.

More than seven years since the return of the Conservative government in 1979, the impact of new policies is clear – despite some setbacks, the New Right has cause for satisfaction. Substantial cuts to public expenditure, together with a political philosophy that advocates a rolling back of State provision in welfare, has prompted a set of policy decisions that have led – and will lead, if left unchecked – to the radical scaling-down of social policies. Housing provision has been drastically curtailed, there has been a serious challenge to the idea of a free and universal Health Service, there have been real cuts in the value of short-term national insurance benefits and other social security payments, the school meals service is seriously threatened, while help for elderly and disabled people has been reduced. The State Earnings Related Pension Scheme is to be cut back substantially and the long-term future of child benefit is uncertain.

Furthermore, unemployment has blighted the lives of well over 3 million people, and many more have been seriously affected. Perhaps even more significantly, there are clear signs that the combined impact of Tory social and economic policies is daily making Britain a more divided and less civilized society. The riots in Brixton and Toxteth and unrest in many other inner city areas are among the most obvious recent indicators of this. No less important, although less visible, is the suffering of the most underprivileged people in Britain.

The time is therefore ripe for a reassessment of social policy – a critical look at past developments; a review of current policy; and a debate about the future. The future of the Welfare State certainly poses a major challenge to the Left, and to the Labour Party in particular. The failure in both 1979 and 1983 to win the debate about social policy was, in large part, one of ideas, a failure to rethink policies in the face of changing social needs, and a failure to explain, to interpret and to enthuse.

The future of the Welfare State is an important question by any standard. Public debate is required, and it needs to be informed by a variety of perspectives. I hope that this book will be of interest to those of different political persuasions, but it does not pretend to be neutral. Rather it argues a case: that the Welfare State is crucial for Britain's future, but that we need to assess critically the nature of social policy and draw on the lessons of the past. If we can build democratic social policies which are both sensitive to different needs and aspirations yet recognize the moral worth of all citizens, then they will become a truly civilizing influence to counter the dark forces of discord and despair.

PART ONE

Social Policy since the War

2 From Consensus to 'Crisis'

Reconstruction has many sides, international and domestic. On the domestic side one can define its aims best by naming five giant evils to be destroyed – Want, Disease, Ignorance, Squalor and Idleness.

Sir William Beveridge[1]

The Conservative election victory of 1979, with all its consequences for Britain's Welfare State, needs to be set in a long-term perspective.

In this chapter the development of social policy from prewar times to the general election of 1979 is reviewed. This period can be divided into three phases. The first, from the Beveridge Report of 1942 to 1951, was a period which saw the construction of the modern Welfare State and was dominated by social reform. The second, essentially the Conservative years from 1951 to 1964, saw the development and growth of the Welfare State and the emergence of much consensus about its role. The final phase, the mid 1960s to the late 1970s, to which this chapter is mainly devoted, was characterized by an increasing sense of anxiety and uncertainty, closely related to economic concerns, but also involving other social and governmental issues.

This review is presented not just out of academic interest but, rather, because what some have termed the 'crisis' of the Welfare State is the culmination of a number of anxieties and uncertainties that, if they are to be properly understood, need to be discussed in their historical context. A political interpretation of historical developments will be discussed in Chapter 5.

The historical legacy

The profound changes in social policies that we are currently witnessing – characterized in Chapter 3 as the Tory attack on the Welfare

State – are taking place over forty years after the inquiry by William Beveridge that led to his famous report, *Social Insurance and Allied Services*,[2] which is in many respects the key document in the modern history of the Welfare State. However, while this chapter reviews the years since 1942, the origins of the British Welfare State date back long before the Second World War.

Modern social reform emerged as a natural corollary of industrialization. But social policy can be traced back to at least the early seventeenth century. Indeed, the Elizabethan Poor Relief Act of 1601 and the New Poor Law of 1834 are the historical antecedents of today's social security system. In the nineteenth century agitation over labour conditions led to factory legislation and there were also major Acts of Parliament concerning State education and, importantly, public health. Social reform in the early twentieth century was boosted by the Liberal government of 1906, which introduced the first old age pensions and laid the foundations of the insurance system. The aims were often radical: introducing his Budget of 1909, Lloyd George declared 'This is a War Budget. It is for raising money to wage implacable warfare against poverty and squalidness.'[3] The interwar years saw some important advances, notably John Wheatley's Housing Act of 1924, but it was not a period of great social reform. However, the mass unemployment of these times highlighted appalling social conditions in much of the country while the Second World War was to create an atmosphere favourable for social change.

Laying the foundations

The Beveridge Report of 1942 defined social security as 'the securing of an income to take the place of earnings when they are interrupted by unemployment, sickness or accident, to provide for retirement through age, to provide for loss of support by the death of another person, and to meet exceptional expenditures . . .'[4] The prime vehicle of support would be through national insurance, with means-tested national assistance playing a residual role for a small minority.

The Labour government of 1945 introduced not only social security measures, but also the National Health Service Act of 1946. Together with Aneurin Bevan's housing policies, and the Education Act of 1944 and family allowances – both products of the Coalition government – this was a period of great social reform which still provides much of the infrastructure of the modern Welfare State.

These social policy measures were matched by – and to a large extent depended on – that cornerstone of postwar politics, full employment. This was a key article of faith and the achievement of this goal was to represent a decisive break with the interwar years. A White Paper on Employment Policy in 1944 accepted the Government's responsibility for the 'maintenance of a high and stable level of employment'.[5] More generally, and in order to achieve the promised full employment, Keynesianism was the order of the day for much of the postwar period and was successfully implemented. Governments, both Left and Right, accepted the responsibility of managing the economy, largely by manipulating demand.

The period from the Beveridge Report of 1942 to the end of the Labour government in 1951 represents the first phase in the modern history of the Welfare State. The second phase, let us say the Conservative years from 1951 to 1964, was different in character.

Development and growth: 1951 to mid 1960s

It was a settling-down period but also a time of growth and development, for while there were no major new policy initiatives (certainly none to rival those of the Attlee government) it was a time of implementation and service expansion.

This period of development coincided with, and was aided by, a period of affluence and economic growth – the so-called 'never had it so good' society, in Macmillan's choice words. Many British households were visibly enjoying the fruits of increasing affluence in the form of domestic technology and gadgetry, a greater variety of – and more convenient – foods, an increasing range of popular entertainment, cars and foreign holidays.

The growth of the Welfare State during this time is indicated by the rising share of total public expenditure devoted to the social services. In 1953 expenditure on the five major policy areas – housing, education, the NHS, personal social services and social security – accounted for 37 per cent of total public spending. By 1963 this proportion had increased to 43 per cent.[6]

In political terms the remarkable feature of this period might appear to be the Tory acceptance of the substantial government intervention in society that a Welfare State entails. But the Conservative willingness to accept – indeed develop – most of Labour's welfare policies can be understood in terms of the 'One Nation' tradition within the Party – the ability (and necessity) of the Conservatives to adjust policies in an age of the mass franchise – and the growing dominance of the 'Progressive Right' and their leaders such as Macmillan, the author of *The Middle Way*,[7] and Butler, architect of the 1944 Education Act. During this time the reformists in the Conservative Party were firmly in control.[8]

Given the economic and political character of the times, the surprise perhaps is not the relative growth of the Welfare State, but the small amount of growth. Indeed, critics pointed to the contrast between private affluence and public squalor. Writing in early 1964, for example, one Fabian critic, Brian Abel-Smith of the London School of Economics, stated that,

Britain's public services are now a bad advertisement for socialism. Deprived of adequate resources, the public sector is forced to protect itself with queues and rationing ... While the private sector is wooing the public with trading stamps, muzak and a battery of packaging devices, in the public sector there is still too often an atmosphere of wartime austerity. You wait your turn and are told what you will have.[9]

The record in some social services was certainly a poor one by any standard.

In retrospect however, and partly because time blunts the memory, the historian is able to point to a large measure of consensus during this period – but it did not always look that way at the time. There were important controversies surrounding social policy, as anyone who recalls the row surrounding the 1957 Rent Act will readily agree. But, in general, there does appear to have been a fair amount of agreement about the need for the Welfare State.

The term 'Butskellism' (amalgamating the names of the Tory reformer and Labour's leader, Gaitskell) was coined by *The Economist* to describe the political atmosphere. And one authority, T. H. Marshall, noted in 1965 that '... in the field of social policy ... there is a growing measure of agreement on fundamentals ... the issues at stake in the sixties turned out to be less concerned with social ideology than with social engineering'.[10]

Even within the Labour Party there was, despite dissatisfaction with the Tory record, much conviction that the postwar reforms were having their effect. Crosland in his influential *The Future of Socialism*, published in 1956, argued that 'Primary poverty has been largely eliminated; the "Beveridge Revolution" has been carried through; and Britain now boasts the widest range of social services in the world; and as a result, the appellation, "Welfare State".' He added that the 'historic objective', by which he meant the 'abolition of primary poverty, and the guarantee of a general subsistence minimum by means of universal social services' has 'largely been attained'.[11] All-in-all during this period there was much cause for satisfaction. It appeared, at long last, that Beveridge's five Giant Evils had been vanquished.

Anxiety and uncertainty: mid 1960s to 1979

If the first phase in the modern history of social policy (1942–51) saw the construction of the modern Welfare State, and the second (1951–64) a period of growth and development, the third marks the change of mood. It dates from the mid 1960s and covers the period up to the general election of 1979. The character of the new phase was largely determined by economic factors – the crisis facing capitalism that intensified during the period and reached major proportions in the late

1970s – but it was also determined by a range of other factors – social, political and governmental. It was a phase characterized by an increasing sense of anxiety and uncertainty in social policy.

Early hopes

The period, however, opened with a flourish of optimism. The grave problems facing Britain – and the wider world – became more and more recognized in the 1960s, but there was also hope that through this recognition and debate they could be tackled successfully. This mood was captured by the Labour Party and particularly its leader, Harold Wilson, who, in 1963, argued for 'the scientific revolution' and referred to 'the Britain that is going to be forged in the white heat of this revolution . . .'[12] Dark clouds were gathering, but for a while at least there was a strong ray of light. The 1960s was not a gloomy decade. Perhaps the idea of the 'swinging sixties' is less helpful than some would like to think, but it was during the 1960s that the Beatles revolutionized popular music, England won the World Cup and Harold Wilson led Labour to victory in the 1964 general election, with a manifesto for the times, urging 'Let's Go with Labour for the New Britain'.

There seemed to be a clear and attractive, radical alternative to the '13 Wasted Years of Tory rule'. The stop–go–stop economic strategy was roundly condemned; social issues such as 'Rachmanism', poverty affecting the elderly and the poor hospital-building programme were highlighted; and Labour was confident that there were answers to the problems. This British mood perhaps reflected the similar atmosphere in the United States which was generated by the brief Kennedy presidency and which found an echo in the later 'War on Poverty'. For a while, this spirit dominated the political climate. There was an idealistic belief in the power of fresh thinking, the bringing to bear of new minds on old problems and a heroic belief in institutional reform, a belief that survived even during the later period when the economic problems crowded out the remnants of idealism. Inquiries abounded and few established institutions or areas of policy were spared the investigations of official committees. There were inquiries into local government,[13] the NHS,[14] devolution,[15] the Civil Service,[16] and also into housing in Greater London,[17] the Rent Acts,[18] public school education,[19] primary education,[20] the personal social services,[21] and several other subjects, notably planning.

It was also a time of minor social experimentation. Educational Priority Areas, recommended by the Plowden Committee, were established[22] and were quickly followed by twelve Community Development Projects.[23] These heralded a growing interest in the problems of urban deprivation and the plight of inner-city areas.

The fast-growing social sciences influenced many of these developments, both through the output of research and the role of individual social scientists. They were active in committees of inquiry, pressure groups, as political advisers and part-time pundits. Given the confidence in the power and rejuvenating quality of reform, new ideas were taken seriously and as Donnison has noted of the planning field: ' "Concepts of Policy Analysis", "Corporate and Inter-corporate Management", and "Public Participation" which found their way into reports such as those by Maud, Skeffington, Peterson, Layfield, and Baines were founded upon an underlying confidence in the capacity and legitimacy of the institution of government itself.'[24]

Although the impact of this period of optimism lasted well into the 1970s, the optimism itself was short-lived. The story is summed up well by the production of the ambitious National Plan published in 1965[25] and effectively abandoned shortly afterwards. Very quickly the new Labour government was dogged by the state of the economy, which seemed impervious to rejuvenation.

Economic problems shifted the spotlight on to the Welfare State: the old confidence of the 1950s in the institutions of the Welfare State and the belief in the effectiveness of social policies began to fade. This loss of confidence was also evident in other areas of life and, indeed, the author of one study of the 1970s argued that, during that decade, 'the old sources of optimism which have sustained the human race throughout the twentieth century ... had begun to collapse on an unprecedented scale'.[26]

At one time or another most things were, at least according to some commentators, in a state of 'crisis' – certainly the economy, but also Parliamentary democracy. The fashionable question was 'Is Britain Ungovernable?' The Labour Party, the Church, the family and marriage, morals, universities and, at different times, recurringly, English cricket and Scottish football – all seemed problematic. The word 'crisis' was used more and more, over-used and abused, the linchpin of a growing volume of pessimistic punditry.

Such prophecies of doom should warn us against any glib analysis in the field of social policy. Nevertheless, during these years of the late 1960s and 1970s, the Welfare State was seen to suffer from a number of major problems and these re-opened a fundamental debate about the future. What were the problems of the third phase in the postwar history of social policy? They related to (a) the economic 'burden' of welfare; (b) the continuation of old problems such as poverty; (c) complexity; (d) a growing concern about the relationship between the individual and the State; and (e) disjointed approaches to social policy.

The economic 'burden' of welfare

Public expenditure

One of the first acts of the new Labour government was to raise old age pensions by 12s. 6d. to £4 a week for single people and by £1 1s. to £6 10s. for a married couple. The autumn Budget also announced increases to other benefits and certain tax increases. However, these, although relatively modest, at an Exchequer cost of some £85 million a year, had serious economic repercussions. As Harold Wilson notes in his record of government:

We were soon to learn that decisions on pensions and taxation were no longer to be regarded, as in the past, as decisions for Parliament alone. The combination of tax increases with increased social security benefits provoked the first of a series of attacks on sterling, by speculators and others, which beset almost every action of the Government for the next five years.[27]

These economic pressures eventually forced the Government into drastic action. In 1966 a package of spending cuts was introduced: prescription charges, which had been proudly abolished in 1964 (and which Harold Wilson himself had resigned over, in 1950), were re-introduced and this about-turn, on a policy of important symbolic significance for Labour, epitomized the change of outlook that so quickly overtook the Wilson administration.

Social policy debate was increasingly dominated by public spending: the costs of the Welfare State and questions about its future growth became acute at a time of grave economic uncertainty. By 1978–9 the five major areas of social policy were to account for 56 per cent of total public expenditure and in that year, largely due to Welfare State spending, 42.5 per cent of all GDP went on public expenditure (having risen to 46.5 per cent in the mid 1970s).[28] This increase in spending on social policy would have surprised many of the early social planners. Beveridge himself estimated that there would be no increase in real terms in the cost of 'health and rehabilitation services' between 1945 and 1965, 'it being assumed that there will actually be some development of the service, and as a consequence of this development a reduction in the number of cases requiring it'.[29]

The growth of social expenditure needs to be interpreted cautiously. It certainly does not inevitably mean that improvements, in real terms, have taken place. Improvements there have been, for example the increasing real value of pensions and other benefits, the introduction of new disability benefits and rent allowances for private tenants, but other factors also have been important. The financial implications of demographic change and particularly the 'ageing' of the population have led to increasing costs in health, social services and social security, more and more expensive technology is being used in the NHS, and there are also the increasing costs of personnel in very labour-intensive services. Similarly, an increasing proportion of men and women retire at the minimum pensionable age, rather than delaying their retirement, and this has led to rising costs. Also growing numbers of children stay on at school beyond the minimum school-leaving age and, of course, there are increasing costs associated with unemployment. Some developments therefore have merely maintained levels of provision for certain groups, while others, such as new health technology and increased staff levels within social service administration, are not automatically linked to increased welfare. And few would argue that the rising cost of unemployment benefit is an indicator of an advancement in human welfare. However, such cautious interpretations did little to affect political debate.

The erratic economy which has been the British experience during the last fifteen years, including periods of nil or very little growth, upset the assumptions of whole generations of social planners. Until the current period, there have always been a few percentages of real growth in social services each year. Of course, there have been debates and arguments about how to divide the expanding cake, both between and within different social services, but these debates took place within the context of expansion. But in 1975 Tony Crosland announced that the party was over, and while some local authorities protested that they had never received their invitations to attend the party in the first place, in the next few years nil growth led to some actual cutbacks in public spending. This increasingly meant tough decisions had to be made about priorities and such a gloomy perspective increasingly determined social policy in the late 1970s.

From the mid 1960s, governments faced increasing economic difficulties. Although these often seemed to relate to particular issues – the strength of sterling, balance of payments, the Public Sector Borrowing Requirement or monetary supply – and while governments often focused their attention on such specific indicators, there were deeper causes at work. Britain's faltering economy must be viewed in the context of worldwide economic turmoil, partly caused, and certainly exacerbated by the oil crisis. By the late 1970s advanced economies were adopting deflationary measures and these deepened Britain's own troubles. But we had some specific national problems of our own. Considered alongside other comparable nations – France, West Germany, Sweden, Japan and the United States – our industrial base was in a serious state of decline and we were adapting too slowly and too late to the technological advances that could have been the stimulus for economic regeneration. The Second World War that had provided that 'stimulus' for many nations did not do so for victorious Britain, which adjusted badly to its post-imperial status. More generally, all Western economies found that the tried and tested strategies, still essentially Keynesian, no longer so predictably or so efficiently manipulated national economies in desired directions. Economic growth, while still experienced for much of this period, could no longer be counted on and, indeed, it petered out in the late 1970s.

The worsening economic climate could not fail to affect the Welfare State and social policy moved to the centre stage of economic and political debates. In more favourable circumstances this would have been a welcome development indeed for those concerned about social welfare, but in the situation prevailing it was sinister. The association between social expenditure and the state of the economy was now at the heart of controversies surrounding future policy and led to the breakdown of any past consensus about the desirability of a large and growing Welfare State.

As the Director for Social Affairs, Manpower and Education of the Organization for Economic Co-operation and Development noted:

The rapid growth of social programmes in the 1950s and 1960s in OECD countries was closely related to high rates of economic growth and, thus, to the successful management of the OECD economies. The lower growth performance of the OECD economies since the early 1970s was bound to disrupt the continuing extension of programmes and the growth of benefits – and in that sense put the Welfare State in crisis.[30]

Analysts from different parts of the political spectrum were discussing the connection between public expenditure (much of it social) and economic performance. In an influential book Bacon and Eltis argued that the public sector absorbed too many resources, so depriving the private sector, with resultant negative effects in terms of productivity, the balance of payments and output.[31] And another book asked the seemingly incredible question: 'Can Government go bankrupt?'.[32] Meanwhile, some Marxist analysts highlighted the 'fiscal crisis of the State'[33] and many questioned critically the relationship between

Welfare State provision and the economic system. Glennerster has noted that:

In the post-war period and notably in the 1960s the social services were seen by a wide spectrum of opinion as the handmaidens of a growing economy, conducive to, and naturally consequent upon, a more prosperous and technically sophisticated economy. By the mid 1970s much academic and political comment saw them as antagonistic to growth, drawing resources from the 'productive' sector of the economy, reducing incentives, curbing initiatives. Welfare was again firmly labelled a 'burden'.[34]

The view that public expenditure is a burden depends, in part, on how measures are taken. Conventionally this is often done by comparing total expenditure with GDP and during the period of the last Labour government there was much wringing of hands when public expenditure appeared to be over 60 per cent of GDP. Indeed, Roy Jenkins saw in the figure a threat to democracy yet, as Ormerod has demonstrated, the calculation of this figure was extremely dubious – transfer payments (that is, social security benefits) were included as part of public spending, but not GDP.[35] But the anxiety about the burden of public expenditure had its effect, leading to expenditure cuts in 1976 which had serious consequences – Ormerod has estimated that 'had the 1975/6 share of public spending been maintained, there would have been £4,700 millions more investment and £3,100 millions more current spending over the period of 1978/9'.[36] In the longer term the concerns about public spending burdens were to help pave the way for the Tory victory of 1979.

Taxation

While direct taxation of income respresents a smaller percentage of total government revenue than might be supposed – indeed the proportion declined from 37 per cent in 1976 to 30 per cent in 1979[37] – it is this tax that is the most 'political' and is the one most publicly discussed. And trends in income tax have made an important impact on debates about the Welfare State and have affected public attitudes towards it.

Frank Field has analysed these trends. He shows that the number of taxpayers has grown from 13.5 million in 1945 to over 21 million – or over 25 million when working wives are included. 'This increase is way in excess of any growth of the working population and highlights the extent to which poorer people have been brought into tax.' The burden of tax has increased more for the poor than for the rich. Furthermore, within each income category, the tax burden has increased most for families with children. In 1981 Field summarized the evidence as follows:

In 1949/50, while a single person began to pay tax at a fraction below 40 per cent of average earnings (now 24.7 per cent), a married couple with one wage packet did not contribute a penny in direct taxation until they earned almost 63 per cent of average earnings (now 38.5 per cent). A two-wage earning married couple without children paid their first income tax when their earnings were equal to the average wage packets (now 63.2 per cent). In the same year, a married couple with two children but only one wage earner, began paying income tax at a fraction below average earnings (now 43.5 per cent).[38]

These tax trends put pressures on workers with families to support (see p. 28), and have altered attitudes to the Welfare State, as we shall argue later. In a very real sense more and more families including those headed by quite low-paid workers were paying for their own social services, or at least a large part of them. Consequently the taxpayer, as voter, was presented with a choice, a choice not widely relevant in 1945, about whether to vote for more social spending or for more money in the pocket. By 1979 the Labour government was growing anxious about this, but had no real answers. But Mrs Thatcher saw her opportunity.

Continuance of old problems

The growing anxiety about the level of social spending and the tax 'burden' would, perhaps, have been less intense if it could have been demonstrated that Britain had a successful, humane and beneficent Welfare State. But other problems that emerged in the third phase cast grave doubt on this. Not least, increasing evidence showed that the

TAX THRESHOLDS AS A PERCENTAGE OF AVERAGE MANUAL EARNINGS IN THE UNITED KINGDOM

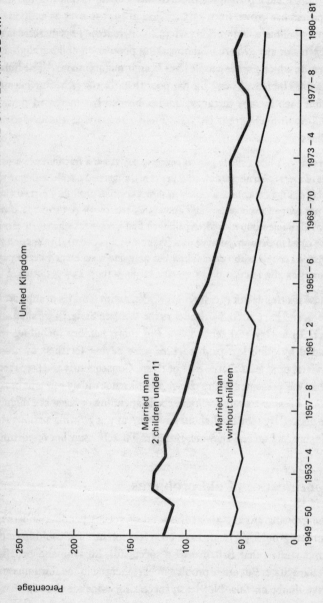

Source: *The Next Ten Years: Public Expenditure and Taxation into the 1990s*, Cmnd 9189, HMSO, 1984

Welfare State was not tackling successfully the old problems of the inter war period. 'Want' or poverty provides the major example.

There was little talk of poverty in the affluent 1950s and in the early years of the 1960s. Many felt that this major problem had been generally abolished, and even if it was still present among some of the elderly and disabled – Hugh Gaitskell argued during the 1959 general election campaign that 'the real challenge to us is whether we're going once and for all to abolish poverty in old age'[39] – then certainly it was not felt to be a problem any more for families, where the head of the household was in work. Scientific confirmation of this feeling seemed to come in 1951 when the third survey for York was published.[40] This found that between 1936 and 1950 the proportion of working-class people living in poverty had been reduced from 31 per cent to less than 3 per cent (according to the definition adopted). A *Times* leader hailed this as a 'remarkable improvement, no less than the virtual abolition of the sheerest want'.[41] This supposed 'virtual abolition' of poverty was assumed to be due to the changed circumstances of the postwar period: full employment, an expanding economy, and the impact of the Welfare State. This view was strong even within the Labour Party and the Party's 1964 manifesto spoke only of 'pockets of poverty'.[42] The complacency about poverty, a product of the so-called 'affluent society', was shaken by the work of a number of social scientists in the early to mid 1960s. The 'rediscovery' of poverty followed studies by Dorothy Wedderburn, Brian Abel-Smith, Peter Townsend and other researchers, many of whom were associated with Richard Titmuss at the London School of Economics.[43]

The 1965 report, *The Poor and the Poorest*, by Abel-Smith and Townsend was particularly influential and its finding that: 'of all the persons in the low expenditure households as many as 34.6% were in households whose head was in full-time work' shattered the myth that full-time employment alone was enough to prevent poverty.[44] During the years that followed further research evidence contributed to the re-emergence of poverty as a key social problem, and campaigners, like the Child Poverty Action Group's Frank Field, fought to push poverty back into the centre stage of British politics: indeed, at the 1970 general election, the Child Poverty Action Group claimed, controversially, that 'the poor had got poorer under Labour'.[45] By the late 1970s, when some 5 million people were dependent on means-tested supplementary benefits, the Government's own Supplementary Benefits Commission was stating that: '... the Supplementary Benefit scheme provides, particularly for families with children, incomes that are barely adequate to meet their needs at a level that is consistent with normal participation in the life of the relatively wealthy society in which they live'.[46]

Unemployment

While 'want' or poverty became an issue once more in the mid 1960s the problem partly changed character and was severely exacerbated in the 1970s by the awakening of another Beveridge giant – long thought extinct – Idleness (or unemployment). For most of the postwar period Idleness was destroyed. This represented an amazing development compared with the interwar years, but one that became an established part of British life.[47]

In the 1950s unemployment seldom rose above 1.5 per cent of the workforce, and in the 1960s it varied between 1.4 and 2.6 per cent. But by the 1970s unemployment was rising significantly: in 1971 3.3 per cent of the working poplation was registered as unemployed and by 1976 it was 5.5 per cent. By the early 1980s it had reached almost 13 per cent.[48] These proportions represent only the registered unemployed and the true number of jobless people was certainly very much higher.[49] There were of course important variations by region and in some parts of the country the unemployment rate was considerable. The postwar Beveridge assumption of full employment – a foundation of the modern Welfare State – was being undermined.

The continuance of poverty exacerbated by unemployment was a major problem and was one focus of attention during this period, but more generally commentators were pointing to the perpetuation of inequalities throughout British society and, very often, the failure of social policies to reduce such inequalities. The attack on inequality was seen by many of its radical supporters as a major objective of the Welfare

State and yet, come the 1960s and the 1970s, social scientists were chronicling the continuation of economic and social problems and inequalities in such vital areas as wealth and income distribution.[50] And in the crucial area of education[51] a number of official reports appeared in the 1960s. They showed up the inadequacies of the education system, not least in terms of buildings.

In housing too the evidence emerging in the late 1960s chronicled a sorry tale of neglect. Local authority housing had been starved of resources and, between 1953 and 1963, local authority housebuilding in England and Wales declined from 203,000 to 97,000 dwellings.[52] And, following the decontrol of private rents, insecurity and harassment were becoming increasing topics of anxiety, culminating in the activities of Perec Rachman. The Milner Holland Committee on housing in Greater London concluded that 'we are satisfied that abuses are general, and too numerous to be dismissed as isolated instances or in any way insignificant. While they do occur, their nature is such as to constitute a serious evil which should be stamped out.'[53] The physical conditions of much housing were also appalling. A survey of England and Wales in 1967 showed that 1.8 million dwellings, or 14 per cent of the total stock, were 'unfit for human habitation'. In addition, there were 2.3 million dwellings that lacked one or more of the basic amenities.[54]

Homelessness also emerged in the late 1960s as an issue of major concern. The BBC Television film *Cathy Come Home* caught the public's imagination and enabled the pressure group Shelter (one of a new type of pressure group to emerge at this time) to campaign vigorously. Two studies of homelessness provided documentary evidence.[55]

Complexity

The growing complexity of the Welfare State was a further subject of concern which contributed to a reduction in confidence that the Welfare State was inevitably promoting human welfare. Indeed, Barbara

Wootton has argued that the 'Giant Complexity' should be added to Beveridge's Five Giant Evils.[56]

The most spectacular examples were found in the methods designed to support family incomes. Since the 1960s a bewilderingly large number of benefits have been introduced for poor families to meet certain financial costs. Such benefits have been introduced by different government departments in an *ad hoc* fashion and, while many have perfectly desirable goals, their combined effect is often far from beneficial and, indeed, is downright confusing for the poor.

Some specific problems result from this complexity. The 'non-take-up' of benefits has been well documented in recent years: large numbers of eligible people fail to claim such entitlements as supplementary benefits, free school meals, rate rebates, rent allowances and free prescriptions.[57] The reasons for non-claiming include ignorance of the existence of some benefits and a fear of stigma, and the complexity of the system – the form-filling and the need to visit several departments to claim different benefits – is one very important factor. The non-take-up problem is not a small one. In 1979, for example, only 55 per cent of eligible persons claimed rent allowances and only 60 per cent claimed free school meals. Moreover, only half of those entitled to Family Income Supplement received it.[58]

The complex inter-relationship between entitlement to benefit and the tax system has also produced problems. We now have a welfare system where one government department, the Inland Revenue, judges some people to be well enough off to pay income tax, while other government departments judge many of the same people to be so poor that they need help, either in cash or kind.

The fact that many of the poor pay tax is a major reason for what has become known as the 'poverty trap', a term that made its way into dictionaries in the 1970s and which occurs when a combination of income tax, national insurance contributions and benefit reductions result in a loss at the margin as income rises, of sometimes more than 100 per cent.[59] Specific problems of non-take-up and the poverty trap have led to the expending of much energy and resources in the search for solutions to these problems. The complexity of our Welfare State led to the development of new institutions – a host of information, advice and aid centres – and new professions – welfare rights workers, for example – which, although welcome developments, were clear signs that all was not well. There are over a hundred DHSS leaflets on social security provisions and one of these is a leaflet that lists all the other leaflets. And an attempt to produce a multi-purpose benefits claim form had to be abandoned at the pilot stage. By then the leaflet had too many pages.[60] Even for the academic expert or social service administrator it is a complex system. For those in need – the one parent family, the elderly widow or the low income worker – it is confusing and appears to lack humanity.

Complexities within social security also affected many elderly people in the 1970s, over a quarter of whom received supplementary benefit, while many others, some millions, received housing benefits. The overlap between these two benefits created many problems. Should an elderly person receive supplementary benefits or would she or he be 'better off' on rent and rate rebates? The calculation was not a simple one to make, many people were on the wrong benefit and were therefore worse off than they might be. In 1975/6, officials combed through over 1 million files and transferred some 90,000 supplementary benefit claimants to rent and rate rebates because these increased their net incomes. But it was reckoned that about three times as many people drawing rebates in the early 1980s would be better off on supplementary benefits, and conversely, that about 100,000 households on supplementary benefit would gain from a transfer to rebates. But, as David Donnison, the last Chairman of the Supplementary Benefits Commission, commented, 'no one is telling them'.[61] This overlap has now been superseded by a unified housing benefit, which itself has plumbed new depths of confusion and complexity, obscurity and obfuscation.

The supplementary benefits scheme is also complex because of the proliferation of discretionary benefits that occurred in the 1970s. Designed originally to tackle 'exceptional' needs, these benefits increased dramatically in numbers – heating benefits, for example, increasing from some 194,000 in 1971 to over 1 million by 1976.[62] Such proliferation helped millions of claimants, young and old alike, with their weekly budgets but it had serious side-effects: it involved social security with more and more detailed inquiries into personal circumstances and has undermined the concept of rights that was meant to underpin the 1966 Social Security Act, which saw the transfer from national assistance to supplementary benefits. As Barbara Wootton has noted, a regular *Supplementary Benefits Handbook* is published in order to explain the complexities of supplementary benefits 'hopefully subtitled', as she puts it, 'A Guide to Claimants' Rights'.

... this volume runs to 125 pages of text plus 4 appendices, costing (in 1980) £2.40. The first 87 pages explain the 'normal' rules governing assessment and payment of allowances, after which three further pages give eight separate instructions about how to claim an 'urgent need payment for day-to-day living expenses', outside the normal rules.[63]

The individual and the State

The complexity of social security was just one example of a wider concern about the relationship between the individual or the family on the one hand, and the State and bureaucracy on the other. The notion of a 'Welfare' State assumes that government departments and other State agencies promote human welfare and that professionals and other staff are employed to serve the public. The proponents of the Welfare State firmly believed in the wisdom, efficiency and humanity of State intervention. By expanding State services and State institutions, and by developing bureaucracies and professions, it was felt that human welfare would increase, and hence age-old problems finally wither. All this was very much in the Fabian tradition, much influenced by the Webbs, and its paternalistic spirit was captured by Douglas Jay in his paperback *The Socialist Case*, published in 1947: 'For in the case of nutrition and health, just as in the case of education, the gentleman in Whitehall really does know better what is good for people than the people know themselves.'[64] The electors of 1945, implicitly at least, believed in this and voted for a programme which was to involve massive State intervention in many areas of their families' lives.

The generation of radicals that were active between the wars and the early postwar period felt that more government action was required to tackle the problems caused by the wrongdoings of the private market. By contrast today, much radical energy is taken up with the exposure of the alleged sins of *public* institutions – social security offices, planning departments, housing departments and other agencies. In general, there has been a growing anxiety about the relationship between the 'Welfare State' and the individual citizen. This anxiety relates to some specific concerns.

The size of government bodies

During the 1960s and 1970s a number of inquiries concerned with health authorities and local government[65] argued the case for the reform of governmental institutions. Invariably, they concluded that larger structures were required. Thus local government in London was re-organized, resulting in the basic unit of local government being the London borough with an average population of 250,000. Elsewhere in England and Wales local government was reorganized, again resulting in larger local councils, while the many discussions about the organization of the NHS were eventually to result in area health authorities (only to change yet again in 1982), invariably much larger than the hospital management committees that they largely replaced.

As more experience of these institutions in practice was gained, many critics argued that the reforms had produced more remote, and seemingly less caring, units of government.

Bureaucracy and professionalism

Since the birth of the modern Welfare State there has been a vast increase in both the size of administrations dealing with education, health, housing and other services and also the number of professionals and para-professionals engaged within it. Many have come to question whether, invariably and inevitably, this growth can be equated with an increase in human welfare. Indeed, many of the reorganizations, particularly within the NHS, seemed to be concerned more with the welfare of bureaucrats and professionals than with the consumers of the service. Of course, this critique needs to be evaluated carefully, rather than accepted at face value. Good arguments can be made as to why administrations have grown within certain sectors. The 'bureaucrats' will always be an obvious target for the conservative and the enemy of the Welfare State. But there was also a radical concern about these developments. Was the growth of bureaucracy out of control? The *Guardian* voiced some of the anxieties in an editorial in 1980:

A recent study based on EEC statistics showed that Britain employed 5.3 million public servants (defined to include local government workers but not 'revenue generating' staff like postmen or steel workers). On this definition, West Germany employs 3.6 million public servants and France 3.1 million. Are the French and Germans really worse served than us? Another example: Our Inland Revenue employs 78,970 people, or roughly the same number as all the Federal tax-gatherers in the United States. Yet our population is only a quarter the size, and we have far, far less income to tax.

Or some British examples: in 1959, there were 1.6 million local government employees. Last year there were 2.9 million. Are we now 82 per cent better served? And even if we were, public sector labour productivity would not have increased a jot. The education system employed 717,000 non-teaching staff last year, compared with 398,000 in 1965. Have our educational standards risen correspondingly?[66]

Another example is the personal social services. While it can be readily accepted that many professionals have gained in terms of income and status from the reforms following the Seebohm Report, it cannot be argued authoritatively that consumers have benefited to the sum total of the energy and resources involved in the reorganization. And within the field of health there is a growing concern that in too many areas medical developments are pursued because of the interest of medical practitioners and scientists, often using expensive technology and techniques which may not always involve the best uses of scarce manpower and resources, given the pressing needs of patients. Heart transplant surgery is the well-known example, but there are many other areas where similar developments have taken place. By contrast, areas of pressing concern – geriatric medicine and mental handicap for example – have been starved of resources, talent and medical status.

Housing and planning provide further examples. An earlier generation of socialists put much faith in the development of council housing. This would ensure high-quality housing for the people, at a reasonable rent. It would be properly managed by the local authorities and allocated according to need. The implementation of this strategy has required the growth of housing departments and bureaucracies to serve them. While a good deal of nonsense is written about council housing – a Martian would conclude from much comment that all council tenants live in twenty-storey blocks of flats where the lifts are permanently broken – it remains the case that most council tenants have relatively little control over the management of their dwelling or estate. The well-known complaint that council tenants cannot often even choose the colour of the paint for their front doors indicates wider grievances. Similarly, postwar developments have often shown planners and architects in a very bad light indeed. Schemes for housing estates, multi-storey buildings and new towns have all too often been way out of scale with human needs and preferences. Only rarely have the customers, the people themselves, been consulted. Too many local authority housing estates have been opened with much applause – even architectural awards – only to quickly degenerate into living hells for the tenants themselves. In recent years high rise buildings (and even low rise 'deck access' flats) built at vast expense in the 1960s and 1970s, and which are still being paid for, have been demolished by their local authorities.

More hopefully, however, in nearly every important field of social policy, there have been countervailing forces at work, all urging either by words or through demonstration projects the need to bring the individual and his or her concerns and needs into the centre stage of social policy. In housing, for example, there has been a greater emphasis on improvement, and less on large-scale housing construction programmes. There has been a developing movement of housing associations and housing co-operatives, many of which involve tenant participation. Within the local authority housing sector, interest in tenants' participation has developed and a number of pilot schemes

have been carried out.[67] And in the field of health there has been a
reaction against technology, specialization and hospitalization. There
is more emphasis on health education, prevention and community care.
Self-help groups, particularly among women, are springing up.

In education, the late 1960s and 1970s have witnessed growing
interest in developing a closer partnership between home and school,
parent and teacher. Active parent–teacher associations, the Educational
Priority Programme, and the reports of committees of inquiry, like
Plowden and Taylor, all bear witness to this. The Taylor Committee
for example argued that: '. . . every parent has the right to expect schools'
teachers to recognise his status in the education of his child by the
practical arrangement they make to communicate with him and the
spirit in which they accept his interest'.[68]

Within the planning field too, there has been more popular involve-
ment with the planning process. Schemes are challenged by residents'
associations and community groups. It is becoming increasingly difficult
for professionals to treat communities as if they were simply the lines
and dots that they appear to be on the map. And within social security,
organizations like the Child Poverty Action Group and the Claimants'
Unions have acted as a countervailing force to the social security system.
There has been more emphasis on rights and the need for proper
representation before tribunals. There have been calls for and some
progress towards better explanation and communication.

Moreover, the concern about the power of the State has led to
an extraordinary mushrooming of organizations, initiatives, quangos,
services and new professions, to advise, help and aid the consumer. They
include the National Consumer Council, the Electricity Consumer
Council, local Community Health Councils, a range of pressure groups
and advice services of all kinds. In some London boroughs – sometimes
in close proximity to each other – there will be a housing advice centre,
a consumer advice centre and a law centre. Moreover, the office of the
Ombudsman has been established to take up complaints against public
bureaucrats.

Most of these bodies are very useful and some have done important
work. The value of others is more doubtful and their development may

contribute to the growth of bureaucracy rather than challenge or humanize it. Certainly many of these initiatives, however worthy, are signs that all is not well, that the relationship between the citizen and the State is not right: they are symptoms of the disease, not a cure.

Disjointed approaches to social policy

Apart from the complexity of the modern Welfare State, there is also a major question about the adequacy of the government machine. Critics contend that central government adopts a narrow approach to its tasks and responsibilities which is increasingly lacking in relevance to present-day needs. Indeed, a characteristic of the third phase of postwar social policy has been a growing awareness of the connections and interactions between different social and economic problems and, hence, the need for a more co-ordinated and comprehensive response to these problems. The traditional interest in, and study of, specific problems and policy areas is now complemented by an interest in broader questions. What sort of issues are these? Some are 'new' and are the product of a range of social, economic, demographic and legal changes. They include the needs of very elderly people – a group that is increasing both numerically and proportionately; inner city decline (a catch-phrase that subsumes a range of social problems, population and economic rundown, and physical decay); and the needs of one parent families, not only a generally disadvantaged group, but also family units which are often ill-served by governmental systems which are based on an increasingly outmoded concept of the typical nuclear family, with a male bread-winner at its head.

Social scientists have contributed to this more analytical perspective which has, in part, been prompted by our failure to tackle some of the old, and seemingly very specific, problems, such as educational disadvantage. Following this example, it is now generally recognized that home and environmental circumstances can often be as important (or more important) a factor affecting educational opportunities than teachers, schools and teaching aids. Whatever the policy implications of this may be, they will certainly be many and varied and need to be followed up by several departments and agencies and not just by the Department of Education and Science and local education authorities. In general the last fifteen years have seen an increasing emphasis on the needs of client groups, the spatial distribution of problems and opportunities, and a more thorough investigation of causes.

One of the specific anxieties of this third phase of the Welfare State therefore concerns the ability of government (at both local and national levels) to adapt its own machinery to cope with contemporary social problems. This anxiety did not appear to be present (at least to such a degree) in the 1940s and 1950s. Then, most of the problems on political agendas concerned specific subjects – housing, education, health – and although such problems often seemed difficult to cope with, it was generally felt that systems of governments and methods of administration were, by and large, the appropriate ones.

Today, although many important problems are adequately matched by the departmental systems we have, there are others that inevitably cut across departmental boundaries, that do not have single solutions, and depend for their resolution on a corporate response and comprehensive programmes from government. And the last involves, among other things, a positive and effective partnership between central and local government.

A number of examples of the disjointed approach to social policy come to mind. Thus the DHSS and Department of Education and Science have failed to plan jointly adequate provision for the under-5s; there have only been half-hearted attempts to 'plan' for the range of housing, health and welfare needs of the elderly; the increase in heating costs and the concern about cold conditions has led, not to a comprehensive government response, but rather to a series of often ill-thought-out and hastily conceived policy responses from the DHSS, the Department of the Environment and the Department of Energy; there is a glaring mismatch between the Department of Industry's industrial strategy (with its regional approach) and the DoE's inner city policy; while government's inability to plan a coherent and adequate social security system (properly related to the fiscal system) has led to the growth in the late 1960s and 1970s of the complexity and confusion which has already been discussed.

The reasons for Whitehall's narrow approach to contemporary problems cannot be fully explored here, but they include failure to set up adequate strategic planning systems, both within and across departments; the narrow perspectives that Civil Service administrators bring to their tasks (the term 'generalist' being, arguably, misleading); the failure of Cabinet to deal with longer-term issues due to a concentration on immediate problems and the lack of interest and time devoted to social policy by prime ministers.

It would be wrong, however, to suggest that the Executive alone is responsible for the disjointed approach to social policy. The work and procedures of Parliament (and perhaps the often narrow interests of many MPs) make it an institution that is sadly unable to ensure that Whitehall develops processes and mechanisms that match the real problems that face the British people. It remains to be seen whether the select committees will rectify this problem, although these match rather than cut across departmental boundaries. Similarly, it is arguable that growing specialization means that there are few academics who are equipped (or even interested enough?) to comment on broad policy issues. And while the sheer growth of knowledge leads social scientists (quite understandably) to retreat into specialization, this trend is exacerbated by the obsession of some (but certainly not all) research funders with the collection of 'new' data to the neglect of broader studies and policy analysis. The Government's own importance as a funder of social research is likely (because of the tying of grants to the study of short-term problems) to increase the move towards specific investigations. (Which research institute today is authoritatively monitoring, evaluating – and acting as a forum for discussing – the important changes now affecting social policy?)

New initiatives

Nevertheless, there were, in the 1970s, some glimmers of hope and examples of a recognition within Whitehall that all was not well. Thus the Central Policy Review Staff's Joint Approach to Social Policy was based on the need for 'improved co-ordination between services as they affect the individual' and the Think Tank called for 'better analysis of, and policy prescriptions for, complex problems – especially when they are the concern of more than one department'.[69] However, while the Joint Approach to Social Policy team within the Central Policy Review Staff produced some useful reports,[70] and while its location within the Cabinet Office was a potentially powerful one, its impact on Whitehall social policy-making was not substantial. Moreover, although it can be argued that many of its most important contributions took place behind closed doors (through briefings to Cabinet and so on) and so cannot be publicly demonstrated, the Joint Approach to Social Policy quickly ran out of steam and political interest in it (never strong) was almost completely lacking even by 1979, when the new Administration dropped the initiative altogether.

The problems of the inner city provide a further example. In 1977 the DoE recognized that new forms of government were required if problems were to be properly diagnosed and tackled.[71] The Department's inner city policy recognized that 'The best results are likely to be achieved through a unified approach in which the different activities and services of government are brought together. Concerted action should have a greater impact.' It also accepted that: 'The activities of central government have themselves at times been over-compartmentalised', but promised 'to develop a more co-ordinated approach to urban problems'. In particular, new 'partnership' schemes (involving active co-operation between central and local government) were started in seven inner city areas. This was potentially an exciting development and the concept of 'partnership' set a useful precedent for other policy areas. However, even before the policy was handicapped by spending cuts and economic recession, the traditional barriers to be overcome (not least within Whitehall) were formidable and the experience of comprehensive approaches to problems of urban deprivation in recent years did not augur well for the new strategy.[72]

A further example is provided by David Donnison's work at the Supplementary Benefits Commission. What used to be a very inward-looking and conservative part of government, and one that dealt with very specific income maintenance services, began to view its own responsibilities quite differently. The supplementary benefits system was revealed as an arena in which a range of social issues come together and the Commission's 'boundary' problems were some of the most important it had to cope with. For example, its 1977 Annual Report included recommendations for a new national housing benefit and for a fuel subsidy system which had important implications, not only for the Commission's parent department, the DHSS, but also for the DoE and the Department of Energy. However, Donnison found that the obstacles to radical reform, from some of the DHSS officials, from DoE and, inevitably, the Treasury, were immense.[73] This was not atypical: during the late 1960s and 1970s new ideas and initiatives were floated and sometimes developed, but without strong political backing innovators in Whitehall were easily outgunned and out-manoeuvred by the sheer weight of departmental traditions, vested interest and inertia.

Public attitudes towards the Welfare State

The election of the 1945 Labour government was made possible by the electorate's desire for positive peace and social reform. There was strong public backing for a Welfare State; it was issues such as housing, social security and full employment that were on people's minds, and Labour was regarded as the party that would deliver effective policies. How have public attitudes towards the Welfare State changed in the period since 1945, and up to the 1979 general election?

During the 1950s, when the Conservative Party won three successive general elections, each time with increasing majorities, Britain experienced relative economic stability and increasing affluence. Personal consumption was a more important concern for many than community provision, and a cartoon, after the 1959 election results were known, has Harold Macmillan addressing a refrigerator, a car, a washing machine and a televison: 'Well, gentlemen, I think we all fought a good fight.'[74] However, the evidence suggests that the Welfare State retained its popularity in the 1950s and, indeed, satisfaction with social services and the belief that they were successful may have worked against Labour because many voters felt that no radical changes were necessary. Nevertheless, one survey in 1960 found that 50 per cent of people reported a willingness to pay more taxes for social benefits. This view was expressed more or less equally by Labour and Conservative voters, the middle class and the working class, with some 40 per cent unwilling.[75] Thus in the 1950s it would appear that there was a good measure of support for the Welfare State, but other issues were given higher priority by many electors.

Support for the Welfare State remained high in the early 1960s. Indeed, during the run-up to the 1964 election social policy issues seemed to re-emerge as politically important. A 1963 national survey asked over 2,000 people 'What do you yourself feel are the most important problems the Government should do something about?' While 17 per cent of respondents mentioned economic problems, 25 per cent mentioned social welfare, 24 per cent housing, 9 per cent education.[76] Commenting on this evidence, Butler and Stokes note: '... there can be no doubt of the salience of the values associated with welfare issues, especially housing and pensions, during this era'. And they noted: 'how one-sided the public's support for increased outlays for the social services was in the early 1960s', observing that the responses were overwhelmingly angled towards spending more on pensions and housing. Fewer than one in ten touched 'restrictionist themes', such as confining family allowances to the needy. Generally, 'the public mood in this period was, in this field at least, strongly interventionist'.[77] Furthermore, the strong interest in welfare issues favoured the Labour Party, for of those in favour of expanding services, 51 per cent regarded Labour as better able to achieve this as against only 18 per cent plumping for the Conservatives. Moreover, these results were associated with actual voting intentions, for the swing to Labour between 1959 and 1963 among the group which wanted social services expanded and preferred Labour to handle the issue was as high as 9.6 per cent.[78]

How did public opinion move in the period leading up to the 1979 general election? So far in this chapter we have discussed a number of particular causes of anxiety about the Welfare State that came to the fore between the mid 1960s and the late 1970s. Some were the concerns of relatively small groups, others found echoes among a wider public. Thus concern about the public expenditure 'burden' usually came from politicians on the Right, businessmen and some academic economists; anxieties about the failure to tackle poverty were voiced by academics, social administrators, some social workers and by those associated with the Child Poverty Action Group and other pressure groups; concern about the divide between the citizen and the State was articulated by numerous commentators in the media and by some consumers of public housing, health and other services.

More generally, the public at large was increasingly interested in the trade-off between taxation and services – between public expenditure and private consumption – and interest was quickened among families and the low paid by the increasing importance of taxation. Public concern of this kind about the Welfare State is mirrored by opinion poll findings although, inevitably, the evidence is ambiguous. Interestingly, the findings reported in *Political Change in Britain* show a change of attitude during the early years of the Wilson government. In response to a question about public spending, 77 per cent supported more spending in the autumn of 1964, but only 54 per cent in spring 1966. However, this still shows a high degree of support for social service spending, and Butler and Stokes refer to these findings as 'interesting evidence that the public desire for this expansion was partially satisfied between 1964 and 1966'.[79]

During the 1970s social welfare issues were overshadowed by economic problems and during the two elections of 1974 social policy concerns do not seem to have significantly helped Labour to victory. 'The related issues of inflation and rising prices seemed to dominate the voters' concerns' was the authoritative verdict on the October result of that year.[80]

By the 1979 general election the British people had experienced a rough economic patch and attitudes towards some aspects of social policy were hardening. Indeed, as early as 1974, one poll found that, even among 'Labour identifiers', support for spending more on social services had declined by 28 per cent since 1964.[81]

Public attitudes to welfare however have been misunderstood. In fact, as one recent study makes clear, support for such services as the NHS remained high.[82] However, the implications of some drift away of support for the Welfare State were important and were not lost on the new Tory leadership. And it was related to a more specific concern that came to grip the popular imagination and mass media reporting of social policy in the late 1970s – scrounging. Concern that the treatment of those dependent on the public purse is too favourable has a long history, probably as long as the Welfare State itself. But this reached a new level of intensity in the late 1970s. In an important study, Peter Golding and Sue Middleton have analysed the syndrome.[83] One case illustrates the issue. In July 1976 an unemployed Liverpudlian, Derek Deevy, was on trial at Liverpool Crown Court. He was charged with three specimen indictments for obtaining supplementary benefit by deception, the three charges totalling some £57. A figure of £500 was mentioned in the charge for the total overpayment to him, but during the case Deevy himself estimated that he had fraudulently claimed £36,000. It was this figure which gripped the imagination of the Court, the media and the public. In particular Deevy's luxurious life style was strongly featured in newspaper stories: '£10,000-a-year life-style for Dole Fiddler'; 'Six years for Dole Cheat Who Spent £25 a Week on the Best Cigars'; 'Incredible Reign of King Con': '£200-a-Week Tycoon on Social Security'; 'King of the Dole Queue Scroungers'.[84]

The Deevy case led to a mass media search for similar scrounging incidents and also to more general – and also hysterical – criticisms of the Welfare State for its many failings. Iain Sproat, a Conservative MP, argued that, 'we have seen only the tip of the iceberg'[85] and this was the general view – it was assumed that very large numbers of people were fraudulently claiming supplementary benefit. While the mass media's role in promoting public fears about social security abuse should not be underestimated, Press stories found fertile ground in popular concern.

Certainly, many political canvassers on doorsteps throughout the country found that this aspect of Welfare State politics was the one that particularly interested many voters. However, Press and public concern also focused at times on different areas of policy. The tragic death of Maria Colwell in 1973, and too many similar cases in the years that followed, drew attention to the performance of social workers in particular and social services departments in general. For example, in 1980 the *Daily Mail*, in a leading article, stated, 'Yet another baby has died because of the stupidity and neglect of professional social workers' and the same newspaper headlined its news story: 'Carly, victim of do-nothing welfare team'.[86]

There certainly seems to be evidence that particularly extreme cases of social security abuse were related in the popular mind to more general anxieties about social policies. As Golding and Middleton argued:

The Deevy story in July 1976 opened the floodgates. All the pent-up anxieties and prejudices fomented by recession, unemployment, dropping tax thresholds and growing economic uncertainty burst through in a great surge of anti-welfare cant and venom ... What started as an anxiety about abuse of the welfare state by excessive or illegal exploitation of it, was turned rapidly into a more general suspicion of the entire apparatus and the philosophy on which it is constructed.[87]

Conclusion

The British Welfare State entered a new phase in the mid 1960s and, despite initial optimism and reforming zeal, it was a phase characterized increasingly by a sense of anxiety and uncertainty about the future. The old confidence, and consensus, about social policy withered away. In large part this was due to the state of the economy, and certainly about industry's capacity to deliver the goods. The economic cake could no longer be relied upon to grow steadily larger each year, the capitalist dream was turning into an economic nightmare, and the expectations and hopes of a generation of politicians, planners, public officials and social reformers evaporated. The words of Tony Crosland, written in the affluent days of the mid 1950s, seemed later like a cruel joke:

With personal consumption rising by 2–4% a year and likely to double in twenty years, it will really not much matter a decade from now whether we plan to produce rather more of this and less of that, or exactly what prices are charged for this commodity or that. The level of material welfare will soon be such that marginal changes in the allocation of resources will make little difference to anyone's contentment.[88]

Crosland looked forward 'as our traditional objectives are gradually fulfilled' to our turning attention to 'more important spheres – of personal freedom, happiness, and cultural endeavour' and the final section of his book was entitled 'Cultural and Amenity Planning; and the Declining Importance of Economic Problems'. In practice, things turned out very differently. And Donnison summed up the situation in this way: ' "Middle England" is not ready to be convinced by research and Blue Books that benign public services will – or should– create a more humane and a more equal society. Yet the old evils of capitalism (unemployment, low wages and exploitation) for which Crosland pronounced a requiem are still very much alive.'[89] Indeed, by 1974, Crosland himself was saying that 'extreme class inequalities remain, poverty is far from eliminated, the economy is in a state of semi-permanent crisis and inflation is rampant'.[90] In 1975, he declared 'the party is over'.[91]

This chapter also shows that anxieties about the burden of public spending raised a related question about the level of income taxation. Had we reached the limits of direct taxation? Lower income groups and families with children had borne the brunt of increasing taxation and this fact has altered the political outlook for social policy.

Social policy in the later 1960s and early 1970s was also influenced by other factors. Research showed that the Welfare State had not been as successful in tackling poverty as had once been thought. Similarly, there was the growing evidence of the perpetuation of inequalities within education, health and income. Forty years after they first appeared on the national horizon, Beveridge's 'Five Giants' still stalked the land. In particular 'Idleness', or unemployment, was increasing.

Added to the re-emergence of old problems, the Welfare State had grown increasingly complex, not least in the field of social security, and other problems highlighted a growing divide between citizen and State. No longer was it assumed that the State always knew best, nor even that it was necessarily a force for the promotion of human welfare. And there were concerns about the government system and its capacity, given its conservatism, secrecy and heavily departmental mould, to tackle the urgent issues on the policy agenda.

These were some of the crucial anxieties about the Welfare State that emerged during the period and gained in intensity up to the 1979 general election. These anxieties provoked uncertainty about the future of social policy. All this prepared the way for the emergence of the new Toryism and its tough new brand of social politics.

PART TWO

Rolling Back the Welfare State

3 Counter-Revolution:
The Tory Attack on the Welfare State

... and when he saw him, he passed by on the other side.

The Gospel According to St Luke[1]

Growing anxieties about the Welfare State broke the postwar consensus about social policy and led to a renewed politicization: the issues at stake in the late 1970s and the early 1980s were to become more concerned with social ideology than with social engineering. Given the crisis facing the economic management of faltering capitalist societies, and the inherent political nature of social policies concerned with the distribution of income, wealth, services and opportunities – and therefore power – in society, this was perhaps hardly surprising. Both major political parties were affected by the gathering storm within the Welfare State, but they reacted differently to it and drew different conclusions. Labour's reaction was stilted and lacked confidence. The Party, and the Labour government, was still committed to the Welfare State but recognized its defects. The Callaghan government was concerned about public spending and the 'burden' of taxation: it introduced its own cuts in public spending. In many respects it accepted, albeit partially, the analysis of the enemies of the Welfare State and did not substitute its own. Faced with the crisis, it wavered: Labour in 1979 offered no comprehensive strategies and certainly no new vision for social policy in the 1980s and beyond.

The rise of the New Right

To appreciate the Conservative Party's approach to the Welfare State in the run-up to the 1979 general election, it is important to understand the profound break with the past that occurred when Margaret Thatcher became leader in 1974. It heralded a revolution within the Tory Party and augured badly for the Welfare State. Politically it was unexpected. Crosland, for example, in the mid 1950s had written that the reforms of the postwar Labour government were *not* vulnerable to 'a few years of Conservative reaction'. He argued then that 'wholesale counter-revolution' was unlikely. 'It is not, for one thing, in the nature of the British Conservative Party, which for all its clamorous fringe of backwoodsmen usually entrusts its leadership to cautious, realistic Peelites.'[2]

Crosland argued the British Conservative was 'attached to the *status quo*, whatever the status quo may be; and his function is less to reinstate the past than preserve the present'.[3] He also added, in words which were to describe adequately pre-Thatcher conservatism: 'Any Government which tampered seriously with the basic structure of the full-employment Welfare State would meet with a sharp reversal at the polls; and this knowledge acts as rather a strong inducement to politicians not to tamper.'[4]

The purpose of quoting Crosland's *The Future of Socialism* is not to mock his prophecies – far from it, for Crosland was one of the most thoughtful socialists of the postwar period – but rather to suggest the shock to the political system that the advent of Thatcherism was to induce. Let us consider the nature of the change by first reviewing the change in Tory ideology that took place in the run-up to the 1979 general election.

A characteristic theme in postwar Conservative politics has been the modernization and adaptation of Party philosophy and policies to the needs of the time, be they social, economic or political.[5] Following the 'One Nation' tradition of Disraeli, there has been an acceptance of the need for social reform, a desire for accommodation rather than confrontation. Many would argue with Crosland that this was a political necessity in an age of the mass franchise and the rise of the Labour Party. To survive, the Conservatives needed more than the votes of the old landed interests, the owners of property and of higher income groups. As Andrew Gamble noted, 'This Conservative wish to have their appeal to the electorate on a national rather than a class perspective is central to their whole electoral strategy.'[6]

Since the war there has always been a tension between the supporters of this approach – the 'Right Progressives' – and those who wish to turn the clock back. During most of this period, the former were dominant and under Churchill, Eden, Macmillan, Douglas-Home and Heath, the Conservative Party pursued (albeit with some important exceptions) the 'Middle Way'. But we are now clearly in a new era. The defeat of Mr Heath in 1974 and the ascendancy of Mrs Thatcher changed Conservative policy at a time when economic problems and acute anxiety about the levels of public expenditure opened up long-camouflaged ideological divisions in British politics. Partly because of disillusion with the Heath years, the Tory Party is now radically different from what it was some years ago and it has led to a new type of Toryism in office.

Evidence of this shift comes in the speeches of Sir Keith Joseph and Margaret Thatcher, the two dominant figures in the Conservative Party of the late 1970s, delivered prior to the 1979 election. The titles of Sir Keith's two volumes of speeches are themselves significant. In 1975 *Reversing the Trend: A Critical Reappraisal of Conservative Economic and Social Policies* was issued, followed in 1976 by *Stranded on the Middle Ground*,[7] an apt contrast to Harold Macmillan's *The Middle Way* published in 1938.[8] Joseph argues that 'it is clear that the middle ground way was not a secure base but a slippery slope to socialism and state control.'[9] The implications of Joseph's analysis are clear, for while he claims to have been 'converted to Conservatism' only in April 1974 ('I had thought I was a Conservative but now I see that I was not really one at all'[10]) his conversion is, arguably, really to Liberalism – the old-style *laissez faire* variety, long rejected by the modern Liberal Party. His 'conversion' to Conservatism in fact flies in the face of the modern Tory tradition. But it has strongly influenced his Party; his thoughts were shared by his leader and they decisively influenced the strategy of the 1979 Tory administration.

These views have been echoed by Margaret Thatcher. Speaking before an American audience in 1975, she argued that 'amidst our well published difficulties a vital new debate is beginning, or perhaps an old debate is being renewed, about the proper role of government, the welfare state and the attitudes on which it rests'. The debate centred on 'the progressive consensus' – 'the doctrine that the State should be active on many fronts in promoting equality, in the provision of social welfare and in the redistribution of wealth and incomes'.[11] The Conservative leader has made it abundantly clear that she is not part of this so-called 'consensus'.

Thus the progressive Right lost control of the Conservative Party – at least for the time being. Those who accept some measure of social reform as an essential component of modern Toryism have been replaced by those with a profound distrust and dislike of the Welfare State – a very product of the much despised 'Middle Way'. They argue that the Welfare State has weakened the nation and its people, that it encourages the shirkers and scroungers, and that its existence imposes major tax burdens, particularly on the hardworking and innovative. This dulls enterprise and creativity, inhibits investment and thus restricts the workings and benefits of market capitalism. The way out of this impasse involved scaling down the Welfare State and the recognition that the private market can and should provide such services as education, pensions, housing and health care.

The economic context

The New Right's approach to social services can only be understood in the context of the new Tory economics. It is a return to Selsdonism, but a more sophisticated Selsdonism, including the new magic formula, monetarism. The Conservative Party advocates the liberalization of the economy – including wage bargaining (except for the public sector) and prices – within the discipline of strict control over the money supply. It entails a smaller direct role for government and a belief in the virtues of enterprise and more or less unfettered capitalism. The strategy was summed up in *The Right Approach*:

The Conservative approach entails living within our means, paying our way in the world, mastering inflation, reviving the wealth creating part of the economy and encouraging all those on whom it depends. This approach means less bureaucracy and less legislation, lower taxes and borrowing, higher profits leading to more investment and more employment, and rewards for enterprise and hard work.[12]

Thus compared to the Labour government's conservative stance on the Welfare State in 1979, the Tories under new leadership were waiting with a 'new' ideology and a package of slogans, ideas and prejudices that were in tune with the mood of the times and which helped to bring them victory at the polls.

While Welfare State issues did not dominate the 1979 election campaign, some of the major themes clearly related directly to social policy. Furthermore, some of the Conservatives' specific social policy objectives were popular with the electorate. Indeed, many *Labour* voters supported Tory policies, as a poll undertaken during the course of the 1979 campaign showed. Thus 63 per cent of Labour voters thought the next government should 'reduce supplementary benefits for strikers on the assumption that they are getting strike pay from their union'; and 75 per cent supported the sale of council houses with discounts. As Anthony King commented on these results, 'seldom can a major party have penetrated so deeply into the political thinking of the other side's staunchest supporters.'[13]

These then were the political and economic ideas which inspired the new Tory government's approach to social policy. The key economic imperatives were to reduce taxation and public spending and therefore, in one sense, there was no 'social policy' as such, but rather decisions about social policy were simply determined by economic considerations. But this is partly a wrong interpretation. The economic objectives of the new Toryism tied in neatly with the political aim of scaling down the Welfare State by encouraging others to provide welfare – the voluntary bodies, the community, the family and the private market. The aim was to move towards, in Titmuss's phrase, 'a residual Welfare State' for the poor and deprived.[14]

Thus economic, political and social objectives involve making a reality of long-held Tory prejudices – the backwoodsmen were out of the closet – in favour of such measures as increasing charges for services, expanding means testing, encouraging the private market in areas like health and education and shifting the burden away from the social services and on to the family and 'the community'. These objectives meant pushing aside any pretence to build 'One Nation', but this was necessary if a revitalized market economy was to rise from the slumber of consensus politics. During the early years of the Conservative government, ministers stopped apologizing for the cuts and rather presented their policies in a harsh and 'realistic' language, which encouraged Reg Prentice to state: 'If we have to apologize for anything, it is for cutting too little and too late.'

The Conservative record

How should we assess the Conservatives' social policy record? This review starts by looking at policy objectives in general and then considers the impact of measures on the major services and benefits.

The government's 'social policy' has been largely determined by its macro-economic objectives, strongly reinforced by a political prejudice against the whole notion of a Welfare State. And yet, the economic objectives have not been achieved. Indeed, all along the line, there have been failures. The 'burden' of taxation has *not* been lifted: in fact it has been increased for all except the rich. Moreover, public expenditure, far from contracting, has actually *increased*, but in ways which bring little comfort to those in need. Indeed, public spending as a proportion of the nation's wealth has *increased*. Let us consider these points in more detail.

Taxation

What has happened to income taxation during the Tory years? Despite election pledges, and an early flourish when the standard rate of taxation was reduced, the burden of taxation for the vast majority of people has

Table 3.1 Income tax and national insurance contributions as a percentage of gross income: changes 1978/9–1986/7

| | Married couple plus 2 children | | |
	1978/9	1986/7	Change
50% of average earnings			
(a) Income tax	6.6	8.8	+2.2
(b) NIC	5.9	7.9	+2.0
(c) Income tax + NIC	12.5	16.7	+4.2
75% of average earnings			
(a) Income tax	14.7	15.0	+0.3
(b) NIC	6.1	8.3	+2.2
(c) Income tax + NIC	20.8	23.3	+2.5
Average earnings			
(a) Income tax	19.1	18.3	−0.8
(b) NIC	6.2	8.4	+2.2
(c) Income tax + NIC	25.3	26.7	+1.4
Twice average earnings			
(a) Income tax	25.9	24.1	−1.8
(b) NIC	4.0	5.8	+1.8
(c) Income tax + NIC	29.9	29.9	+0.0
Five times average earnings			
(a) Income tax	48.1	41.3	−6.8
(b) NIC	1.6	2.4	+0.8
(c) Income tax + NIC	49.7	43.7	−6.0
Ten times average earnings			
(a) Income tax	65.3	50.6	−14.7
(b) NIC	0.8	1.2	+0.4
(c) Income tax + NIC	66.1	51.8	−14.3

Sources: Hansard, col. 188, 3 December 1981; col. 152, 17 February 1982; col. 530, 26 March 1986.

For the assumptions used, see Hansard. In particular, it should be noted that *no* tax reliefs, other than the standard allowances, are allowed for.

increased. Details are shown in Table 3.1. This table just gives one family type, the married couple with two children, but the picture for other groups is similar. It demonstrates that personal taxation, that is, the combined effect of income tax and national insurance contributions, has increased since 1979. Indeed, the position for much of the period (until tax thresholds were raised in the 1985 Budget) was worse than that shown in Table 3.1. In the tax year 1978/9, a married couple with two children on average earnings would have paid 25.3 per cent of their gross income in taxation and national insurance. Eight years later, in the year 1986/7, the percentage was 26.7 per cent – an increase of 1.4 per cent. For those on lower incomes, the position is even worse. At half average earnings, the percentage of gross earnings going in taxation was an extra 4.2 per cent over the period, while for those on 75 per cent of average earnings, the percentage change was 2.5 per cent. Even for those earning twice average earnings, the tax burden was not eased.

It is only at much higher income levels that a reduction is apparent. For those earning five times average earnings, the tax burden for a married couple and two children declined by 6.0 per cent, while for the very rich on ten times average earnings, the percentage reduction was a substantial 14.3 per cent.

The general failure of the Conservative government to reduce the burden of taxation remains the case when one takes a broader view of taxation. After including VAT and other indirect taxes from central government, the evidence shows that the burden of taxation has *not* been significantly reduced for most people since 1978/9. Indeed, a married couple with two children on average earnings paid 38.5 per cent of their gross income in income tax, national insurance contributions, VAT and other indirect taxes in 1978/9; it was as high as 41.4 per cent in 1981/2; and the estimate for 1986/7 is 38.9 per cent.[15] And all this is just not good enough for a Party whose 1979 manifesto stated unequivocally: 'We shall cut income tax at all levels to reward hard work, responsibility and success.'[16]

A further way of examining the real gainers from Conservative tax policy is provided by Table 3.2 which shows the position to 1984/5. This looks just at income tax and reveals the truth behind Tory rhetoric about tax cuts. In particular it shows the impact of higher tax-rate reductions, from 83 to 60 per cent. While the 5 million poorest taxpayers

Table 3.2 Conservative tax cuts: the gainers, 1978/9–1984/5

Range of total income in 1984/5	No. of units paying tax in 1984/5	Overall		Reductions in income tax					
				Due to real changes in allowances etc.		Due to indexation		
(£)	(million)	Amount (£ million)	Average per tax unit (£)	Amount (£ million)	Average per tax unit (£)	Amount (£ million)	Average per tax unit (£)
Under 5,000	5.0	2,370	320	120	20	2,250	305
5,000–10,000	8.8	5,130	580	870	100	4,260	480
10,000–15,000	4.2	4,060	970	840	200	3,220	770
15,000–20,000	1.4	2,570	1,835	520	370	2,050	1,465
20,000–30,000	0.7	2,480	3,480	550	770	1,930	2,710
30,000–50,000	0.21	1,640	7,700	510	2,400	1,130	5,300
over 50,000	0.065	1,260	19,400	760	11,700	500	7,700
TOTAL	20.4	19,510		4,170		15,340	

Source: Hansard, 4 April 1984, cols. 543–4.

(those with incomes under £5,000) gained an annual average £320 per tax unit ('gains' more than offset by other tax changes) as the result of Tory measures since 1978/9, at the other extreme the very rich (the estimated 65,000 taxpayers with incomes over £50,000) gained an annual average of £19,400 – an amount sixty-one times that received by the poorest! The table also demonstrates just how significant, in overall terms, has been the redistribution of income to the rich: in 1984/5 those with incomes above £20,000 paid £1.82 billion less than would have been the case if tax cuts had not been introduced even after excluding the effect of indexation, and therefore showing only the impact of real changes to taxation.

Public expenditure

Prior to the 1979 election, the Conservatives linked the reduction of taxation to the cutback of public expenditure. Moreover, the latter was crucial to the overall economic strategy, for as the 1980 White Paper on Public Expenditure made clear: 'The Government intend to reduce public expenditure progressively in volume terms over the next four years.'[17] This change of direction was central to the achievement of economic objectives which were 'to bring down the rate of inflation and interest rates by curtailing the growth of the money supply and controlling Government borrowing; to restore incentives; and to plan for spending which is compatible both with the objectives for taxation and borrowing and with a realistic assessment of the prospects for economic growth.'[18]

In practice, however, things have turned out rather differently, as the frantic notes which crept into the next two White Papers indicate. In 1981 the document noted that the level of spending was higher than that planned in 1980 and 'higher than the Government would wish in the light of their financial and economic objectives. The Government regard this development as one which requires the most serious attention during the 1981 Annual Survey . . .'[19] A year later, in 1982, the White Paper noted: 'The Government's revised expenditure plans for 1982/83 onwards are higher than the cash equivalent of those in the March 1981 White Paper. For 1982/83 ... the planning total is £115 billion, some £5 billion more than the earlier plans.'[20] And this story holds true for later years. As Terry Ward, the Specialist Adviser to the House of Commons Treasury Select Committee, noted in 1984: 'The present government has published five White Papers since it took office in 1979. Each one has shown an intention to hold down public spending in real terms. So far none has succeeded.'[21]

The last Labour government, in its 1979 Expenditure White Paper, planned that, in 1982/3, £120 billion would be spent (expressed at 1983/4 prices). In the early flush of victory, the Conservatives planned to reduce this to £106.4 billion,[22] an 11 per cent reduction on Labour's plan. In practice, however, the amount actually spent in that year turned out to be £113.4 billion,[23] less than 6 per cent below the allegedly profligate Labour government's plan.

What has gone wrong for the Conservatives? In order to understand the position fully, it is important to make a technical point about public expenditure figures. Since the White Paper of 1982, the Government has moved over to measuring expenditure in terms of *cash* prices, rather than in volume terms as previously. This makes the task of analysing public spending trends very difficult, as cash prices take no account of inflation and therefore do not reveal a true picture of what is occurring. As the House of Commons Treasury Committee has observed: 'We are in no doubt that volume estimates reveal information useful to Parliament in a way that cannot be matched by cash estimates alone which do not even measure inputs.'[24] Another adviser to the House of Commons Committee has observed: 'a serious deterioration in the standards of information given in Public Expenditure White Papers in the 1970s'.[25] However, since the Expenditure White Paper of 1982, one statistical table has been included which shows general expenditure trends in 'cost terms', which means that cash figures have been adjusted for general inflation. Unfortunately this only gives a general approximation of how expenditure on the different areas of policy is actually changing, as the prices of goods and services change more quickly or slowly in different policy areas (for example, the cost of weapons may increase at a different rate from the cost of school books or certain items of the health budget). Nevertheless the 'cost' figures are an advance on mere cash figures and they certainly show the broad picture that is emerging. (Unfortunately, the detailed expenditure on specific programmes are only available in 'cash' terms.)

To add to the difficulties of following expenditure trends in recent years, the Conservatives (embarrassed by their failure to hold back spending) have deliberately massaged official information so as to prevent a clear picture emerging. Thankfully, the House of Commons watchdog on Treasury Affairs, the All Party (in fact Conservative majority) Select Committee has monitored these manoeuvres. In particular they have shown how the changed treatment of sickness and housing benefit, national insurance surcharge, national debt interest and the treatment of the proceeds from the sale of assets all contribute to an artificial reduction of official spending statistics. As the Select Committee note, when these factors and inflation *are* allowed for: 'Public expenditure is shown to have risen by 12.3% over the five financial years to 1983/84.'[26] In other words spending has increased to a greater extent than is suggested by official figures. In fact, the Select Committee (after adjusting for the factors excluded by the Government) show that, in cost terms (1982/3 prices) expenditure increased from £110.4 billion in 1978/9 to £124 billion in 1983/4, instead of the £106.9 – £114.6 billion increase presented by the Government.[27]

These total figures in isolation hardly suggest a wholesale slaughter of the Welfare State. So what happened? Has the new-style Toryism had a change of heart and renewed the Party's long-standing, always cool, on–off love affair with Britain as 'One Nation'? No. The figures overall tell us little and are seriously misleading in that they understate the damage done to social policy over the last six years. Peter Shore, then Shadow Chancellor, summed it up when he noted in the House of Commons that 'The Government are achieving much more a distortion of the pattern of public expenditure than the overall and massive reduction that they had originally planned.'[28]

Table 3.3 presents public expenditure in real terms by programme.

Table 3.3 Planning total in real terms by programme (£ million, base year 1983/4)

	1979/80 outturn	1984/5 est. outturn	Expenditure changes: 1979/80–1984/5 (%)	1987/8 plans
Defence	13,405	16,467	+23	16,050
Overseas aid and other overseas services	2,949	2,390	−19	2,360
Agriculture, fisheries, food and forestry	1,461	2,017	+38	1,600
Industry, energy, trade and employment	5,822	6,856	+18	2,940
Arts and libraries	587	636	+8	620
Transport	4,761	4,554	−4	4,080
Housing	6,569	2,979	−55	2,250
Other environmental services	3,833	3,592	−6	2,990
Law, order and protective services	3,746	4,837	+29	4,770
Education and science	12,994	13,125	+1	12,110
Health and personal social services	12,933	15,087	+17	15,410
Social security	28,204	36,221	+28	37,500
Other public services	1,736	1,772	+2	1,710
Common services	1,462	948	−35	1,050
Scotland	6,613	6,817	+3	6,230
Wales	2,569	2,516	−2	2,490
Northern Ireland	3,615	3,875	+7	3,910
Adjustments				
Special sales of assets	−1,451	−1,909		−1,910
Reserve				4,250
General allowance for shortfall		−477		
PLANNING TOTAL	111,809	122,301	+9	120,370

Source: *The Government's Expenditure Plans 1985/6–1987/8*, Cmnd 9428-II, HMSO, 1985, Table 2.6.

This also shows the total percentage change in programmes between 1979/80 and 1984/5. A more detailed discussion of some of the points contained in the table is included later in this chapter. Here some broad conclusions can be noted.

The dismal economic record lies at the heart of any explanation of rising public expenditure and of particular importance is the public cost of *unemployment* which has led to increased spending on social security. As Table 3.3 shows, public expenditure in real terms on social security increased from £28 billion in 1979/80 to £36 billion in 1984/5 – up 28 per cent. Expenditure on benefits for the unemployed increased (in cash terms) from £1.47 billion in 1979/80 to an estimated £6.54 billion by 1985/6.[29] Added to this sum are the costs of employment and training programmes made necessary by rising unemployment. Indeed, the Department of Employment's budget (much of it related to unemployment) rose from £1.2 billion in 1979/80 to £3 billion in 1984/5.[30] Thus the overall public expenditure costs of unemployment must be in the region of £8 billion per annum and this takes no account of the costs of more 16-year-olds staying at school (for want of a job) or the effects of unemployment-related demands on health and welfare services or law and order provisions.

Defence has also consumed larger amounts of public expenditure, rising from £13 billion in 1979/80 to £16 billion in 1984/5 – up 23 per cent. Apart from general Tory ambitions to spend more on defence, these figures are partly due to a commitment to NATO to increase defence spending in real terms by 3 per cent per annum up to 1985/6. Also, the extra costs associated with the Falklands War are significant, accounting as they do for an additional £552 million in 1985/6.[31]

There have also been substantial real increases in police and other law and order services. During the Conservative years, expenditure has increased here by 29 per cent and while some £3.7 billion was spent in 1979/80, the total in 1984/5 was £4.8 billion.

The other side of this picture is also revealed by the table. The major victim has been expenditure on housing. Expenditure on education has been very seriously constrained and only rose by 1 per cent in real terms over the period. Overseas aid has also declined significantly.

The significance of these trends is that, not only is the Government spending less than was planned for by the last Labour administration, but in addition a greater proportion of its total expenditure is going on the cost of keeping people out of work and on other areas of policy – cruise missiles and more police for example – which have nothing to do with welfare in the sense of providing hospitals, schools, housing or social services. To conclude, we can note that the Conservatives have also failed to decrease public expenditure as a proportion of the nation's wealth, as measured by GDP. The proportion increased from 39.5 per cent in 1979/80 to 42.5 per cent in 1984/5 (having risen to 46.5 per cent in 1982/3).[32]

The impact of Tory policies on the key areas of social policy: housing, health, personal social services, education and social security is now assessed.

Housing

Housing has always been centre-stage in the party political battle and, true to form, it is housing that has been the major victim of Tory social policy. Certainly public expenditure cuts have hit housing harder than other sectors, as Table 3.4 shows. The total housing expenditure programme has been reduced by more than a half in real terms over the period.

Fortunately for housing ministers the presentation of specific plans in cash terms camouflages the extent of decline, but even using these misleading figures, which do not allow for inflation, shows the direction of the trend. For example, central government subsidies to local authority housing, which stood at £1,247 million in 1979/80 and £1,423 million in 1980/81 had decreased to £360 million by 1984/5. Similarly, capital expenditure on land and new dwellings has declined even in cash terms from £1,168 million in 1979–80 to £705 million by 1984/85. Conversely, total sales and repayments brought in £1.6 billion in 1984/5, mainly owing to the sale of council houses.[33] Thus the Government's public expenditure targets have been realized not only by spending less on housing, but also by the receipts gained by selling off some of the existing stock.

Table 3.4 Housing: some key indicators, 1978–83

	Local authority rents (gross unrebated) as % of average weekly earnings, England & Wales	Housebuilding (new starts), UK (000s)				Council house sales, England & Wales
			Public	Private	Total	
1978/9	6.6	1978	110.9	161.6	272.5	30,620
1979/80	6.4	1979	83.5	148.2	231.7	42,460
1980/81	6.6	1980	59.4	101.5	160.9	85,700
1981/2	8.2	1981	40.3	118.9	159.2	106,485
1982/3	8.8	1982	56.1	144.6	200.7	207,050
1983/4	8.4	1983	51.9	174.2	226.1	146,450
1984/5	8.3	1984	43.0	162.0	205.0	106,930

Source: The Government's Expenditure Plans 1985/6–1987/8, vol. II, Cmnd 9428, HMSO, 1985, Table 3.72; *Social Trends*, 15, HMSO, 1984, Tables 8.16 and 8.18; *Social Trends*, 16, HMSO, 1986, Table 8.15.

One of the aims of Tory housing policy has been, simply, to restrict public housebuilding and this has been dramatically successful.

The impact on housebuilding has been dramatic, as Table 3.4 shows. Already under the Labour government, housebuilding was in decline (total public sector dwelling starts having reduced from 180,100 in 1976 to 110,900 in 1978).[34] But more was to come from the Conservatives. By 1980 total public sector housing starts were down to 59,400 and in 1981 the figure was 40,300. In 1984 the number started was 43,000.

A depressed economy also reduced private housebuilding and this declined from 161,600 in 1978 to 101,400 in 1980, but there was a revival, and starts stood at 162,000 in 1984.

Sale of council houses

The Conservatives have been long-standing advocates of selling council houses, but in the past this ambition has been thwarted, in the main, by Labour housing authorities. However, the return of the Conservatives in 1979 brought with it a more determined approach to the question. In their manifesto, the Party pledged: 'In the first session of the next Parliament we shall therefore give council and new town tenants the legal right to buy their homes.'[35]

And the Conservatives kept their word: in May 1979, for example, the secretary of state removed restrictions placed on sales by the last Labour government providing more generous discounts than ever before. And under the Housing Act 1980 'right to buy' clauses were included aimed mainly at putting pressure on Labour local authorities to sell. Tenants now needed simply to ask local authorities for the 'right to buy' form and the local authority had to comply. In 1984 discounts were raised to a new upper limit of 60 per cent for tenants of twenty-five years' standing, and local authorities were instructed to make available 100 per cent mortgages where necessary. In 1982 the average discount given by English local authorities was £7,300, representing over 40 per cent of the average market value of £17,000.[36] The case of Norwich was to show that the Conservatives meant business: here the secretary of state went to the High Court in order to obtain permission to take over the sale of council homes in that city – the effect was to force the council to administer the policy itself.

The policy is having a major impact and, indeed, has serious implications for meeting housing need in the future. The impact on the local authority housing stock is substantial. For England alone, almost 600,000 dwellings were sold between April 1979 and the end of June 1984.[37] In 1982, for example, the proportion of existing dwellings sold or leased was 4 per cent in just that one year.[38] And between 1979 and 1983 the stock of local authority or new town dwellings in the United Kingdom decreased by 56,000 from 6.84 to 6.28 million.[39] If this policy is pursued with vigour – as it will be – by the Conservatives in power throughout the 1980s, it would transform the quantity and quality of the public housing stock by 1990. And the impact would be more significant than even the figures suggest for most homes sold are houses rather than flats – in 1984, 94 per cent of sales in Great Britain were houses[40] – and these houses are more likely to be desirable ones, on the best housing estates, in suburbs rather than inner city areas.

Rent levels

Another means of reducing public expenditure is to increase the real level of public sector rents and this has been achieved: in 1978/9 gross unrebated rents, in England and Wales, were on average £5.90 per week; by 1985/6 they were £15.66. This represented an increase in real terms and thus, while rents represented 6.6 per cent of average weekly earnings in 1978/9, they comprised 8.1 per cent by 1985/6.

One major consequence of the policy of raising rents in real terms has been to bring profits into local authority housing. In general, for England and Wales, rate fund contributions to local authority housing have declined, and in some local authorities – an increasing number – housing accounts are actually in surplus and are now subsidizing the rate fund.[41]

Another consequence of the Government's rent policy is an increasing problem of rent arrears: by the end of March 1984 rent arrears in England and Wales totalled £188 million.[42]

The Conservatives introduced a new 'unified' housing benefit scheme administered by the DHSS rather than the DoE, and involving the amalgamation of supplementary housing payments and rent rebates and allowances. The former Supplementary Benefits Commission advocated such a reform, but warned that this would only be satisfactory if extra resources were available.[43] Needless to say, the Government ignored the warning and introduced a scheme of much complexity, which in many cases puzzles both administrators and householders alike.[44]

The privately rented housing sector has also been under scrutiny. Measures have been taken in order to increase rents, despite the fact that much of this property is the poorest in the country. For example, rents can now be raised every two years, instead of three, when 'fair' rents are registered. Similarly, the phasing-in periods for rent increases have been curtailed and fair rents are now also applied to some 200,000 properties which lack basic amenities which had previously been exempt from the 'fair' rent legislation and subject instead to low controlled rents. Moreover, since 1980, new types of tenure have been introduced which lack traditional security of tenure and protection against rent increases.[45]

The overall impact of Conservative housing policy is to restrict the housing opportunities of those most in need. Certainly the number of people on council waiting lists is increasing. And in some local authorities, councils have virtually stopped building. This, combined with the policy to sell council houses, represents a grim situation for those in need of council housing.

A further effect is on the quality of existing housing stock. After years of progress, brought about by the combined impact of slum clearance, new building and improvement policies, the quality of Britain's housing stock is now deteriorating at a rate which is causing grave concern. The Association of Metropolitan Authorities, for example, has predicted that one in six English dwellings will be unfit and seriously in need of repair by the mid 1980s.[46] The 1981 English House Condition Survey revealed that the number of dwellings requiring repairs costing £7,000 or more (at 1981 prices) increased by nearly 200,000 − 22 per cent − since 1976. And in 1981 1.1 million dwellings were 'unfit for human habitation' − no reduction since 1971.[47]

Health

The Conservatives have failed to hold down expenditure on health and this presents a dilemma for the Government. As Table 3.3 shows, spending on health (and personal social services) in cost terms, increased from £12.9 billion in 1979/80 to £15.1 billion in 1984/5. Yet these increases are occurring at a time when up and down the country 'cuts' are being made to the NHS. Health authorities have been struggling hard, but often unsuccessfully, to cope with the day-to-day demands of providing adequate health care. During the 1980s an increasing number of reports in national and local newspapers gave testimony to the impact of expenditure cuts on the NHS. Seldom a week goes by without some new report of a hospital facing closure, wards which have been shut, research threatened or specialist units facing the axe – and lives in danger as a result.

This paradox of increasing expenditure and 'cuts' is explained, in part, by the pressure of demographic change and the increasing numbers of frail elderly people in the community: in 1982/3 (for England) health costs per head were £965 for those aged 75 or over, against only £140 for those aged 16–64.[48] Increasing concern about the services for other groups, including the mentally ill and mentally handicapped, has grown and added to the demand on scarce resources.

The increasing use of expensive technology in medicine is an additional pressure on finances and is a further reason why health costs are rising. Moreover, the NHS is an extremely difficult institution for the Government to control, unlike, say, benefit levels or the number of council houses built each year; decisions about health expenditure are taken by thousands of doctors, nurses and other health workers in response to demands made on them by the sick. For all of these reasons, therefore, as Table 3.3 shows, the health and personal social services increased in expenditure in real terms by 17 per cent between 1979/80 and 1984/5.

In its 1982 White Paper on Public Expenditure the Government stated that: 'Plans for future health spending must, however, be formulated with strict regard to the total of public expenditure which the economy can sustain. The Government believe that the best way of meeting new needs is by increasing the efficiency of the health service.'[49] Accordingly the Government asked health authorities to contribute 'efficiency savings', which the Social Services Committee of the House of Commons expressed serious doubts about. 'If authorities save money by greater efficiency, well and good: if they do not, however, the result will be that they have fewer resources. There is some suspicion that "efficiency savings" are becoming a regular euphemism for "expenditure cuts".'[50]

The Government's plan to allow only a 1 per cent real growth in hospital and community health service expenditure can be evaluated in the context of expert opinion within the DHSS. A report in the *Financial Times* in August 1983 shows that DHSS officials calculate that demographic factors warrant an increase of nearly 1 per cent a year and that, after taking account of the impact of medical technology, spending in real terms would have to rise by at least 1.5 per cent per year to avoid slippage. Moreover, another Civil Service report estimated that expenditure increases of 2–3 per cent a year were required to secure desired improvements in treatment, both on the frontiers of medicine and for the mentally ill and mentally handicapped. The report also questioned whether efficiency savings of 0.5 per cent a year could be achieved on a sustained basis.[51]

In its 1984 Expenditure White Paper, the Government state that over the three years up to 1986/7, plans provided for growth in resources of about 1 per cent per annum, in order to allow for demographic pressures and other demands on the NHS.[52] However, the Government assume very low rates of pay increases within the NHS and their limited view of what extra resources are required to meet adequately the needs of an increasingly elderly population will mean severe pressure on the health services over the coming years.

Expenditure cutbacks have had serious effects on the quality of health care, as a number of grim reports testify. A few examples, from many available, illustrate the point. In August 1983 it was reported[53] that a London hospital, Whipps Cross, was turning away patients living outside its own self-imposed 'catchment area', in order to meet a cut of £350,000 in its budget. Later in that same month, another report described how children needing surgery for conditions ranging from hernias to ear defects and babies suffering from kidney, heart and neurological conditions were being affected by the cuts at Guy's Hospital. The head of paediatrics, Professor Robinson, commented: 'We had to restrict emergency admissions and a decision had to be made over every acutely sick child needing intensive care.' Some twenty children were reported to have been turned away in a five-week period.[54]

Elderly patients are also suffering from expenditure constraints and pressure is placed on them and their families to leave hospitals. As one hospital consultant noted: 'We are finding more and more that we are having to press reluctant relatives to take back patients.'[55] And the President of the Royal College of Nursing, which published a list of ward closures, ambulance service cuts and closures or postponements of services for the old, mentally ill and mentally handicapped, has said: 'This Government is demanding too much, too quickly; these cuts cannot be imposed without standards of care – and patients – suffering.'[56]

Another example concerns heart pacemakers. A consultant cardiologist at the Westminster Hospital spoke out about the effects of cutbacks in 1983: 'The situation is approaching where some patients will require pacemakers and will not be able to get them, and some of them will die.'[57] And, in March 1984, the Presidents of the Royal Colleges wrote to *The Times* to express their concern: 'Without adequate funding the future development of preventive medicine, health care and improvement from advances in medicine will be threatened.'[58]

Charging

There have been two significant developments in the past three years that signal a move away from the traditional concept of the NHS: increased charges and private medicine. Both represent the Government's attempt to deal with the expenditure implications of increasing demographic and medical pressures.

Britain in recent years has moved away from providing a free Health Service, open to all, regardless of income. Charges have increased substantially. Prescription charges which had stood at 20p per item since 1971 were increased by the Conservatives three times in an eighteen-month period – to 45p per item in July 1979, to 70p in April 1980, and to £1 in December 1980. After several more increases the charge was £2.20 in 1986.

Dental charges too have been increased significantly. Between May 1979 and April 1985 the maximum charge for routine dental treatment increased from £5 to £17 plus 40 per cent over that figure. For more complicated treatment, the maximum charges have increased from £30 maximum in May 1979 to £115 in April 1985. There can be no doubt that such steep charges deter some from seeking treatment. The British Dental Association commissioned a Gallup poll to ask a representative sample of people: 'Within the past year did you ever put off arranging a dental check-up because of what you might have to pay for your treatment?' The results showed that 18 per cent of women had delayed check-ups, compared with 11 per cent of men, and 17 per cent of class DE, against 11 per cent of class AB. As the Association states '. . . it must surely be a matter of concern that more than one adult in seven is delaying dental treatment because of cost.'[59] Similarly, optical charges have increased. Maximum charges for lenses were £15.15 in May 1979, but stood at £16.50 in April 1984. Moreover, the Government intended to 'end the general supply of NHS glasses, other than to exempt groups'.[60] (Since July 1986 these groups have been provided with spectacle vouchers.)

For all family practitioner services, the clear strategy is to increase income from charges as a proportion of total expenditure and this is succeeding: in 1978/9, income from all health charges represented £144 million: by 1988/9 it will be an estimated £530 million.[61]

Private medicine

The growth of private medicine represents one of the most serious – and sinister – features of Tory social policy. The number of subscribers to private medical insurance increased by 16 per cent in 1979; 26 per cent in 1980; and 13 per cent in 1981. During 1982 the increase was much smaller – just over 3 per cent – and in 1984 it was 3 per cent. However, the overall development has been significant: 'By the end of 1984 nearly 4.4 million people were covered by private medical insurance – nearly 8 per cent of the population. This compares with 1.6 million in 1966.'[62] In 1982, 23 per cent of professionals were covered by private medical insurance, against only 2–3 per cent of unskilled manual workers.

The boom in private health insurance has not been sustained in recent years: the sector is still growing, but the growth rate declined. Faced with the slowing down of membership and rising costs in 1982, the major provident associations sought government help to boost 'private' medicine. As reported in *The Times*, they were pressing the Government for tax reliefs on premiums at least for those over 75. Derek Deamerell, Chief Executive of the British United Provident Association, said that 'If the Government really want to see growth continue some sort of incentive has got to be applied.'[63]

The general trend towards private medicine has not only been welcomed by the Conservative government, but actively encouraged. In 1982, for example, the then Minister of Health, Dr Gerard Vaughan, said that he would like to see private health expand to provide a quarter of all health care: 'It would be very nice if we got to something like three-quarters State and a quarter from the private sector.'[64]

The Conservative administration have abolished the Health Services Board which was charged with the responsibility of removing pay beds from the NHS. They have also relaxed controls on the development of private hospitals and encouraged the health authorities to use the private sector. Consultants' contracts have been renegotiated so that they can undertake private work without losing their NHS salary and also Civil Servants have been circulated with offers of private health insurance at special rates.[65]

Early in this administration, the Conservatives ceased taxing individuals on the premium paid by employers for private health insurance. At present, however, only those earning below £8,500 are exempt from tax and there is pressure to abolish this limit. Certain NHS services, including cleaning, have also been privatized – a move which has caused much concern about standards.

Britain under the Tories has experienced some modest increases in real expenditure. However, given demographic and other pressures, the NHS is in a poor state of health in the mid 1980s, and both increasing charges and the growth of private medicine are poisoning the principle of a free, universal health service. These two developments are also significant for what they indicate for the future: the NHS has seen nothing yet. The promise of Mrs Thatcher that 'The NHS is safe with us'[66] was the most unassuring reassurance in the history of British social policy.

Personal social services

After a period of real growth following the Seebohm Report and the creation of social services departments, personal social services are now facing serious financial constraints at a time when the economic recession and cutbacks in other areas of policy are adding to the workload of social services staff. Moreover, demographic trends continue to challenge the ability of departments to provide adequate services. In particular, as with the NHS, the increasing numbers of frail, elderly people in the community have particular implications for demand and expenditure: in 1982/3 for England, the estimated expenditure per head for personal social services among the over-75s was £305 compared with only £50 for the population as a whole.[67] In addition, an increased recognition of the needs of the mentally ill and handicapped, and concern about children at risk, all combine to put intensive pressure on overstretched statutory services.

What has happened to expenditure on personal social services since the 1979 election? In brief, the story is one of successive attempts by the DHSS to curb spending, attempts which have been, in part, successfully thwarted by local authorities. However, despite overall growth in most areas, some services have been cut, and the future could be bleak.

In the Government's 1980 White Paper on Public Expenditure it stated 'for 1980/81 the assumed level of current expenditure is 4½ per cent below that for 1978/79. In subsequent years annual growth is 2 per cent, sufficient to maintain the level of services for the increasing numbers of elderly and of children in care.'[68] However, in 1980/81, expenditure was, in fact, higher (by 3.4 per cent in real terms) than that for previous years. And the next expenditure White Paper, for 1981, was ambiguous in its wording, seeming to argue both the need for restraint and recognizing the pressure on services:

The figures for both current and capital expenditure in future years reflects the Government's call for additional savings in overall local authority spending. It is, however, for local authorities themselves to determine the actual level of expenditure of individual services recognising for example demographic pressures arising from the increasing number of elderly people in the population, and the need to protect as far as possible services for the most vulnerable.[69]

While the Government has recognized demographic pressures on budgets, it is becoming clear that, in reality, the sums allowed for this are inadequate and also that increasing costs within personal social services are far outstripping the 2 per cent increase suggested by the DHSS as necessary for demographic change. Therefore as Webb and Wistow have argued in one study: '... even a constant rate of growth can involve cuts in service cover nationally if, as seems likely, the 2% rate of growth failed fully to reflect increases in needs'.[70] And the evidence shows that services are being affected. Thus for 1980/81 only five out of eighteen services were unaffected by the cuts: 'Residential services for all client groups, except for mentally handicapped, were reduced, as were most community care services.'[71] This evidence backs up the concern of the Association of Directors of Social Services, expressed in 1980, that: 'Further cuts may well foreshorten the lives of the elderly.'[72]

As for the future, it seems uncertain that local authorities will be able to thwart continuously the plans of central government to cut services. As the most authoritative study of this subject has recently concluded:

the real crisis could yet be to come. A continuation of the general pressure on local government expenditure must soon undermine the ability of local authorities to protect the PSS. Assuming that the easy adjustments have been made, cuts in existing service and in service cover would become inevitable in a service in which all clients fall within the 'most vulnerable' category.[73]

A detailed study of personal social services shows how they have failed to keep pace with the growing number of elderly people in the community. While the elderly population aged 65 and over increased by 9.9 per cent between 1975/6 and 1982/3 (and the population aged 75 and over by 21.7 per cent) services fell behind. Although, in absolute numbers, home helps and meals on wheels grew, in real terms they *declined*. Measured against each 1,000 of the population aged 75 and over, the number in residential care declined by 14 per cent; and home helps and meals on wheels by over 13 per cent.[74] Provision for the elderly has failed, by a large measure, to keep pace with population growth. So much for the rhetoric of community care.

Financial constraints inevitably distort provision. Thus cutbacks in building will mean fewer places in residential homes for the elderly, while the cost of institutional care for children may mean that some children will be given foster care as an alternative, despite this lessening the chances of a return to their natural parents.[75] More generally, pressures on social services departments' budgets mean that not enough attention will be given to supporting parents with difficulties and the child may thus be removed – too quickly – from home into care. The judgement as to when and whether to remove a child from his or her own home is too difficult already for it to be influenced by budgetary imperatives.

And yet, the chairman of the inquiry into the death of 2-year-old Lucy Gates, in 1982, warned in his report that: 'If in the present economic climate more money cannot be made available for supporting families at risk in their own homes, then, if these children are to be safeguarded more may have to be separated from their parents.'[76]

Disturbing evidence has also come to light to show just how shallow is Britain's policy of 'community care' for mentally ill people. A series of articles in *The Times* showed that in practice an increasing number of mentally ill people were simply left to wander the streets without care or support. John Wilder, the Chairman of the Psychiatric Rehabilitation Centre, commmented that some 'end up on the streets, or struggling to get by with their families. Sooner or later, if they are not helped in time, they commit suicide or die of exposure.'[77] The closure of up to one-third of Britain's mental hospitals will, it is feared by professionals, add to the problem. And Dr Patrick Campbell, a hospital consultant, stated: 'My fear is that many of those already discharged have disappeared on

to the streets, or live in appalling squalor because of community neglect.
Now the hard rump are to go, and I cannot see any way to prevent the
same thing happening to them.'[78]

The social services have the task of coping with society's victims and
those in need of the most help. In recent years a number of groups with
particular needs increased dramatically in numbers. These include the
unemployed, the very elderly and one parent families. Providing an
efficient patch-up squad is hardly an adequate response to these trends,
but starved of adequate resources it will not even be efficient, and the
results of inefficiency will be the most tragic victims of the 1980s, when
the Government sought to walk by on the other side.

Education

The Conservative government has looked to the vital area of education
to make substantial expenditure cuts. Education and science received
almost £13 billion in 1979/80, but only £13.1 billion five years later in
1984/5 – and the amount is planned to decline to only £12.1 billion by
1987/8. As in other areas local authorities have had different ideas, and
their own spending patterns have thwarted the Government's aims to
some extent.

Schools

By happy coincidence for the Conservative government, the determination to reduce expenditure occurs at a time of falling school rolls and
this provides a handy camouflage for financial objectives. It has enabled
the closing of some schools and the reduction in the number of teachers.
However, it is indicative of this administration's approach to education
that the pupil–teacher ratio at 17.8 in 1984/5 is to remain at approximately the same level up to 1987. In Scotland the ratio is actually on
the *increase* from 17.0 in 1983/4 to 17.8 by 1988/9.[79] Thus, far from
using the opportunity of falling school numbers to reduce the ratio and
to improve educational standards, the number of teachers employed in

the school system is declining dramatically: the number was, for England, 441,000 in 1978/9, 406,000 in 1984/5 and is planned to reduce to between 386,000–390,000 in 1987/8. For Scotland and Wales, it is a similar story.[80]

The under-5s are subject to serious constraint in expenditure, and gone are the hopes of increasing provision in this most crucial area. Moreover, the Conservative government was embarrassed by the discovery that, under the 1944 Act, local education authorities could not close nursery schools as they had a statutory duty to provide schools for those under 5. The Government acted quickly to remove such a duty and, through the Education Act 1980, merely gave local authorities *power* to establish and maintain nursery schools. Thus the stage is set for a State retreat from pre-school education.

Expenditure constraints have had a marked effect on school books and equipment. For example, in 1984/5, £2 million less was spent on books than in 1983/4.[81] Moreover, it was revealed in the *Sunday Times* in 1980 that at least thirty-three local educational authorities were paying more for children to attend public schools than on books for children in their own secondary schools.[82] One effect of expenditure cuts is that parents are being asked to pay for books and other items of equipment. Indeed, the former education secretary, Mark Carlisle, encouraged this by saying that he was 'a believer in the 50–50 system, whereby the community pay up a certain amount of money and the State puts up a certain amount of money'. He told a conference of head teachers that parents should be encouraged to help pay for their children's books and other school resources.[83]

The Government's own school inspectors have voiced their concern about the effect of expenditure cuts on school standards. In a forthright report for the year 1981 the inspectors showed just how serious was the deterioration of the education service as a result of expenditure cutbacks.[84]

Widening inequalities The report noted that 'there are growing differences in access to education both for comparable pupils and for pupils with different needs. Both the academically able and the less academic, particularly the slow learners, are affected in some degree, the latter more obviously than the former and at every stage from the primary school to the sixth-form.'

Falling standards For primary schools, the inspectors stated that 'it is unlikely that existing standards, particularly in numeracy and literacy, will be maintained or that it will be possible to achieve comparable educational standards in all primary schools. It is even less likely that they will be able to secure improvement or implement new policies.'

Curriculum reduction 'In over one-third of the authorities, and especially in the shire counties, district inspectors report changes in the curriculum for secondary school pupils in the form of reduction in the ranges of courses offered. These changes affected pupils of all abilities to some extent but particularly the less able.'

School books 'Shortages of text-books and deficiencies in school libraries affect particularly the setting of appropriate homework and may generally diminish the pupils' part in their own learning.'

The less able 'District inspectors report that in twelve LEAs [local education authorities] sixth-form courses have been cut back, particularly, but not only, those designed for the less academic pupils.'

Parents' financial contributions The inspectors also show how the principle of the free education system is being undermined. 'In virtually all LEAs parents are contributing to schools in cash, kind or labour, to an increasing extent.' In some authorities such funds were being used for the purchase of books. The inspectors concluded that 'This trend is leading to marked disparities of provision between schools serving affluent and poor areas.'

Teacher reductions Within primary schools, the report noted that 'Increasingly when teachers leave, they are either not replaced or are replaced by teachers on short-term contracts or by redeployed teachers who may not fit the school's needs in terms of curricular cover or the age and ability range of the pupils to be taught.'

The inspectors reached a clear overall conclusion: 'these characteristics add up to a serious threat to the maintenance of standards and to desirable improvements'.

School meals

The school meals service has been decisively reduced and has been a major victim of cuts. The charges for school meals have been dramatically increased. Although in several areas the local education authorities have continued to subsidize school meals at a significant level, real expenditure decreased by 35 per cent between 1979/80 and 1984/5.[85]

The Education Act 1980 removed the duties of local authorities under the 1944 Education Act and subsequent regulations to provide meals of a standard price and of a prescribed nutritional standard for all school students, and to provide free school meals for needy children. Rather, the new Act leaves local authorities free as to what to provide and how much to charge for it. Schools now need only to make available at midday, without charge, a meal for children whose parents are in receipt of supplementary benefit or Family Income Supplement, 'such provision ... as appears to the authority to be requisite'. As a consequence it is estimated that some 174,000 children lost their entitlement to free school meals.[86]

More generally, the impact of rising school meal charges, and falling standards, has been to decrease dramatically the number of meals in total being served in schools. The number of pupils receiving school meals declined from 4.8 million in 1978, for England, to 3.5 million by 1980, a level it approximately maintained in 1983. This means that, whereas 64 per cent of English pupils received a meal in 1978, this was true for only 51 per cent in 1983. The proportion of pupils receiving a *free* meal has however increased from less than 14 per cent in 1978 to 17.4 per cent by 1983, as a result of the recession increasing the number of families dependent on supplementary benefits.[87]

Many have voiced their concerns about the effect of school meal charges on nutritional standards and thus on the health of Britain's schoolchildren. This is associated with a trend towards the privatization of school meal provision. Moreover, the stationing of ice cream vans and hot dog stalls outside Britain's schools has become part of the architecture of Tory education policy.

Higher education

A further vulnerable area is higher education. The Government is now actively planning for the 'contraction of higher education', as the 1982 Expenditure White Paper puts it.[88] Adequately qualified young people are now being turned away from university. Entrants to higher education, as a proportion of those with qualifications, declined from 87.1 per cent in 1981/2 to 83.3 per cent in 1984/5.[89]

The concern to reduce opportunities for youngsters to go to university is leading to several thousand redundancies among university staff. Huge sums of money are being paid out in redundancy payments under a special scheme. Thus at one extreme, a professor or senior lecturer aged 49 with twenty-four years' service would receive an immediate £55,000 plus a pension on reaching 65 of just over £4,500 per annum and a further sum of nearly £14,000.[90] Government has announced that it is to give the University Grants Committee £50 million to help to meet the cost of redundancies. This is in addition to the £10 million already set aside by the Committee.[91] Thus the nation is having to devote substantial resources to destroying part of its education system. Such is the financial logic for a Government that has turned its back on Britain's future.[92]

Social security

Social security has been a further victim of Tory policy. This government has taken every opportunity to cut back on the value of benefits paid and this at a time when the impact of recession has made more individuals and their families dependent on social security.

Social security has presented the Conservatives with severe difficulties, however. It is not an easy budget to reduce substantially: many groups have statutory rights to benefits of different kinds and there is no easy means of controlling access to these. Moreover, even apart from the recession, demographic and social factors are increasing the number of people, particularly the elderly and one parent families, who are dependent on social security. The Conservatives have done well however, given their objectives, to cut benefit levels whenever they could get away with it. This can be demonstrated by looking at three important groups of the population: elderly people, children, and those dependent on unemployment or supplementary benefit.

Elderly people The elderly have been among those most hit by cutbacks. One of the earliest acts of this government was to de-index the link between pensions and earnings: from November 1980 pensions are only protected against price inflation. The effect of this has been significant. Thus, comparing the pension for a married couple at November 1985 with the rate that would have applied if pensions had increased in line with average earnings, the amount is £61.30 against £63.45 that should have been due – a weekly equivalent of £2.15.[93]

Children The young have also been hit by Conservative measures. The most significant 'cut' here has been in the real value of child benefits for most of the Tory years due to the lack of commitment to increase it in line with inflation. In November 1985, for example, the benefit increased by just one-third of inflation. Among those out of work, families with children have suffered from a decision in 1980 to change the method used for up-rating the child additions awarded to those dependent on National Insurance benefits. Since then those on such benefits have received child additions which have not kept up with inflation. For those on unemployment benefit, they have gone altogether, and such families now have to draw more of their income from means-tested supplementary benefit. As one commentator noted: 'To refer to this process as an anomaly is over-charitable: the Government is deliberately fiddling the figures.'[94]

The unemployed The unemployed and those dependent on benefits have been hit particularly hard by Tory measures. These include cuts in the real value of short-term benefits and invalidity benefits by 5 per cent. This was only restored in November 1983. In addition, unemployment and supplementary benefits paid to the unemployed have been taxed since 1982. In general, policy changes have resulted in the unemployed losing several pounds a week. In addition to these reductions there has been the abolition of the earnings-related supplement to unemployment and other short-term benefits as from January 1982. For those qualifying for this benefit, the loss is substantial – an average of over £11 per week in 1982.[95]

The above brief description demonstrates the impact of Conservative social security measures on some major groups in the population. However, there have been other changes too, for example, responsibility for sickness payments has been transferred to employers for the first twenty-eight weeks of sickness. Consequently, the estimated number receiving sickness benefit by 1987/8 will be 40,000 compared to 395,000 in 1982/3.[96] Also a new structure of supplementary benefits has been introduced and an estimated 1.75 million people are worse off as a result.[97] In addition, in order to cut administration costs, child benefits for new mothers are now paid monthly in arrears. In all, it has been estimated that Conservative 'cuts' to the social security budget total approximately £2 billion.[98]

The most significant impact of the Conservative government on social security, however, was not so much the cuts in benefits – important though they were – but rather the fact that more people became dependent on such benefits during these years. Thus the number drawing unemployment benefits rose from 550,000 in 1979/80 to 965,000 in 1985/6.[99] And unemployment also swelled the numbers dependent on supplementary benefit. For those below pensionable age the numbers receiving supplementary benefit totalled 1.2 million in 1979/80 and the total was over 3 million in 1985/6. Altogether, including both pensioners and younger claimants, the number of people receiving supplementary benefit rose above 4 million for the first time during the Conservative years.[100]

Overall, the Conservative years have been poor years for a growing number of families. The Government has released less information about low incomes, but the little that there is shows the trend: between 1979 and 1983 the number of families in, or on the margins of, poverty (with incomes less than 40 per cent above the supplementary benefits level) increased from 1.1 to 1.9 million and the children in such families numbered 2.4 million in 1979, but 3.9 million by 1983. The totals affected must be considerably higher in the mid 1980s.[101] And more children were living in families subject to the means test. In 1979, 1.2 million children were in families drawing either supplementary benefit or FIS; by 1982 it was over 2.4 million. The proportion of children affected by these means tests has doubled since 1979.[102]

The future

So far in this chapter, the major areas of social policy have been discussed and the impact of specific Conservative measures briefly assessed. After more than six years of Tory government what does the balance sheet look like? What is the character of Tory social politics? How radical will Conservative social policy be in the future? And what will be the wider impact on society? This chapter concludes by discussing these questions.

The Government's economic strategy has clearly been a failure. Its only success has been to reduce substantially the rate of inflation and this is really only indicative of the general depression within the economy at large. While ministers try hard to point to an economic revival, it is record levels of unemployment, the collapse of much industry, and bankruptcies that have become the key indicators of the new monetarism.

What of the Government's social strategy? This is in very much better shape, and while the New Right have had many disappointments and are impatient for further onslaughts on the traditional Welfare State, from the Tory perspective important progress has been made in recent years and the scene is now set for further advancement.

Not all commentators would agree with this view,[103] and they would point to record levels of public expenditure and real increases in expenditure on the NHS to show that, despite the rhetoric, Thatcher's social policy is not so dissimilar from that of previous Conservative (or even Labour) governments. Some 'wets' within the Cabinet take comfort from this kind of analysis. These commentators would dismiss the possibility that any of the radical suggestions for dismantling the Welfare State – for example a major advance towards private medicine – are serious starters.

This analysis is not only complacent but is seriously misleading. The evidence in the real world – families suffering from unemployment, the effect of health cuts, higher rents and pressures on school budgets – reveals a more alarming picture than some academic analysts seem to see when studying the distribution of percentage points in government Blue Books. The attack on public housing has been a major success for the Tory government. Also, the contraction of the school meals service and the introduction of penal prescription charges are only two more direct hits which can be pointed to. Moreover, expenditure constraints within both the Health Service and the education system are undoubtedly convincing many people that the State system is not for them and they are turning instead to the private sector. The proposed decimation of State Earnings Related Pensions is the latest indicator of Tory intent. In addition, the general ideology of this Government and its contempt for the public service, and for those working within it, has seriously undermined morale and has contributed to a view that somehow the Welfare State is an outdated institution which needs to be replaced by something new and fresh for the future.

Tory social strategy

It is possible to point to a clear Tory social strategy and this needs to be emphasized as a complement to the anger and frustration up and down the country about specific cuts and threats to particular services and institutions. Public opinion will only be mobilized effectively in favour of a just social policy if these particular frustrations can be seen in the wider context that is emerging.

What is the nature of Conservative social strategy? As noted earlier it is a move towards a 'residual welfare state' to use Titmuss's term, that is one: '... based on the premise that there are two "natural" (or socially given) channels through which an individual's needs are properly met; the private market and the family. Only when these break down should social welfare institutions come into play and then only temporarily.'[104] It has a number of distinct characteristics. First, a belief that the role of the State in human welfare should be minimal, that for the majority of citizens, the provision of health care, education, housing, pensions and welfare should be by the private sector with the State's role confined to those – the weak, the very frail, the destitute and the irresponsible – who cannot be so provided for. It follows that State services that are available should be less well-resourced than those available privately. The Poor Law principle of 'less eligibility' has returned with a vengeance in the 1980s. Moreover, the Government says that access to State services and benefits should, wherever feasible, be guarded by a means test and charges should be levied. In past years more people have come under the means test, and charges in such diverse areas as health, school meals, housing, welfare and recreation have been increased substantially.

The second characteristic of Tory social policy in the 1980s is the encouragement of alternative sources of welfare provision, and this centres around the ideological trinity of private market, voluntary sector and the family. Over the last six years private medicine has expanded significantly, aided and abetted by the Government. Similarly, State apparatus and new legislation has enabled private markets to make substantial inroads into public housing and, via the Assisted Places Scheme, into State education.

The voluntary sector has also been encouraged by this administration. Indeed, the prime minister apparently seeks to revise the respective roles of the State and voluntary bodies in a modern society, having declared: 'I believe that the voluntary movement is at the heart of all our social welfare provisions. That the statutory services are the supportive ones underpinning, where necessary, filling the gaps and helping the helper.'[105]

Finally, there is the family, with a significant role to play in the programme of a Conservative leader who once declared, 'We are the Party of the family.'[106] Given the public expenditure costs of pre-school education and, more significantly, the provision of services for the elderly, 'family care', which in reality nearly always means female care, has a crucial role to play if the Government's economic objectives are to be achieved. Quite simply, with the woman's place in the home, State services can contract (or at least hold steady).

Barriers to success

Before considering the future development of Tory social strategy, it is useful to consider why it has not made more progress since 1979. The Conservatives have certainly found that there have been some substantial obstacles barring the way to the achievement of a residual Welfare State. This is, in part, the story of the complex number of factors that determine the nature of social policy and public spending on it. First, the Government's ambitions have been thwarted by demographic pressures. A rapidly ageing population, and in particular the growth in numbers of those over the age of 75, have put severe pressures on social security, health and welfare budgets. While individual cutbacks can be carried out – and have been – the pressures of demography are a serious handicap to any government wishing to wield the axe on public spending.

Second, there are many services which react to the 'demand' of consumers. The NHS is a major example here and it is clearly difficult for government, in Whitehall, to restrict expenditure decisions which are in practice taken by tens of thousands of individual professionals, and workers, in a wide variety of institutions, in response to the needs of millions of patients.

Third, much of the Welfare State is based on legislation, some of it dating back several decades. Any reforming government has to amend or abolish this legislation if major changes are to be made. The Tory government has not been backward in making some major legislative changes, but these have often provoked both Parliamentary and public opposition and put the spotlight on what is going on. It is therefore far easier for government to tackle those areas of policy, which depend not on legislation but on rules and regulations. Thus subtle, and often very complex, changes have been made to supplementary benefit provisions which are not easily understood by the public, but which have major effects on poor claimants and achieve spending reductions.

A fourth point – and a very important one – is that many parts of the Welfare State – education, personal social services, public transport and housing – are in effect determined and implemented by local government. A detailed reading of the Public Expenditure White Papers issued by this Conservative government in part reveals the story of central government expenditure ambitions thwarted by determined local authorities, often Labour controlled. The Conservatives' desire to cut back on the spending programme within personal social services, to take one important example, has been seriously undermined by decisions taken by scores of local authorities. The contemporary history of public transport policy provides another major example here. Several of the new breed of Labour local authorities have been determined to revitalize public transport and to charge fares which ordinary people can afford. This policy goes right against the grain for current Tory ambitions and for this and other reasons the whole future of local government has been placed in doubt during the early 1980s.

A fifth factor has been the quite unprecedented amount of 'leaking' of secret Government papers by concerned public officials during these years. This may have thwarted the development and implementation of radical attacks on social policy. The leak of papers from the Central

Policy Review Staff, the Family Policy Group papers, and a whole range of documents relating to social security cuts and other proposals have seriously embarrassed the Government and have alerted a range of groups – Tory wets, the Labour Opposition and the public at large – to the possibilities of further onslaughts on the Welfare State. The vicious sentence of imprisonment for leaking documents relating to the political presentation of cruise missile deployment meted out to Sarah Tisdall really represented the Establishment's vengeance for a whole series of leaks, as did the unsuccessful prosecution of Clive Ponting. Like the jury in that case, many individuals were not prepared to accept that the interests of the Conservative government were necessarily to be equated with the interests of the State.

Finally, and of great importance, there has been the clear evidence of public concern about the effects of Conservative social policies. Earlier, it was argued that back in 1979 the Conservatives seized the initiative on social policy and were able to present a package of proposals, policies and prejudices that seemed to be in tune with the public mood. After several years of experience of Conservative social politics, the mood has changed or rather, perhaps, it is now clear that the public is in fact very anxious to preserve certain parts of the Welfare State, not least the NHS. For example, in September 1985, a Gallup poll showed that 80 per cent of respondents thought that the Government was spending too little on the NHS. Also, in February 1985 Gallup found that 59 per cent favoured more public expenditure on services, even if it meant higher taxes. Only 16 per cent wanted to see tax cuts even if it meant cutting services.[107] It is within this context of a number of formidable barriers to a successful implementation of Tory social strategy that we need to consider the likely development of future policy.

Future policy?

To date, the Conservative social strategy has made significant progress and is certainly intact. However, from the viewpoint of the administration itself, and from its monetarist vanguard, there have been serious disappointments. As Leon Brittan noted in September 1982: 'This Government has been more successful in applying brakes than most but even we have not yet been able to put the machine into reverse' and he added, ominously, 'radical options have not been ruled out.'[108]

Indeed they have not, as two major leaks of Government papers showed. If confirmation were needed that Tory intentions for the Welfare State involved a drastic transformation, it came in a paper from the Central Policy Review Staff, the Cabinet Office 'Think Tank'. This paper was circulated with other Cabinet documents on 7 September 1982 and was leaked to *The Economist*, which noted that 'it came with the seal of approval of the Treasury, which recommended that it form the basis of a six-month study of public spending strategy for the rest of the decade'.[109]

Education Ideas included the end of State funding of higher education. Instead, fees would be set at market rates – £12,000 for the average three-year course. Some 300,000 State scholarships could be made available, together with student loans for those with entry qualifications but without scholarships. The Central Policy Review Staff document also said there would be great savings if the State no longer had to provide for primary and secondary school education, but recognized the political difficulties of abolishing State schooling. However, it considered a move to a system of educational vouchers for parents, which they could cash at schools of their choice to pay for their children's education. But the Think Tank was doubtful whether vouchers would cut State spending. However, savings would be made by allowing teacher–pupil ratios to rise.

Social Security Savings would be made if all social security payments – including pensions – were no longer index linked with inflation.

National Health Service The document suggested replacing the NHS with private health insurance. This could save £3–£4 billion a year out of the 1982/3 Budget of £10 billion. There might be a need for a compulsory minimum of private insurance for everyone. Meanwhile, savings could be made by charging for visits to the doctor and more for drugs.

In another paper for the same Cabinet meeting, the Chancellor of the Exchequer, Sir Geoffrey Howe, argued that a failure to shift spending on social policy would have severe consequences for the Government's fiscal strategy.

While those concerned with the Government's image were quick to argue that the Central Policy Review Staff report had no real official status and was of little consequence, it was no aberration. Rather, it simply became the most quoted evidence from a long line of indications that many within the Conservative Party wished to destroy Britain's Welfare State. Thus the Chancellor's deputy, the Chief Secretary to the Treasury, Mr Leon Brittan, had some months earlier argued that while 'some minimal level [of social provision] has to be provided' . . . 'we have to begin to rethink both the way that the basic services are financed and delivered *and* the way that people choose, and Government provide, services above the basic level'. And his own conclusion was clear: 'An answer in health, as in education and other services, may be to try to create a greater variety and flexibility in provision, to allow and to foster a great variety in financing methods and delivery systems'. He felt that there might be scope for 'public and private facilities coexisting and supplementing each other, together with an increased reliance on private insurance, vouchers and the like'.[110]

The leaking of the Central Policy Review Staff document to *The Economist* proved to be a major political embarrassment and one which Mrs Thatcher was quick to try and smother. Again, *The Economist* provides the background – 'On Friday, 1 October Downing Street briefed Sunday newspaper correspondents on Mrs Thatcher's supposed reaction to the Think Tank. She was said to be against its report and had shelved it. Several Sunday and Monday papers carried a story along these lines.'[111] The *Observer*, for example, on 3 October headlined its story 'Mrs T is angry at cuts hint'.

The Conservative Party was anxious to close down the public debate, not least because its own Party Conference was about to open in Brighton and it would be a major break with Tory tradition if their own

Party Conference was to have a full, frank and critical debate about policy. Yet the argument would not go away and the background story in *The Economist* reveals that Mrs Thatcher's anger was more about the publicity given to the Central Policy Review Staff document than with the major thrust of its proposals. And, while Tory 'wets' were able to prevent discussion of the paper at the Cabinet meeting, it was clear that hardliners in the Cabinet, including Mrs Thatcher, meant to return to the issue.

Confirmation that wild ideas were still very much on the Cabinet agenda came in February 1983 when the papers from the Family Policy Group were leaked to the *Guardian*.[112] Some of the Group's more whimsical ideas gained notoriety overnight – training children to manage their pocket money and encouraging banks and schools to look for further ways to promote saving – but the papers revealed a determination to recast radically the Welfare State. The ideas being discussed within the Group included encouraging mothers to stay at home; and the encouragement of families to provide more care: 'what more can be done to encourage families ... to reassume responsibilities taken on by the State'. The papers also revealed a strict approach to State pensions: 'enable individuals to have more responsibility for their own pensions'. The leaking of the Family Policy Group papers provoked both derision and strong opposition and, once again, the Government was left in an embarrassing situation. However, the Central Policy Review Staff documents and the Family Policy Group papers show the high-level attention that has been given to the question of social policy within the Conservative government. It demonstrates that it was trying to learn the lessons of its first term in office. How to reduce public expenditure on social services substantially? That is the question for the future and the Government's determination to provide an answer is undermining Britain's Welfare State in the 1980s.

During the general election campaign of 1983 – and unlike the one in 1979 – the future of the Welfare State loomed large as an issue, although the Labour Party failed to make it a key factor in the minds of the electorate. However, a series of stories, based on leaked official documents, appeared in the *Guardian* and *Time Out* which raised a number of fears about the future of social policy. Although some of the leaked documents were clearly simply floating proposals, which might not (in some cases would not) be implemented, their effect was to fluster the Conservative government and force a number of denials from Conservative leaders. Thus, we often heard during the campaign that the NHS was safe with the Conservatives.

Since the 1983 election, however, there have been clear signs that the Conservative government is anxious to reassess the Welfare State and that they are taking a long-term view of it. For example in January 1984, in an interview she gave to the *New York Times*, Mrs Thatcher said that Britain faced a 'time bomb' over social security spending. She said she would not sit by and 'do nothing' about the cost of pensions and the NHS.[113] The present Chancellor of the Exchequer, Nigel Lawson, is a major ally of Mrs Thatcher in terms of her social policy objectives and he is likely to be tougher-minded about public expenditure than his immediate predecessor.

Social Security reform

The Government's reviews of social security[114] and subsequent legislation are further indications of the Conservative administration's overall strategy and, if successfully implemented, would represent a decisive break with the past in some important areas. The reviews were much-trumpeted as 'the most fundamental reappraisal of the Welfare State since Beveridge' and can be seen, in part, as a more systematic and determined drive to produce the changes that both the Central Policy Review Staff review and the Family Policy Group were seeking. However, any suggestion that they were indeed fundamental reviews can be quickly dismissed. They were not based, for example, on any thorough appraisal of crucial social trends since Beveridge's time and, hence, some key issues – about divorce and care within the family, for example – were ignored. Moreover, by dividing the social security field into traditional territory – pensions, housing benefits, child support and supplementary benefit – the reviews were, from the start, set on a narrow path and some key issues were avoided.

· Particularly absurd was the separation of social security from parallel debates about personal taxation policy. Some important questions, such as the future of the married man's tax allowance, were therefore not integrated into thinking about the future of child support, to take just one illustration. The omissions were made obvious when the Government published a second Green Paper on family taxation in 1986. It should also be noted that the reviews, despite their ostensibly 'public' nature, were dominated by ministers themselves, their political supporters and allies in the private sector.

What will be the impact of the new proposals? In practice they are a curious mixture of administrative convenience, mean-minded expenditure cuts and clear attempts to reduce living standards, both now and in the future. Most important is the decision to reduce the role and scope of the State Earnings Related Pension Scheme, a far from egalitarian measure when it was introduced originally but one nevertheless which did offer certain groups the prospect of better pensions in retirement – particularly those on low incomes, many women, and disabled people – the very categories who are, and always will be, ill-served by the private pension industry.

Regarding supplementary benefits, it is not so much the structure that is wrong with the new proposals, but the implementation. The Government propose a new system of Income Support to replace supplementary benefits. This will have regard to special groups – pensioners, families, single parent families and the long-term sick and disabled – through the payment of premiums. The existing system of weekly extras will be scrapped. Income Support, states the Green Paper: '. . . will provide people with a reasonable level of income which they will be responsible for managing as they will. The system will not provide in detail for every variation in individual circumstances.'[115] Now in theory this is the right strategy: the poor should not have to rely on extras to maintain a minimum living standard, particularly when this involves divulging detailed, and often personal, facts about their lives. But this will only work if the basic benefit is adequate, and substantially more than the existing level of supplementary benefit. In practice, Income Support will not be adequate, nor could it be given the cost-cutting nature of this reform. In these circumstances the abolition of weekly additions will provoke real hardship. Moreover, the proposal to establish a new Social Fund 'to provide for the exceptional circumstances and emergencies faced by a minority of claimants and to help those who find difficulty in managing their resources and budgeting'[116] implies a return to Victorian values with a vengeance. Poor people need cash, not counselling.

The Government's review process was heavy with rumour that child benefits would be means-tested. In the event the Government backed away from their convictions in this area, doubtless put off by the adverse reaction to this leaked proposal: the 'Party of the family' had second thoughts and, indeed, proclaimed: 'The principle that we should give financial support to those who bear the extra responsibility of bringing up children is one to which this Government are committed.'[117] Again, however, the practice is crucial. And, following the review, the up-rating for child benefit, from November 1985, from £6.85 to £7 was a mere one-third of inflation. The stage is therefore set for a slow, but decisive, deterioration of child benefit in the future: indeed if the level is maintained at just one-third of inflation, the real value of child benefit would reduce by one-quarter over five years, 40 per cent over ten.[118]

Other 'family support' proposals are equally worrying. Instead of Family Income Supplement there will be a new Family Credit. Unlike Family Income Supplement (that was drawn by mothers at the Post Office) the new Credit will be paid by employers and therefore go to the father in two parent families. This redistribution of income within low income families from 'purse to wallet' will be exacerbated by the withdrawal of free school meals (and welfare food) from such families. The mothers in poor families, who bear the brunt of making ends meet, will lose the right to draw Family Income Supplement and have the new burden of paying for, or making up, school meals.* The result will be a major redistribution of resources away from mothers in poor families. In addition, those currently above the Family Income Supple-

* In July 1986, and at the eleventh hour, the Government gave way to pressure and announced that mothers would after all receive Family Credit.

ment level who nevertheless qualify for free school meals for their children will now lose this entitlement.

How radical will the Tory Cabinet be on other aspects of social policy? On the more optimistic side, it seems likely that some of the more harebrained schemes, such as the introduction of educational vouchers, have been ruled out, partly because of their impracticality and partly because of likely popular resistance. However, even here, Mrs Thatcher has recently spoken in support of such a scheme. Similarly, the public support for the NHS, and the way in which Tory politicians have been forced into a defence of it by the Labour Opposition, might make it difficult for major restructuring in that direction. Nevertheless, the DHSS has plans to reform general practitioner services and to encourage the development of private practice. High prescription charges are an important move away from a free, universal health service. There are likely to be others.

Since the Falklands War, and as a result of two major shuffles of her ministerial team, the 'wets' are now in a clear minority and their most formidable spokesmen – Ian Gilmour, Francis Pym, James Prior and others – are now on the back-benches and, at present, relatively powerless.

Moreover, through legislation, such as that relating to the sale of council houses, the Conservatives now have the authority to enact certain aspects of their policy programme. In addition, and of great significance, the Conservatives have moved decisively against local government in order to remove this formidable barrier to success. Through the introduction of rate-capping, the abolition of the GLC and the metropolitan counties, and by a determination if necessary to introduce 'commissioners' to take charge of rebel local authorities, the Government show that they mean business. In other ways too, the Conservatives have not wasted time in recent years to equip themselves, and the State machinery, to ride roughshod over opposition. The building-up of an increasingly armoured police force is not unrelated to the future battle over the Welfare State.

The scene is therefore set for a crucial confrontation in the 1980s between those who support the notion of a Welfare State, as a major means of helping ordinary men and women and their families, and those who see the time as ripe for a major assault on social policy as a means of achieving the kind of capitalist society they yearn for. Precise predictions are difficult, and unnecessary. Much will depend, however, on the shape and character of opposition to Tory measures. There is a need for local campaigns to oppose specific cuts, a wider national campaign to demonstrate the nature of Tory ambitions, and an alternative vision for the future of social policy.

PART THREE

Reassessment: Successes and Failures

4 Inequality

... what thoughtful rich people call the problem of poverty, thoughtful poor people call with equal justice the problem of riches.

R. H. Tawney[1]

It has been argued that the Welfare State entered a new phase in its history during the mid 1960s, one increasingly characterized by anxiety and uncertainty, if not actual crisis. The Tories reacted better than the Left. Labour was defensive, often conservative, and uncertain of its ground *or* its message. The Conservative Party, however, with a New Right leadership, analysed the situation in terms of *too much* State welfare and won the 1979 election on a shrewd platform of *less* bureaucracy, *less* public spending and *lower* taxation. They sought at the same time to reassure the electorate that those in need would not be harmed.

Chapter 3 analysed the Tory record, discussed the new brand of Conservative social politics and looked at the Right's policy agenda. It is an awesome one not only for those with most to lose – the poor, the unemployed, the sick, elderly people and those struggling to raise families – but also for 'One Nation' Tories, progressives, radicals and socialists who care about the Welfare State and the need for a united society. But what should be the positive response to Thatcherism? Clearly something more than a 'return to 1979' is required, but what would an alternative social strategy look like?

Later these challenging questions are taken up, but the discussion is preceded by a reassessment. How should radicals judge the performance of the Welfare State to date? To consider the question this chapter focuses on the impact of the modern Welfare State. It discusses how social policies have affected both absolute standards, as well as inequalities. Chapter 5 then considers critiques of the Welfare State from both the Right and Left. Chapter 6 goes on to review the ways in which demographic, social and employment trends are changing British society and hence the context for policy.

Success or failure?

In his account of the postwar Labour government, published in 1954, Clement Attlee talks of the 'remarkable advance' that had been made in many directions and he remarked '... I always feel cheered when I look at the children and babies of today and compare them with those of past times'. He concluded that 'during these years a peaceful revolution has taken place. Broadly speaking, there has been a great levelling-up of conditions.'[2]

Significantly Crosland, writing of the postwar government, has argued:

Wars are only permanently revolutionary if followed by Left-wing Governments which dig in, consolidate the changes, and use them as a basis for further advance. This was the historical task of Mr Attlee's Government. Just how successfully it was accomplished, people perhaps scarcely realise today. Memories are feeble; the changes are quickly taken for granted and accepted as part of the status quo; and it becomes impossible to recapture former moods and hopes.[3]

Nevertheless, has the Welfare State lessened inequalities in Britain? This is the key question which this chapter considers and it is a crucial one for socialists, for the attack on inequality and the move towards a society where resources are distributed equitably according to need are crucial objectives that distinguish democratic socialism. And the postwar Welfare State, together with progressive taxation and full employment, was to be a major instrument in the move away from inequality.

What is the record since the war? We noted in Chapter 2 that whereas many socialists thought that the movement was in the right direction in the 1950s, doubts came to the surface in the mid 1960s and gained strength throughout the 1970s. The purpose here is to review the evidence in certain key areas: income, health, education, and housing.

Income

At the heart of Labour's postwar social policy was the desire to establish a more equitable distribution of income and the chosen instruments were to be income taxation, progressively levied, and social security. What then has happened to income distribution in the decades since the end of the Second World War? Does the evidence support the oft-voiced view, for much of the period, that the trend has been towards equality? Table 4.1 presents some evidence for three periods since the war.

Table 4.1 Percentage shares of income before and after income tax, received by given groups

Percentage share	1949	1970/71	1981/2
	Before income tax		
Top 1	11.2	6.6	6.0
Top 10	33.2	27.5	28.3
Next 40	43.1	49.0	49.2
Bottom 50	27.3	23.5	22.7
	After income tax		
Top 1	6.4	4.5	4.6
Top 10	27.1	23.9	25.6
Next 40	46.4	49.9	49.2
Bottom 50	26.5	26.1	25.2

Sources: The Wealth Report (1983), based on *Royal Commission on the Distribution of Income and Wealth*, Report No. 1, *Initial Report of the Standing Commission*, Cmnd 6171, HMSO, 1975; *Social Trends*, 15, 1985, Central Statistical Office, Table 5.17.

It is noticeable that the poorer half of the population has not improved its position in the thirty years since 1949. Indeed, whereas the bottom 50 per cent received 27.3 per cent of all gross income in 1949, their share was only 22.7 per cent in 1981/2. And, despite the impact of supposedly 'progressive' taxation, the effect on the rich was almost insignificant: the top 10 per cent received 27.1 per cent of post-tax income in 1949, 25.6 per cent in 1981/2. The pips never squeaked because they were never pressed. Similarly, our tax system has failed to bring significantly higher incomes to the poorest. In 1949 the bottom half of income earners gained 26.5 per cent of after-tax income, against 25.2 per cent in 1981/2.

Commenting on postwar trends the Royal Commission on the Distribution of Income and Wealth noted that:

The overall impression from the figures is of a reduction in inequality but, if the decline in the share of the top one per cent is ignored, the shape of the distribution is not greatly different in 1976/77 to what it was in 1949. The major part of the fall in the share of the top one per cent is balanced by an increase in the shares of other groups in the top half of the distribution.[4]

To bring all these statistics into more easily understood terms the comments of Playford and Pond are helpful:

The richest 1 per cent, having average incomes in 1978/79 of almost £22,000 a year, had a larger share of the total income than the poorest fifth of the population between them. The richest 10 per cent (average incomes almost £11,000) had a larger share than half the population (26.1 per cent compared with 23.5 per cent) and ten times as much as the poorest tenth.[5]

The evidence so far reviewed only includes income taxation and it has been observed by the Royal Commission that: 'The progressive effect of direct taxation is largely offset by the regressive effect of indirect taxation. Thus the tax system has little effect on the overall shape of the distribution.'[6]

Three other factors should be briefly mentioned which make their own impact on income distribution. The first is fringe benefits which have rapidly increased in size and scope during the 1970s. For example, superannuation and fringe benefits, for a managing director, as a percentage of average salary plus bonus and commission before tax increased from 12 to 36 per cent between 1974 and 1978.[7]

The second factor is tax avoidance and evasion. By its very nature, good evidence on this subject is hard to come by, but in 1979 the Inland Revenue Board's chairman, Sir William Pile, reported that undisclosed income might amount to as much as 7.5 per cent of GDP or an annual total of £10 billion. By 1981 this percentage amounted to £16 billion which represented a tax *loss* of £4 billion or about one-fifth of the entire income tax yield.[8]

Avoidance and evasion are, of course, practised by workers in different occupations. However, it is particularly prevalent among the self-employed, and the overall effect would appear to further distribute real income in favour of the better-off.

Finally, there is the differential impact of price inflation on groups in society. This produces further inequalities. For example, Piachaud found that for the period 1956–74 prices rose for the poorest 5 per cent by 26 percentage points more than for all families and by 30.9 percentage points more than for the richest 5 per cent.[9] Further evidence from the Low Pay Unit's separate indices for low and high paid workers also shows the adverse effect of price rises on relative income.[10]

Wealth

What has happened to the distribution of wealth since the war? As with income, this is a complex question to answer. Definitions of wealth vary (should one include, for example, pension rights?) and there are also problems about, and shortcomings in, evidence. The aim here is to summarize the key trends – other studies provide more detailed accounts.[11]

Atkinson and Harrison have produced statistics on inequality for a period of a half century from the early 1920s to the early 1970s. They show that the share of wealth of the top 1 per cent has declined, but that the redistribution of wealth that has taken place has occurred within a very narrow band affecting mainly the top 20 per cent, who in 1972 still owned 85 per cent of all wealth.[12] As Atkinson has noted: 'What redistribution there has been is not between the rich and the poor, but between the very rich and the rich.'[13] Consequently while the wealth shares of the bottom 80 per cent of the population had increased marginally, the fifty-year period that experienced the mass franchise, the rise of the Labour Party, and the advent of progressive taxation, ended with 80 per cent of the people still owning only 15 per cent of the wealth.

What happened to wealth inequalities in the 1970s, a decade that followed six years of Labour government in the 1960s and witnessed a further five years, years moreover of a government committed to shift 'the balance of power and wealth in favour of working people and their families'?[14] Improved estimates are available for the 1970s and beyond and these are shown in Table 4.2. The table gives three separate measures in order to include the effect of occupational pension rights and State pension rights. The inclusion of such rights is open to debate, for while these increase future command over resources, they are hardly the same as money in the bank. Moreover, while the inclusions make the distribution appear more egalitarian, other future rights, as Pond notes, such as rights to education, inheritances and earnings, are excluded. Be that as it may, even with the inclusion of pension rights the bottom half of the population still owned only approximately one-fifth of the wealth.

What do these statistics mean in real terms? Pond explains:

The scale of the inequality becomes clearer if we consider the actual amounts of wealth involved. In 1979, total marketable wealth was estimated at just under £500 billion. If equally distributed, each member of the population aged over eighteen would have had average net wealth (after paying off their mortgages, debts and other liabilities) of around £12,000 at 1979 prices. Each household would have net wealth, on average, of over £30,000 in 1979. The actual situation was rather different. Those in the bottom half of the distribution had average wealth of only £1,200 each or £3,000 per household – less than a tenth as much as if wealth had been equally shared. Meanwhile, those in the top half of the distribution had an average wealth-holding of £23,000 each (almost £60,000 per household). A sharper illustration of Disraeli's 'two nations' would be difficult to contemplate. Half the population had an average twenty times as much wealth as the other half.[15]

Table 4.2 Distribution of wealth in the United Kingdom (percentages and £ billion)

	1971	1979	1983
Marketable wealth			
Percentage of wealth owned by			
% of population*			
Most wealthy 1	31	22	20
Most wealthy 2	39	28	27
Most wealthy 5	52	40	40
Most wealthy 10	65	54	54
Most wealthy 25	86	77	78
Most wealthy 50	97	95	96
Total marketable wealth (£ billion)	140	453	745
Marketable wealth plus occupational pension rights			
Percentage of wealth owned by			
% of population*			
Most wealthy 1*	27	19	18
Most wealthy 2	34	24	23
Most wealthy 5	46	34	34
Most wealthy 10	59	45	46
Most wealthy 25†	78–83	70–74	69–73
Most wealthy 50†	90–96	88–92	89–93
Marketable wealth plus occupational and State pension rights			
Percentage of wealth owned by			
% of population*			
Most wealthy 1	21	13	12
Most wealthy 2	27	17	16
Most wealthy 5	37	25	25
Most wealthy 10	49	35	35
Most wealthy 25†	69–72	56–9	57–60
Most wealthy 50†	85–9	79–83	80–84

Notes: * Aged 18 or over. † Estimates vary with assumptions.
Source: *Social Trends*, 16, Central Statistical Office, HMSO, 1986, Table 5.22.

Poverty

This discussion of income and wealth has focused on the position of the top people in society, for this is where economic resources are concentrated. This focus is justifed, for while much attention is given to the characteristics and problems of the poor, too little attention is focused on the rich.

However, the poverty of millions of British people is as much an indication of inequality as excessive income and wealth.

How many of the British population are in poverty? The quoting of statistics about the numbers of families in poverty begs the question, what is poverty? Some will argue that, compared with, say, the 1920s or 1930s or with conditions in the Third World, poverty no longer exists in Britain. This raises the issue of whether poverty should be measured in absolute or relative terms. Egalitarians, of course, accept the relative approach and consider the standards of living of low income groups against those generally enjoyed within society. As Peter Townsend has argued: 'people's needs, even for food, are conditioned by the society in which they live and to which they belong, and just as needs differ in different societies, so they differ in different periods of the evolution of single societies.'[16]

We need, then, to measure poverty relatively, but let us start by considering those dependent on supplementary benefits as providing a basis for estimating the numbers in poverty. There are both large numbers of old and young alike who receive these benefits – almost 4.8 million persons in 1985/6.[17] Together with dependants, this represents about one in seven of the total population. However, many people fail to claim this entitlement to supplementary benefit and, furthermore, a significant number of household heads earn wages which are less than they would receive if on benefit. Hence, the numbers in poverty are clearly larger than just those receiving supplementary benefits.

Moreover, we must not readily accept that the supplementary benefit level provides a reasonable basis for assessing poverty in contemporary Britain. These benefit rates have developed in an often *ad hoc* manner and are widely regarded as being grossly inadequate. An answer to the

complacent assertion that supplementary benefits provide a reasonable
minimum income comes from Piachaud's study of the minimum costs
of bringing up children in contemporary Britain.[18] The diet assumed
more milk and vegetables, and less meat, than children actually consume, and *no* snacks whatsoever between meals. He included small
sums for only two presents a year and very small sums for entertainment
and the cost of one week's cheap holiday. In the case of an 8-year-old,
his estimate came to £11.42 in May 1981, of which £7.06 was for food.
For all ages of children, Piachaud's estimates are significantly higher
than the supplementary benefit age-related rates.

Overall the study demonstrated that supplementary benefit rates for
children are some two-thirds of the estimated minimum, and that
therefore these rates would need to increase by about 50 per cent to
provide adequately for the minimum costs. This important finding
affects estimates about the incidence of child poverty in Britain, and
shows that these underestimate the extent of poverty. This study also
strengthens the view of the Supplementary Benefits Commission that:
'. . . the supplementary benefit scheme provides, particularly for families
with children, incomes that are barely adequate to meet their needs at
a level that is consistent with normal participation in the life of the
relatively wealthy society in which they live'.[19]

Not only is the distribution of earnings very unequal but, at the
bottom, earnings are very low indeed. Taking as a base £100 per week
(£2.50 an hour for part-timers), figures for 1983 show that among full-
time male workers (21 or over) 12 per cent, or 1.1 million employees,
were low paid. When overtime payments are excluded the figures are
17.7 per cent or 1.6 million. For females in full-time work (aged 18 or
over), the numbers who are low paid are significantly higher: including
overtime, 3.4 million women (24.5 per cent) are low paid; without
overtime the figures increased to 4.0 million (29 per cent). Altogether
then there are some 4.5 million full-time workers in Britain who are
low paid (two-thirds of them women, including overtime pay), and for
those working part-time there are an additional 2.7 million females and
400,000 males who are low paid.[20] The combined impact of a number
of trends, but primarily low pay and unemployment, means that large

numbers of people now live in, or close to, the poverty line (that is, 40 per cent above supplementary benefit level). As noted in Chapter 3, this includes some 1.7 million families, with 3.6 million children.

The contrast between the salaries of the highest paid company directors and the wages of Britain's lowest paid workers is worth making. The differences are stark. They represent some of the most miserable measurements of greed and deprivation. Thus the *weekly* salary of Britain's highest paid company director (£10,875) is over two-and-a-half times the *annual* salary of a cleaner (£4,253).[21] It is also highly significant that, while Britain's top paid directors are male, Britain's lowest paid workers are female.

The impact of social security

Within this context of stubborn inequality and continuing poverty, what has been the effect of social security measures? Social security benefits have shown an increase in recent decades. For example, taking supplementary benefit paid to a couple with two children, the level was 50 per cent of average net earnings in 1948, 64 per cent by 1968, and 67 per cent by 1984. Moreover, the ordinary supplementary benefit scale rates for a married couple have increased in real terms (measured at 1983 prices) from £20.37 in 1948 to £42.74 in 1984. Another example is child support (formerly child tax allowances and family allowances, now child benefits). Looking at the value in real terms (at October 1980 prices) in 1950/51, the combined value of child support for a two parent family with two children aged under 11 (where the man was on average earnings) was £5.70; by 1970/71 it was £7.60. While the position fluctuated during the 1970s, the situation in the mid 1980s was far better than in earlier decades.

Social policy therefore has had a beneficial effect on the position of the poorest in absolute terms. However, it is the failure of policies to bring about greater equality that is chronicled in these pages. What has been the impact of the Welfare State in other policy fields?

Health

The NHS has a special place in socialist politics, epitomizing the belief that the very best medical care should be available, according to need and regardless of income. In Aneurin Bevan's words 'a free health service is pure socialism and as such it is opposed to the hedonism of capitalist society'.[22]

The desire to eradicate health inequalities gave impetus to this social reform. What is the record forty years on from the establishment of the NHS?

Overall improvements

The health of the people has improved dramatically, compared to pre-NHS times, as evidence on mortality testifies. Expectation of life at birth in 1931 was 58.4 years for males and 62.4 years for females. By 1981, the respective figures were 69.8 years and 76.2 years.[23]

Since the 1930s also, maternal deaths have declined dramatically: from 4.54 deaths per 1,000 live births in 1930–32, to 0.88 in 1950–52 and to 0.17 by 1970–72. There have been similarly dramatic decreases in infant mortality rates. Taking the age-group 0–4 years, deaths per 1,000 among males declined from 22.3 in 1930–32 to 7.7 by 1950–52 to 4.6 by 1970–72. The respective figures for females are 17.7, 6.0, and 3.6. Improvements continued to take place in the 1970s. Thus, perinatal mortality rates decreased from 22.5 deaths per 1,000 (legitimate) births in 1971, to 11.3 by 1981.[24]

While a number of factors help explain these substantial improvements – public health measures, economic progress generally, and improved medicine – can it be doubted that the role of the State in health care, in general, and the advent of the NHS in particular, have not been crucial factors?

Health inequalities

But has the NHS been a force for *equality?* There is a mass of material to help answer this question, but fortunately 'Inequalities in Health' (the Black Report) published in 1980 summarizes the most important evidence.[25]

Let us take a closer look at mortality trends. Death rates for those aged 15–64, analysed by social class and sex, reveal the massive inequalities between social classes: in 1971, men from social class V were subject to 9.88 deaths per 1,000 compared with only 3.98 among social class I – two-and-a-half times as great.[26]

For some, tragically, the impact of social class strikes early, as the infant mortality figures demonstrate: in 1981 still births and deaths in the first week of life are almost twice as likely in social class V as in social class I (at 15.6 per 1,000 live births, against 8.3).[27] Furthermore, while infant mortality for all classes has declined in recent decades, the class gradient is still present. Indeed, between 1950 and 1973, the perinatal mortality rate declined by 45 per cent for those of professional class and 49 per cent for those of managerial class but by only 34 per cent for those of unskilled manual class.[28] In 1981 infant mortality (deaths under 1 year) were 7.7 (per 1,000) for social class I, compared to 16.0 for class V.[29]

Social class also affects the final stages of the life cycle. As we have seen, more middle- and upper-class men and women will survive into old age than working-class people. For both men and women the risk of death before retirement is seven-and-a-half times as great for unskilled manual workers and their wives than for professional men and their wives.[30] Indeed, life expectancy at birth varies considerably: 'A child born to professional parents, if he or she is not socially mobile, can expect to spend over five years more as a living person than a child born to an unskilled manual household.'[31]

A similar picture is present when illness is studied. There is a strong association between class and reported illness throughout all socio-economic groups.[32]

In summary, the evidence leads to a clear conclusion: inequalities in health continue and are a significant aspect of inequalities within Britain. As Sir John Brotherston has stated 'For the most part the evidence suggests the gaps remain as wide apart as a generation ago and in some instances the gaps may be widening.'[33] To show what this means in human terms, the Black Report estimated that if the mortality rates of class I applied to classes IV and V during 1970–72, the dates for which the most recent evidence on mortality exist, 74,000 lives of people aged under 75 would not have been lost. This includes nearly 10,000 children, and 32,000 men aged 15–64.[34]

Education

Inequalities within the education system were well recognized by prewar socialists. G. D. H. Cole, for example, in his *Plan for Democratic Britain*, argued that 'The British class system has its roots in economic exploitation; but it is powerfully reinforced by the structure and working of the educational system.'[35] Accordingly, education occupies a special and strategic place within socialist social policy, for it has been seen as a corner-stone of a more equal and fair society. Through State education, it was believed, standards would rise and age-old inequalities would be abolished.

Rising standards

How has the development of State education affected education standards during the period that has seen a progressive raising of the school-leaving age, the growth of secondary education, the coming of comprehensive schools and an expansion of higher education?

Higher proportions of older children are now educated. For example, of all children aged 15–18 only 6 per cent were at school in 1931; by 1951 the proportion had grown to 12.5 per cent, and by 1968 it was 30 per cent of the age-group.[36]

Pre-school education has also expanded. While in 1971 under-5s in school were just 20 per cent of all 3- or 4-year-olds, by 1984 the proportion was over 45 per cent.[37] Moreover, thanks to the raising of the school-leaving age, the proportion of 16-year-old children in full-time education increased from almost 36 per cent in 1971 to some 45 per cent by 1983/4.[38] Academic results have also improved: in 1973/4, 48 per cent of boys and 51 per cent of girls left school with at least one 'O' level (graded A–C, or the equivalent) but by 1982/3, the respective proportions were up to 53 per cent for boys and 59 per cent for girls.[39] Pupil–teacher ratios also improved: in the United Kingdom the ratio was 23.2 in 1971, but only 18.6 by 1984.[40] As with health, however, rising absolute standards have not meant greater equality.

Education inequalities

Halsey and his colleagues in the Oxford Social Mobility Study surveyed approximately 10,000 men in 1972 and thereby provide some fascinating data about educational opportunity and attainment during the period from the 1930s to the end of the 1960s.[41] Their conclusions make gloomy reading for those who thought that the development of State education during this century was likely to have major effects in reducing inequalities in Britain. They show that 'class inequalities are cumulative at each successive stage of the educational career'.[42] Thus, among those from social classes I and II, 58 per cent obtained 'O' level, 27 per cent 'A' level and 20 per cent attended university, against 12, 3 and 2 per cent respectively of those from working-class backgrounds.

The results show the persistence of educational inequalities over time. Whereas for the 1913–22 period, less than 1 per cent (0.9 per cent) of working-class boys attended university, this proportion increased in later decades, but still stood at only 3.1 per cent for those born in 1943–52. Over this period the percentage of young people entering university from upper-class backgrounds also rose, from 7.2 per cent for those born in 1913–22 to 26.4 per cent for those born in the years 1943–52.

The evidence is clear: despite a massive growth in State education, and despite important absolute improvements, this has not resulted in lessening inequalities. Indeed: 'a service-boy in our sample was four times as likely as his working-class peer to be found at school at the age of 16, eight times as likely at the age of 17, ten times as likely at the age of 18, and eleven times as likely to enter a university'.[43]

Halsey's Oxford study covered a period which did not allow it to measure the impact of comprehensive education on inequalities. However, the stubbornness of inequalities, the often half-hearted nature of 'comprehensive' education, the persistence of private schools, and the ability of the middle class to gain most from the most expensive forms of State education do not hold out a great deal of hope. The middle class's ability to do better from the State education system is demonstrated by Le Grand who, for 1973, analysed public expenditure on education by socio-economic group (SEG):

when all the different sectors of education are taken together, the top SEG received over one-and-a-quarter times the mean public expenditure and about one-and-a-half times as much as the lowest SEG. This arose because, although people in the top SEG received slightly less state expenditure on primary and secondary education for pupils under 16 (presumably because they made a greater use of private education) they received substantially more expenditure in all the other sectors.[44]

Indeed, the highest social groups make use of the most expensive sectors of education: for universities they received over five times the expenditure received by the lowest group. This evidence backs up the view of Glennerster that 'the main beneficiaries of the education explosion of the 1960s have been the middle class since the fastest expansion took place in that sector which was and remains predominantly theirs – higher education'.[45] Certainly, Halsey and his co-researchers have argued that 'secondary education was made free in order to enable the poor to take more advantage of it, but the paradoxical consequence was to increase subsidies to the affluent'.[46] Whatever else, the growth of State education has certainly not produced egalitarian results for, as Halsey's study shows, 'school inequalities of opportunity have been remarkably stable over the forty years which our study covers'.[47]

Housing

Since the 1930s there has been an important improvement in housing standards, and much of this gain has been the direct consequence of public initiatives – slum clearance, improvements, and local authority housebuilding – many of which have been taken by Labour when in power, either at central or local levels. There has been an improvement in space standards since the early 1930s: the proportion of households living more than 1.5 persons per room declined from 11 per cent in 1931, to 5 per cent in 1951 and only 1 per cent by 1971.[48] Similarly, the proportion of households sharing dwellings fell from 19 per cent in 1931, to just over 14 per cent by 1951, and was down to 5 per cent in 1971.[49] Moreover, the proportion of people lacking basic amenities declined dramatically: in 1951, for example, 22 per cent of households either shared or lacked a water closet; by 1971 it was only 5 per cent.[50]

In more recent times progress was maintained. Taking the stricter measure of one person or more per room, 14 per cent of all households were living at this standard in 1971, but only 9 per cent by 1982. And for basic amenities, while in 1971 12 per cent lacked sole use of a bath or shower, only 3 per cent did so in 1983. Similarly, those lacking sole use of an *inside* water closet in 1983 were less than a quarter the number who were in this position in 1971 – 3 per cent against 13 per cent. Furthermore, while 66 per cent of all households were without central heating in 1971, the proportion had declined to 36 per cent in 1983.[51]

Housing inequalities

At first sight, therefore, it would appear that there has been a radical move in the direction of housing equality in the period since the war. Certainly the last comprehensive official review of housing sounded an optimistic note: 'In 1951, there were nearly ten million households in England and Wales . . . living in physically unsatisfactory conditions or sharing accommodation. By 1976 the figure had probably fallen to about 2.7 million and there was no longer an absolute shortage of houses.'[52]

In terms of the traditional 'basic amenities', there certainly *has* been a trend towards equality. The 1982 *Social Trends* concluded that 'Households headed by semi-skilled and unskilled manual workers showed the biggest improvements in housing conditions during the 1970s'.[53] But to consider only basic amenities is inappropriate for the 1980s and is similar to measuring poverty by means of standards of living pertaining in the 1930s.

Measuring housing quality today ideally requires the consideration of modern amenities: housing space, fitness and immediate environment. Not all of the statistics we require are available, but those we do have reveal massive inequalities.

First, let us consider modern amenities, that is those amenities that have grown in use and popularity since the war and which many of the better-off would regard as important or even 'essential'. Central heating is the most important not just because of its ability to produce overall comfort in the home and therefore enable all of the dwelling to be properly used (rather than have all of the varied activities of a household clustered in only one or two rooms) but also because it is almost certainly associated with the decline in cold-related deaths among the population as a whole.[54]

Access to this modern amenity is clearly very unequal. Thus, for 1982, while 87 per cent of professional households have central heating, this is true for only 44 per cent of households headed by unskilled manual workers. A similar picture emerges for other modern amenities. For example, while nearly all (96 per cent) of professional households have a telephone, this is true for only 50 per cent of unskilled manual workers. For washing machines and deep freezes the variation is much the same.[55]

There is also a firm association between class and housing tenure. In 1982, 89 per cent of professionals were owner occupiers (either owning outright or with a mortgage), as were 86 per cent of employers and managers. This contrasts with only 35 per cent of semi-skilled manual workers and 27 per cent of the unskilled. Moreover, it is significant that unskilled manual workers were some six times as likely as professionals (6 per cent compared to 1 per cent) to be renting unfurnished private housing, accommodation which is normally associated with the poorest amenities and conditions. And, despite the dream of some social planners that public housing would be occupied by all social classes, the reality is polarization: only 1 per cent of professional households were in local authority homes, compared with 60 per cent of unskilled manual workers.[56]

The differences in tenure are also reflected in the distribution of housing *type*. In 1982 while 51 per cent of professional households lived in detached houses, this was true for only 2 per cent of unskilled manual workers. Conversely, 28 per cent of the unskilled lived in flats, maisonettes or rooms, compared with 9 per cent of professionals.[57]

The suitability of housing depends, in part, on the presence of children, and again class differences are to the fore. Middle-class children are more likely than those from working-class families to be living in houses. Indeed, in 1977 9 per cent of children from unskilled manual households lived in flats on the second floor or higher, against only 1 per cent of children from employers' and managers' households, and no children from professional households.[58] Similarly, there are great inequalities in terms of the size of homes and the space available to individuals.[59]

The inequalities in housing space are reflected in sleeping arrangements for children. The National Child Development Study has produced some important findings. In its reports on 11-year-olds based on an inquiry carried out in 1969, it found that more than 90 per cent of 'disadvantaged' children shared their room, compared with less than half of the children in the 'ordinary' group. And three out of ten among the disadvantaged shared with at least three others. More importantly, the studies revealed that over half of the disadvantaged children shared their bed with someone else compared with only one in eleven of the ordinary group. Furthermore, 'one in twenty-two disadvantaged children both shared and wet their bed ... and if we but knew how many of the brothers and sisters wet the shared bed, no doubt this picture would look even more disturbing; some of the "dry" disadvantaged children would also be found to be sleeping in a wet bed'. The authors note that bed-sharing among children brings an inevitably increased likelihood of disturbed sleep and cross-infection and they concluded that 'Even when disadvantaged children were in bed, the nature of their sleep was likely to be very different from that of ordinary children.'[60]

Successes and failures

This chapter has reviewed evidence about incomes, wealth, health, education and housing. What conclusions can be drawn about the impact of the Welfare State on the life chances of ordinary people? It is a mixed conclusion and an understanding of this is important if wise judgements about the future of social policy are to be made.

Some of the evidence documents important gains for working-class people in areas like health, education and housing. The years after the war were a period when, for the first time, many working-class people gained access to decent housing with hot and cold running water, baths and inside lavatories; when their children, often for the first time, went to secondary school and more and more of them achieved educational qualifications; when the incomes of the poorest rose in absolute terms and *also* relative to average earnings; and when poor people, no matter how poor and no matter how ill, obtained the very best medical care from the NHS.

The improvement in absolute standards among the working-class community also meant, in a very real sense, that there was increasingly *equal* access to some of the basic goods and services within society. No longer were housing amenities, secondary schooling and health care the sole prerogatives of the better-off. Indeed a letter to *Labour Weekly* made the point well. Arguing against the writer who had stressed the failure of the Welfare State to reduce inequality, he noted: 'The Welfare State has reduced inequalities. As a youngster of 14 in 1908 I remember it was only the well-off who could afford to visit a doctor. Today, thanks to the Welfare State and to Labour governments, that inequality does not exist.'[61] Analysts might respond to this (with ample evidence) that the middle class do better from the NHS, but the point is well made and illustrates the need for a meshing together of some perceptions of the performance of social policy.

Miliband has argued that the Welfare State did not 'for all its importance, constitute any threat to the existing system of power and privilege. What it did constitute was a certain humanization of the *existing* social order . . .'[62] Evidence on inequalities undoubtedly supports the first part of this statement. But it is wrong to dismiss too lightly the 'certain humanization' that Miliband refers to. We need to remember that this means such tangible things as better housing, fewer mothers dying during childbirth and fewer of their babies dying in the first weeks of life, and healthier children. As Gough has argued 'to concentrate solely on its "negative" aspects, as do certain critical theorists, is to lose sight of the very real gains that a century of conflict has won'.[63]

However, if the evidence of the Welfare State's success is clear, the same is true for its failure. Inequalities are unshaken. Britain remains a greatly divided society.

Table 4.3 brings together some of the evidence reviewed in this chapter to form an index of inequality. It shows the different standards and life chances enjoyed by the richest people in Britain as against those experienced by the poorest. Thus, the top 10 per cent of income earners received, after tax, as much income as the poorest 50 per cent; the richest 10 per cent have thirteen times as much wealth as the whole of the poorer 50 per cent, babies born to mothers from unskilled manual-worker families are over twice as likely to die in the first year of life as those from professional families, and an earlier death (between 15 and 64 years) is two-and-a-half times as likely to be the lot of the unskilled, compared to the professional. And in housing, professionals, compared to the unskilled, are almost three-and-a-half times as likely to be owner occupiers, and twice as likely to have central heating. Conversely, the unskilled manual worker family is over five times more likely to have to raise children in a flat. And in the crucial area of education, children from the better-off classes, compared to those from the working classes, are almost five times as likely to get 'O' levels, nine times as likely to achieve 'A' levels and ten times as likely to receive a university education.

This chapter focused on one form of inequality, namely that associated with class or income. Inequality is traditionally understood in these

Table 4.3 Indices of inequality: comparative life chances of the rich and poor

Indicator	Year	'Rich' definition/rate	'Poor' definition/rate
Income (% of total after tax)[a]	1981/2	Top 10% 25.6	Bottom 50% 25.2
Wealth (% of total)[b]	1982	Top 10% 54	Bottom 50% 4
Death (per 1,000 live births)			
Infant mortality (under 1 year)[c]	1981	Professional 7.7	Unskilled 15.8
Premature mortality[d] (15–64 years)	1971		
Males		3.98	9.88
Females		2.15	5.31
Housing (%)	1982	Professional	Unskilled
Owner occupiers[e]		89	27
Flats, maisonettes or rooms[f]		9	22
Children in flats[g]		4	22
Central heating[h]		87	44
Education (%)[i]	1930s–60s	I and II	VI–VIII
One or more 'O' Levels		58	12
One or more 'A' Levels		27	3
University education		20	2

Sources: (a) *Social Trends*, 15, Central Statistical Office, HMSO, 1985, Table 5.17; (b) *Social Trends*, 16, Table 5.22; (c) Hansard, 15 May 1984, cols. 143–4; (d) Peter Townsend and Nick Davidson (eds.), *Inequalities in Health: the Black Report*, Penguin, 1982, Table 5.10; (e) *General Household Survey 1982*, HMSO, 1984, Table 5.10; (f) *General Household Survey 1982*, Table 5.17; (g) *General Household Survey 1977*, HMSO, 1979, Table 3.31 (figures for 1977); (h) *General Household Survey 1982*, HMSO, 1984, Table 5.28; (i) A. H. Halsey, A. F. Heath and J. M. Ridge, *Origins and Destinations: Family, Class and Education in Modern Britain*, Clarendon Press, 1980, Table 10.5.

terms and class remains the most important determinant of life chances. However, further forms of debilitating inequality exist in Britain and these need to be properly understood when drawing up a future social programme. They include inequalities based on sex and inequalities *within* the home; racial inequality; geographical inequalities, both in terms of large regions and also smaller areas, such as the inner city; inequalities between those with and without responsibilities for children, elderly relatives or other dependants; and inequalities between family types, particularly those affecting a growing number of one parent families.

5 Critical Perspectives

Liberty without equality is a name of noble sound and squalid result.
L. J. Hobhouse[1]

Supporters of the Welfare State have been on the defensive since the advent of Thatcherism and have been uncertain of their ground for a longer time. If now the arguments for welfare are to be stated clearly, attractively and with confidence, something very much more than a return to the position in 1979 has to be advocated. This formidable task involves, in part, understanding the several schools of critical thought that have emerged with strength in recent years. The most obvious of these is the New Right and their position needs to be confronted. There have also been critiques from the Left however, in particular from the Marxists and what might be termed 'democratic' or libertarian perspectives. These help to inform any new approach to welfare that can win popular support in the late 1980s and beyond.

In this chapter, therefore, these critical perspectives are discussed and their implications for radical social policy explored.

The New Right

The triumph of Mrs Thatcher in 1979 heralded not just the return of another Conservative government, but the victory of the New Right over, the Labour Party of course, but more significantly the 'One Nation' Tories as well. As Chapter 3 argued, there was a decisive break with the past and this involved a significant ideology about the role of the State, not least in relation to welfare.

While any thorough assessment reveals New Right proposals

embracing some different positions – Hayek, for example, differs from Friedman about the role of the State[2] – it nevertheless represents a clear ideology in relation to welfare. In essence the New Right's approach is based on ideas about, first, the supremacy of the private market and, second, the necessity of reducing the role of the State. It therefore marks a significant break with traditional – paternalistic – Conservative politics: 'The Old Right was based in political philosophy and on ideas about tradition and hierarchy. The New Right is mainly based in economics and on ideas about individualism and markets. One is a conservative creed while the other is eager for certain kinds of turbulence and change.'[3] Bosanquet has analysed and summarized the philosophy of the New Right in terms of a thesis and an antithesis. The thesis is that: (a) society has inherent tendencies towards order and justice; (b) inequality is the inevitable and tolerable result of social freedom and personal initiative; (c) capitalism is a system which has ensured growth and improved living standards in the long term; (d) the entrepreneur is the key figure in insuring for all the gains to be had from economic growth; and (e) economic growth will first reduce and then eliminate poverty in absolute terms.[4]

The antithesis of the New Right concerns, in part, the concept of politicization, that is, the tendency for the State to increase its power because of democratic pressures. This is partly because in an 'unlimited democracy' 'the holders of discretionary powers are forced to use them to favour particular groups on whose swing vote their powers depend', in Hayek's words.[5] It is contended that this 'politicization' increases both public expenditure and encourages the growth of bureaucracy.

Much of the New Right's energy has been directed against the Welfare State and this is particularly so of the Institute of Economic Affairs, one of the most persistent standard-bearers of the philosophy in recent times. The concept of choice is critical: according to the New Right the Welfare State negates choice, while the private market promotes it: 'The provision of so-called "free" welfare services denies citizens the freedom of choice they enjoy as consumers in the competitive market.'[6] Friedman, however, outlines the disadvantages of 'paternalistic programmes' more comprehensively – they 'weaken the family;

reduce the incentive to work, save and innovate; reduce the accumulation of tax and limit our freedom'.[7]

From this analysis a sustained attack on State provision has developed. The NHS has come in for particular criticism. Long ago D. S. Lees outlined the New Right's approach: '... medical care would appear to have no characteristics which differentiate it sharply from other goods in the market ... medical care is a personal consumption good and as such is a dubious candidate for collective provision'.[8] This conclusion encourages Lees to suggest that 'if the aim is to maximize consumer satisfaction, medical care should be supplied through the market';[9] and to propose that 'some hospitals' be transferred to 'private ownership to provide competition and to enlarge consumer choice'.[10] He also argued that 'Governments should move away from taxation and free services to private insurance and fees'[11] and that 'a means test should be introduced to help with the dwindling minority unable to pay.'[12]

As was discussed in Chapter 3, the ideas of the New Right provided the philosophical and intellectual foundation for the present Conservative government. Several prominent Conservatives – Mrs Thatcher herself, Sir Keith Joseph, Sir Geoffrey Howe and Leon Brittan – have taken their cue, and, indeed, sharpened up the political message.

How exactly would the New Right abolish the Welfare State? First, there would be a reverse income tax, as a means of topping up low incomes. This would be part and parcel of an approach to taxation that would entail reducing taxes so that people 'would thereby be enabled to insure themselves and their families against unemployment, sickness and retirement, and ultimately to pay for services in kind'.[13]

The second stage in the strategy, as set out by the Institute of Economic Affairs, is that, with a reverse income tax in operation, it would no longer be necessary to provide free services '... most families are already paying indirectly for all the welfare services they consume. What possible objection can there be to bringing this payment into the open by direct charging for schooling, hospitals, G.P.s and the rest?'[14]

The third part of the strategy is that 'The reverse tax could gradually be extended to replace ultimately all or most "free" education, medical

care and other benefits in kind that government now supplies to all and
finances from higher taxes on the supposed beneficiaries.'[15]

The Institute reluctantly concedes that minimum standards may be
necessary.[16] A range of specific proposals have been made as a means
of implementing this strategy – including education vouchers, private
health insurance and rent de-control in the privately rented housing
sector.

The arguments of the New Right can be countered in different ways.
Their thesis, for example, that such services as health and education
are no different from other goods and services – apples or shoes, for
example – and that they therefore can be provided efficiently by the
private market can be effectively demolished. Titmuss long ago argued
that: 'Classical supply and demand analysis may help us to understand
the social institutions of very simple and primitive economies. But it is
singularly unhelpful when applied to the immensely complicated play
of forces operating in the field of modern scientific medicine.'[17]
Moreover, it can be shown that in such a complex area as health, the
rules of the simple market-place do not operate: 'There cannot be true
consumer sovereignty in the demand for health care,' argues Bosanquet.
This is due to the fact that the consumer is not paying 'at the point of
consumption. He is paying for insurance or paying income tax. He does
not express his preference by an act of payment.'[18]

In addition, many of the supposed advantages of private medicine
can be challenged. For example, despite the New Right contention that
the NHS is over-bureaucratized and therefore expensive to run, an
OECD study found that the proportion of total expenditure for
administrative costs was lower in the United Kingdom than in either
Europe or the United States: 'General administrative costs were 2.6
per cent of total current outlays in the UK, and 5.3 per cent in the
US.'[19]

What would be the impact of the New Right's 'social' policy? First
and foremost, it would inevitably be a strategy for inequality. Taxation
for the rich would be further reduced and any income provision for the
poor would be set at the most minimum level. Education vouchers
would exacerbate inequalities in the school system. They would enable

rich parents to reduce their own costs of private education, while poor parents would only be able to afford the minimum. Rich parents would simply top up their vouchers to pay for higher standards. Strangely, advocates of vouchers have tried to argue that vouchers would promote greater equality, somehow imagining that poor parents would spend more to top up vouchers than better-off ones.

Within health, the effect would be the same. The poor would receive a low standard of care from a residual public sector, while the rich would be able to afford the best. If fully implemented, the New Right strategy for welfare would soon reflect the worst abuses of the American medical system, with poor consumers being turned away from private hospitals – their credit rating being more crucial under the new morality than their health status. Moreover there would be no place for groups with the highest health requirements – the very elderly, and mentally and physically handicapped people – in the private sector.

Quality of care would also suffer and this would rebound on all consumers – rich and poor. The evidence from the United States indicates many abuses: unnecessary operations and cosmetic surgery are the consequences when profits, rather than professionalism, dictate day-to-day 'care'.

The democratic critique

While from the perspective of the Left – and indeed from a wider constituency concerned about fairness and justice – the New Right scenario for welfare is easily confronted, those aspects of it that have some appeal to public opinion need to be recognized and understood. These concern the critique of the Welfare *State* as overbearing and bureaucratic, uniform and grey. Moreover, this critique from the Right has an uncanny resemblance to the attack on aspects of welfarism that have come from the Left, but to appreciate this point we need to go back a little.

Central to democratic socialism is the belief that it is mainly through Parliament that inequalities can be attacked and social justice achieved.

Indeed, Bevan argued that: 'the issue therefore in a capitalist democracy resolves itself into this: either poverty will use democracy to win the struggle against property, or property, in fear of poverty, will destroy democracy'.[20] However, the recent history of the Welfare State shows that the role of the State is problematic. State interventions in housing, education, health and incomes have substantially changed the conditions of society and have therefore been beneficent, but similarly, State intervention has not always contributed to the enhancement of freedom, and the perception of the State has suffered accordingly.[21] Certainly, many council tenants, health consumers and social security recipients do not regard their relations with the State as wholly positive (to put it mildly). In too many areas – and in too many individual cases – the State (and the professionals and officials who represent it) are viewed as harsh, unsympathetic, intolerant, prejudiced and unhelpful.

Why is this? It is, in large part, due to the ambiguous nature and objectives of social policy. Given the 'mixed parentage' of the Welfare State – parts of it being influenced by socialist ideas, but others by deeply conservative ones – this is not surprising. Even within any one social policy there are conflicting objectives. Social security is a prime example. The supplementary benefit system is concerned to provide cash benefits 'as of right' to those in need, but the officials who administer the system are also charged to insure that the able-bodied are genuinely seeking work and that public funds are properly spent. The system has always had a social control function and this conflicts with – and damages – more liberal objectives.

While it is easy to relate 'social control' to the needs of the 'capitalist system', those who are concerned to translate radical ideas into practice, and practical administrative arrangements, need to wrestle with the difficult task of relating the meeting of social needs to the public's concern for the proper accountability of public funds. Socialists must always point to – and tackle – the much greater abuse of public money through tax evasion, but it is wrong to imagine this means that abuse within social security should not also be tackled. This is an important area, where social policy ideas need to be related to the concerns of the public, if we are to build a Welfare State that has universal confidence. As noted earlier, fanned by the wild stories of the popular Press, the 'scrounger' issue was a significant reason for the public's loss of confidence in the Welfare State during the 1970s, and it probably helped to win support for Tory policies during the 1979 election campaign.

A major explanation for popular wariness about the State's role in many areas of social policy is the way in which welfare is delivered – through large State bureaucracies – some organized centrally, some locally – which in too many areas, and in too many cases, seem remote from the needs of clients and customers. Moreover, some services seem, all too often, to be run more in the interests of the professionals and administrators than those for whom these services were set up.

The growth and administration of welfare organizations can be understood in the context of radical and socialist theory within Britain. The British Labour Party came into being with a profound belief in the power of central government, local authorities and other public bodies to do good, to promote human welfare and to eradicate inequalities. This involved recruiting large and well-trained staff, developing bureaucracies, and drawing up rules and regulations. All this was necessary – indeed desirable – if building homes, running schools and ministering properly to the sick were to be undertaken competently.

This was the socialism of Sidney and Beatrice Webb and Herbert Morrison that spawned a hundred Fabian tracts and gave impetus to the London County Council and many other municipalities. It was the socialism that was, in no small measure, responsible for the concrete achievements detailed earlier.

Faith in this approach faltered in the 1960s and, as was argued in Chapter 2, there has been a growing uncertainty and anxiety about the relationship between the citizen and the State, and an awareness of other potential conflicts: professionalization versus participation, efficiency versus democracy, and bureaucracy versus accountability.

Some of the critique of State services has been exaggerated, and knowingly exaggerated by the enemies of collective action, and we should be wary of the strange ideological alliances that have developed between some of the most Right-wing enemies of the Welfare State and some anarchists, libertarians and power-to-the-people advocates. The ideological climate that favoured Mrs Thatcher's victory in 1979 was, albeit in only a small part, created by some who should have known better. As Donnison has argued: 'Those on the far Right and the far Left who are hostile to the state as such may pull down the institutions around which humane and unifying loyalties can be mobilized – loyalties we destroy at our peril.'[22] Certainly within the labour movement there is a need for more rigour in this area of discussion. Indeed, Elizabeth Wilson has argued:

If the call to 'democratise welfare' is not to remain an empty popular slogan we must consider what it means. Part of the Left critique of welfare in the 1970s reacted so violently against what it saw as authoritarian centralised state provision that it rushed to the other extreme and approached a facile anti-statism in over-emphasising 'grass-roots' alternatives.[23]

The lesson from all this is that while faith in ultimate goals remains steady, socialists must rethink methods and strategy and not make the mistake of confusing ends with means, in the misguided belief that the methods that were right in the 1930s are necessarily right fifty years later.

Modern social policy needs to draw on a second and different radical tradition which found expression in the labour movement itself. Indeed, Halsey has asked how 'the movement which had invented the social forms of modern participatory democracy and practised them in Union Branch and Co-op meeting, thereby laying a Tocquevillian foundation for democracy, was ironically fated to develop through its political party the threats of a bureaucratic state'.[24] Today, the radical tradition is expressed through a number of modern campaigns, organizations and community groups which emphasize the power and rights of the individual to organize human affairs on a small and more democratic scale, through industrial co-operatives, community schools and housing co-ops.

In some respects, the Labour Party is not easily placed to understand some of these questions because, being the party of *labour*, it is better at receiving and implementing the wishes of the staff of welfare bureaucracies than it is at recognizing the anxieties of consumers, who are, in any case, unorganized. (Indeed, in at least some constituency Labour Parties, Welfare State professionals are probably better represented than those who they 'serve'.) However, without adequate and close control, welfare bureaucracies, health authorities, universities, social services departments, or education authorities can grow because of the ambitions and aspirations of senior staff in ways which do not inevitably increase the sum total of human welfare.

The challenge for radicals is to draw on the democratic tradition and to learn the lessons for the future of social policy. This theme is returned to in Chapter 11. The stakes are certainly high: if the New Right are allowed to successfully hijack 'choice' and 'freedom' as part of the vocabulary of dismantling the Welfare State they will be powerful weapons in their campaign for inequality. If, however, they become key concepts in the development of social policy they will be revitalizing ingredients in the renewed search for greater equality.

The Marxist critique

Another major strand of critical thought about social policy is the 'Marxist' analysis, although under this head there are in practice a variety of perspectives. In many ways, it might be better termed the 'socialist' critique, for many democratic socialists have in the past developed much of the analysis. In brief, it is argued that 'the Welfare State' far from being the antithesis of capitalism (and therefore a critical weapon in the battle against inequality) is in fact an integral part of 'welfare capitalism'. Moreover, it is contended that the development of social policy has to be seen in terms of the needs of capital. Thus social policy, far from undermining capitalism, actually sustains and protects it.

This is a thesis central to current debates on the Left in British politics, for the failures of the Labour governments in the 1960s and 1970s have strengthened the view of some Marxists and others that a Labour Party committed to social reform through Parliament is treading a false path, inevitably destined to end up in a political cul-de-sac.

How should democratic socialists judge this critique? This question is best discussed by considering a further one: How can we account for the historical development of social policy in Britain and societies like our own?

The development of social policy

While the early origins of social policy date back to at least the nineteenth century (and in some areas, much longer) there have nevertheless in the modern era been certain parallels between the rise of the Welfare State and the history of the Labour Party. And while it would be a gross oversimplification to say that the Labour Party 'created' the modern Welfare State, it remains true that the key reforming government was the postwar Attlee administration. Furthermore, the Labour Party has been the party most committed to social policy. How, therefore, after all this time, should democratic socialists and radicals evaluate social policy? This key question is not just of historical interest. Rather it is of fundamental importance for the future, for two reasons. First, it is essential for Labour to learn the lessons of the past if it is to produce and implement future policies which will create a more compassionate, equal and just society. Second, it is important to see whether democratic socialism has produced and can produce gains and benefits for working-class people, with all the redistributions of power, income and status that this would entail.

Most traditional accounts of the history of social policy have been basically descriptive rather than analytical. Generally, they do not seek to place events in a social, economic or political context. Some of the exceptions to this consider the Welfare State as a natural consequence of society's economic, industrial and urban development. Titmuss has described this view in the following terms:

Some students of social policy see the development of 'The Welfare State' in historical perspective as part of a broad, ascending road of social betterment provided for the working classes since the nineteenth century and achieving its goal in our time. This interpretation of change as a process of unilinear progression in collective benevolence for these classes led to the belief that in the year 1948 'The Welfare State' was established. Since then, successive Governments, Conservative and Labour, have busied themselves with the more effective operation of the various services, with extensions here and adjustments there and both parties, in and out of office, have claimed the maintenance of 'The Welfare State' as an article of faith.

On this view it could be supposed that speaking generally, Britain is approaching the end of the road of social reform: the road down which Eleanor Rathbone and other reformers and rebels laboured with vision and effect.[25]

This consensus view of social policy does recognize that differences of opinion exist between the political parties, both historically and today, but generally implies that society's values about social services have been clear and unified. On the surface there might appear to be evidence for this interpretation. The foundation of the Welfare State was laid before Labour became a force in the land – it only formed its first majority government in 1945 – and before this pensions, health insurance, State education and local authority housing were well and truly established. Similarly, much of the groundwork for social reform was undertaken by non-socialists. The famous late nineteenth-century poverty surveys were carried out by Booth and Rowntree, both Liberals. And, as for legislation, Marshall has remarked:

The three pillars of the British Welfare State were the Education Act, the National Insurance Act, and the National Health Service Act. They are associated with the names of Butler, Beveridge, and Bevan – a Conservative, a Liberal, and a Socialist. When one remembers the mixed origins of social policy at the beginning of the century it is not surprising to find that the Welfare State, when it eventually saw the light, was of mixed parentage.[26]

Partly as a reaction to the intellectual poverty of many traditional accounts, there has in recent years been a surge of new Marxist writing about the Welfare State which aids immensely an analysis of contemporary social policy. What is not useful, however, is that kind of analysis which, swallowing whole a conspiracy theory, not to mention an excessive functionalism, suggests that social reforms have not merely failed to create a more equal society – a view readily accepted by non-

Marxists and one which was argued in Chapter 4 – but that they can be understood merely as a key tool for capitalist preservation which has thus kept power in the hands of the ruling class. This analysis *is* a powerful one and contains strong elements of truth, but if it were to be accepted whole, without important qualifications, it would suggest that the efforts of the Labour Party since its origins had been a waste of energy at best and at worst a cruel ritual and hoax. This analysis would have us believe that *all* social reform can somehow be understood in terms of the needs and interests of capital, that any working-class victory is somehow really a victory for capitalism (by preventing revolution and hence safeguarding capitalist interests), and that therefore any future reform programme is inevitably flawed.

Any simple-minded conflict view of the Welfare State should be rejected (as it is incidentally rejected by many modern Marxist writers and would have been by the grand old man himself).[27] The story of the Welfare State is a more complicated one than this and involves a number of elements and explanations.

First and foremost it is important to recognize that there is nothing implicitly or inevitably 'socialist' about social policy. Here the general use of the term 'Welfare State' is misleading: there are a variety of such states and some have little to do with welfare. In many respects a Welfare State can be seen as a product of a certain stage of national development and is common to many different kinds of modern societies, capitalist and communist alike. Certainly some of the most politically reactionary regimes had sophisticated 'social' policies. Nazi Germany, for example, offered a relatively generous package of marriage loans, family benefits and maternity provisions, in order to encourage the growth of the Aryan race.[28]

Any modern society will be forced to intervene in certain matters, not least in the fields of public health and planning, as a consequence of industrialization and consequent urbanization. This has led some writers to note a convergence whereby, despite different political orientations, there are marked similarities in the ways in which Welfare States develop across nations.[29]

Social order

This 'functionalist' approach to explaining the rise of modern Welfare States is also useful – although only partially – in understanding the approach of the Right to social welfare. For while, within capitalist societies, the rise of Welfare States can be explained in part by their functional value in providing the fit and educated workforce necessary for modern capitalism, given the need for increased skills and greater productivity, it also serves other functions. One relates to the maintenance of social order and thus political control.

Social security has often played a key role here, as Piven and Cloward have noted:

Relief arrangements are ancillary to economic arrangements. Their chief function is to regulate labor, and they do that in two general ways. First, when mass unemployment leads to outbreaks of turmoil, relief programmes are ordinarily initiated or expanded to absorb and control enough of the unemployed to restore order; then as turbulence subsides, the relief system contracts, expelling those who are needed to populate the labor market.[30]

The history of the English Poor Law provides powerful support for this kind of analysis. Fraser has argued that:

It was undoubtedly fear of social disorder in the two and a half centuries following the Black Death which gradually converted the maintenance of the poor from an aspect of personal Christian charity into a prime function of the state.... Laws against vagrancy were ... the origins of poor relief, and whenever economic conditions prevailed which encouraged men to wander the country in search of employment, the later medieval and early modern English state sought to restrict this mobility for fear of its social consequences.[31]

Nineteenth-century Britain introduced the workhouse, with its odious regime determined by the principle of 'less eligibility', to produce conditions worse than those in the outside world in order to encourage what the Establishment regarded as the feckless and the lazy to work for their living. This approach is echoed today within the supplementary benefit scheme. Similarly, some of the hastily conceived youth employment schemes have been inspired more by a fear of disorder and

other adverse social consequences than by genuine concern to provide
employment for young people.

Military strength

The development of social policy has also been influenced in the past
by military considerations. The 1871 Franco–Prussian War taught
many leaders that successful conflict now involved whole nations and
not just rival armies. The German victory showed the importance of a
fit and literate population. And in Britain a widespread concern about
the high rejection rate of recruits during the South African War on
medical and physical grounds led to the setting-up of a committee on
physical deterioration. Its 1904 report appealed for action to alleviate
overcrowding, pollution of the atmosphere (decades before the passing
of the Clean Air Act), underfeeding, and also the medical inspection of
schoolchildren.[32] In general, war has often led to interest in social
conditions and Titmuss has noted 'the increasing concern of the state
in time of war with the biological characteristics of its people. The
growing scale and intensity of war has stimulated a growing concern
about the quantity and quality of the population.'[33] David Donnison
has recently suggested, however, that the advent of nuclear weapons
may have negated this requirement.[34]

Capitalism and social policy

All of this shows that the factors at work behind social reforms are more
complicated than a simple beneficent desire to help mankind. Moreover,
quite apart from the need to maintain order, more fundamental political
calculations were also of importance. The rise of the Welfare State can
only be comprehended fully in the context of the development of social
class, subsequent class conflict and the evolution of political movements
and parties – in the case of Britain the rise of the modern Conservatives
and the advent of the Labour Party. In the view of George: 'The
strongest continuing influence in the development of the social security
system has been the successful attempt of the dominant social groups

to buttress the existing social and economic order.'[35] There is certainly no shortage of evidence to support this contention. Indeed, arguably, the first measure in the modern history of social security was the introduction of old-age pensions by Chancellor Bismarck, coinciding with the banning of the German Social Democratic Party. And the example of Bismarck was not lost on British politicians. In 1908, for example, Churchill was advising the prime minister to 'thrust a big slice of Bismarckianism over the whole underside of our industrial system'.[36] However, much earlier, in 1885, Joseph Chamberlain, the influential Liberal (and later Liberal Unionist), said, 'I ask what ransom will property pay for the security which it enjoys?' His own answer was that 'society owes a compensation to the poorer classes of this country, that it ought to recognise that claim and pay for it'.[37] The Marxist political scientist, Miliband, has observed that 'in insisting that the "ransom" be paid, governments render property a major service, though the latter is seldom grateful for it'.[38] Balfour, later a Conservative prime minister, developed Chamberlain's point when he remarked in 1895:

Social legislation . . . is not merely to be distinguished from Socialist legislation but it is its most direct opposite and its most effective antidote. Socialism will never get possession of the great body of public opinion . . . among the working class or any other class if those who wield the collective forces of the community show themselves desirous to ameliorate every legitimate grievance and to put Society upon a proper and more solid basis.[39]

While some reforms have undoubtedly been of benefit to capitalism, and while others may have been introduced as a peremptory measure to seduce the working class away from socialism in an era of the mass franchise, a strong element behind social reform has been pressure from working people themselves, pressure which during the twentieth century has been largely exercised through the trade unions and their 'representative committee' in Parliament, which became the Labour Party in 1906. Undoubtedly the rise of the Labour Party has led to reforms, not only, most obviously, by Labour governments, but also by Conservative politicians anxious to preserve their Party as a dominant political force, despite rapidly changing social and political circumstances. In his book, *In Place of Fear*, Aneurin Bevan made the point well:

I am not asserting that when social reformers are moved to ease the distress of poor people they are thinking of the minimum concession necessary to preserve the rule of wealth. What I do contend is that the suffering of the poor was ignored while they lacked the power and status to insist on alleviation.[40]

Bevan here was echoing a point made much earlier by the young Engels, in 1845, when he wrote: 'It is high time, too, for the English middle-class to make some concessions to the working-men who no longer plead but threaten; for in a short time it may be too late.'[41]

In some cases working-class pressure has led to an immediate reform. The introduction of rent control in 1915 is a case in point and certainly an interesting one. The general scarcity of housing in conditions of war had led some landlords to increase their rents, a move which provoked a popular outcry. The areas particularly affected, and those consequently that led the campaign for a rent freeze, were those heavily engaged in war work. Amongst these the 'Red' Clyde stood out – a thorn in the flesh of government. In this area, as in others, the First World War led to an increase in population and with it a demand for housing. The general cessation of house construction and the slackening in the activities of the Local Government Board inspectors made worse a housing situation that was already in 1914 a cause for national shame.[42] The rent increases lit the touchpaper. With the encouragement of the Clyde Workers' Committee, the support of the Glasgow Trades Council and the help of John Wheatley and other Labour members of the city council, a rent strike started which led to several tenants being brought before the small debts court where the men's wages were impounded. When the first case was heard, thousands of workers left their factories to surround the court. A historian who has studied the politics of the Clyde during this period has concluded that: 'the wave of agitation rose so quickly and was so broadly based that . . . the Government promised to bring in a Rent Restriction Bill'.[43] While Middlemas goes on to say that the Glasgow experience was not the only reason for the decision, there is no doubt that this agitation was of great importance. Although the 1915 imposition of rent control was meant purely as a temporary wartime measure, governments ever since have found themselves entangled in the 'rent question'.

The rise of the Welfare State is therefore not a rosy story of problems discovered, followed by a common desire to tackle them, but rather, is one bound up with Britain's economic and political development. Many social reforms have been enacted in order to make capitalism more efficient, others have involved tactical concessions to an emerging, organized working class, while some have been gained through working-class struggle or via the ballot box, as Labour's great victory in 1945 and subsequent reforms testify. This is not to deny that there have been many reformers who, while not being socialists or even radicals, have been moved to demand reform for philanthropic, Christian or humanitarian reasons. It would be foolish, indeed repellent, to assume that every privileged person who is moved to campaign on behalf of the poor and underprivileged had a hidden political motive, as if he or she were some mere agent of capitalism or a simple puppet in some devious political theatre. To argue the history of social policy in this way is unnecessary and stupid and brings into ridicule a socialist analysis that needs to be properly stated and understood.

The story is certainly a complicated one, in part because yesterday's opponents of certain reform measures emerge later as champions of them, or at least accommodate them. As Engels noted, 'that horrid "People's Charter" actually became the political programme of the very manufacturers who had opposed it to the last';[44] and the Establishment has wisely chosen to support limited measures in order to prevent more radical ones being enacted. Bevan certainly understood that: 'capitalism proudly displays medals won in the battles it has lost'[45] and Crosland, writing in the mid 1950s, observed that 'the Conservatives now fight elections largely on policies which 20 years ago were associated with the Left, and repudiated by the Right'.[46]

The history of the modern Welfare State has therefore been intimately associated with democracy. The coming of the mass franchise changed the political landscape and, therefore, ideas about the correct role of government. Sidney Webb had warned that the governing classes must be prepared for a new Parliamentary climate. The dock labourer or tram driver would not regard their new voting privilege as a means of determining the party affiliation of the ambassadors in Paris or even deciding questions of war and peace. Surely, Webb asserted, they would see it as a way of altering 'the conditions under which they live and work'[47] and as Gilbert observed, that fear of socialism was 'the catalyst of social politics'.[48] Indeed, Engels had remarked in 1845:

The question: What is to become of those destitute millions, who consume to-day what they earned yesterday; who have created the greatness of England by their inventions and their toil; who become with every passing day more conscious of their might, and demand, with daily increasing urgency, their share of the advantages of society? – This, since the Reform Bill, has become the national question.[49]

The complex development of Britain's Welfare State is a large part of the answer to that 'national question'. British social policy has been shaped by a range of various social, economic and political forces. The end product is compromise between competing ideologies. It is full of contradictions and based on a range of institutions and policies, some of which undoubtedly reflect, rather than challenge, inequalities, while others, such as the NHS, are based on ethical principles directly opposite to those of capitalism. Around this compromise was built the postwar consensus. The consensus is now over and a re-evaluation must take place.

The State in welfare capitalism

The arguments developed in this chapter raise some important questions about the role of the State itself in relation to its welfare functions or, as some might pose the question, what is the role of the State within 'welfare capitalism'?

Again, following the analysis of this chapter, the issue is complex and one must reject equally the argument that the State is inevitably beneficent or is totally oppressive or manipulative – that is, the State as being 'but a committee for managing the common affairs of the whole bourgeoisie'[50] to quote the *Communist Manifesto* of 1848, simply serving the interest of capital. The former view hardly squares with any honest description of much current social policy, but the latter does not explain the principles and much of the practice of the NHS or the dedicated work of thousands of 'State employees' as hospital porters, nurses, doctors, teachers, council officials or administrators.

To the consternation, no doubt, of the tidy analyst, the reality of the State's role is more complex than many academic accounts would have us believe. Also, it is misleading to regard the State as a homogeneous institution: in practice there are competing interests within and between, say, ministers, Civil Servants, central government and local authorities. Indeed, the present administration has faced not insignificant difficulties because of this: many Labour local councils have thwarted Conservative expenditure ambitions, while the 'leaking' of official documents from within the bureaucracy has alerted the public to many dangers.

For much of the postwar period, what some now regard as the golden years of the 1950s and early 1960s, economic growth enabled Conservative politicians to back their liberal instincts and expand, albeit within limits, many welfare services – in other words, to be beneficent. The economic problems that developed in the mid 1960s and reached crisis proportions by the late 1970s changed all this: the collapse of certainty about economic growth contributed to the advent of a new kind of conservatism and encouraged a new breed of Conservative politicians to have the courage of their illiberal convictions and to roll back the Welfare State. Harsher times called for harsher measures. As Gough has noted:

Capitalism, which in the central countries of Europe and America has permitted the development of the productive forces, political democracy and social rights in the post-war period, may no longer be capable of achieving all three simultaneously. In that case, either accumulation in economic growth or political and social rights must be sacrificed. Either way the nature of the Welfare State would be transformed.[51]

The impact of social policy

We need to turn now to a related, but separate, question: how should socialists evaluate the *impact* of social policy in Britain? In the last chapter it was argued that, in general, social policy had not improved fundamentally the *relative* position of working-class people in Britain. Certainly the performance of the Labour governments in the 1960s and 1970s in the field of social policy were a disappointment by any reasonable standard.[52] Even allowing for economic difficulties and the political problems caused by small majorities or no majorities, there is nothing in the record of these administrations to compare with the social policy achievements of the great postwar government. Related to the lack of achievements, even when the most extreme criticisms are discounted (and after allowing for the growth of social expenditure that occurred during many of the Labour years), no radical transformation of British society occurred. And related to the lack of achievements is the failure of ideas, the lack of any vision for the Welfare State in the changing world of the 1970s and 1980s. It was this lack of new ideas and philosophy that so ill-prepared Labour to fight the 1979 general election.

After forty years of the modern Welfare State, despite the radical reforms of the postwar Labour government and Labour being in power for seventeen of the last forty-one years, Britain is not a fundamentally more *equal* society. Given the enormous growth of State social services during this period – and the large number of State interventions in a range of areas – this is a remarkable conclusion. It testifies to the enduring inequalities of capitalism and the strength of the forces in society which create and maintain inequalities. It also demonstrates the enormous difficulty that confronts any radical government which generally seeks greater equality.

The evidence on inequality has also convinced many socialists and other critics that the Welfare State has failed to help working people, and it is at this stage that it is necessary to introduce a different perspective and to recognize the successes of a Welfare State. For while a focus on relative deprivation and therefore inequality is of prime importance, we should not ignore the impact of social policies on absolute standards in areas like income, health, housing and education. The evidence for this was presented in Chapter 4. Indeed, one of the reasons for conflict within the Labour Party at local levels is, in part, due to this conflict of perceptions. The older generation (usually with working-class backgrounds), whose formative years were often the 1930s and who have spent a lifetime serving the working class as councillors and in other capacities, focus on the achievements of the Labour Party and can see these in terms of better housing, State schooling and the NHS. The younger generation of Labour activists, who are more likely than their predecessors to be of middle-class backgrounds, became active very often during the late 1960s and the 1970s and are well aware of the disappointments of the Labour governments of those years and focus on the perpetuation of inequalities in society and thus easily – too easily – dismiss postwar Welfare State achievements.

There is a sense in which the academic critique of social reforms has been *too* academic. This has led to a cynical atmosphere where every reform has to be shown to be fundamentally flawed. And yet it needs to be emphasized that British society has been significantly transformed by social policies and related measures. While this point is readily appreciated by many people over the age of 50, it seems often to have escaped the attention of many commentators, partly because academics have various axes to grind – which do not include highlighting the *successes* of the Welfare State. The growing number of Marxist academics have a vested interest in showing the inevitable failure of welfare reforms; New Right academics wish to demonstrate the inflexible, bureaucratic and monolithic nature of welfare; while many non-Marxist socialists and radicals focus on failures and criticisms in the hope and belief that this will stimulate the public conscience and lead to better reforms. However, the intellectual climate so fostered meant that in the run-up to the last two general elections there was no body of opinion arguing for the Welfare State from conviction, and hence the New Right, often using evidence from Left-inclined academics and pressure groups, were able to call for a re-evaluation, in essence a retreat, from State welfare. The critique, far from having beneficial results, has become a force for reaction. Thus radical criticism of the complexity of supplementary benefits has led to retrenchment; the criticisms of local authority housing as regulation-bound has helped legitimize the sale of council houses; while attacks on State education and health have re-vitalized the case for private markets in these areas.

The Left critique was not matched by the development of a new social programme let alone the building-up of popular support for a reformed Welfare State. The political beneficiaries of this failure were the New Right – the major victims have been the working class and the poor.

The common feature of New Right, Marxist and libertarian critiques is their pessimism about the role of the State in human welfare: indeed it is regarded as bureaucratic and overbearing, very often denies liberty – and often dignity – infringes choice and, according to the Marxists, has actually preserved, rather than undermined, capitalism.

What are the implications of this for the future of social policy? As for the New Right, their stance is the direct antithesis of democratic social policy. It is important to recognize, however, that some of the things said by the New Right about the Welfare State have struck home with the wider public. Their criticisms of the State have been echoed, in part, by those who wish to make social policy more democratic, accountable and participatory.

The implications of this are pursued in later chapters. As for the Marxist critique, this has been immensely valuable in enabling radicals to analyse better the historical development of social policy in Britain and present-day societies like our own. While avoiding the trap of falling for the conspiracy theory approach, it enables us to understand better the reasons for the perseverance of inequality. It also shows the formidable barriers that stand in the way of implementing a genuine strategy for equality.

6 Social Changes towards the Year 2000: Population, Family and Work Patterns

... all three institutions, family, work and the state, are in a period of flux, and we need to understand both the changes *within* these institutions and the changing relationships *between* all three if we are to have informed discussions, and if these are to lead on to appropriate policy prescriptions.

Study Commission on the Family[1]

The success of future social policies will depend not only on a critical assessment of the past, but also on an understanding of how British society has changed, and will change, as we approach the new century. Some of the most important contemporary developments concern individual, household and family living patterns, on the one hand, and work and employment patterns on the other. Thus three important institutions that affect most people – the family, work, and the State – are undergoing rapid change. Halsey has referred to the need to 'renegotiate' the respective roles of these three – and such a renegotiation involves important social, economic and political questions.[2]

The Tory approach is clear and has particular implications for women and the poor. It involves permanently high levels of unemployment; a desire to return women to the home, to perform unpaid caring tasks; and a diminishing role for the State in the field of welfare. The challenge for socialists and radicals is not only to reverse this trend, but to understand social developments in order to implement appropriate reforms that will lead to a more positive and attractive relationship between employment and home life; equality between men and women; and a more comprehensive view of 'work', whether it is performed in employment, or at home, or in the community. This socialist renegotiation starts, however, with an appreciation of present and likely future trends.

Population changes

At the most basic level, changes in population, not only total population but also within and between certain age-groups, affect social needs and hence, future provision.[3] Table 6.1 shows population figures, by age-groups, from 1971 to 2021. The ageing of the British population is the most dramatic development and the details of this are discussed later in the chapter.

Here, however, we consider trends among the younger age-groups. Starting with the youngest, it can be seen that the number of under-5s declined from 4.3 million in 1971 to 3.5 million by 1986, but that the number is now on the increase: it will rise by some 282,000 in the years up to 1991. If such an increase occurs – and by its very nature predictions here are the most uncertain – it has important implications for health visitors, much of whose work is with young children and for the provision of nurseries, play groups and other day-care services. Thus, the growing number of under-5s in the 1980s poses one challenge for a new government, not least because of the priority many would give to this area of policy.

The total number of school pupils in the United Kingdom has fallen from 11.3 million in 1976 to 10.1 million in 1983 and is projected to decline further to below 9 million in 1991.[4] *Social Trends* describes the changes as follows:

Between 1976 and 1983 the total number of pupils in public sector schools aged 5 or over fell by about 12 per cent – the number in primary schools fell by 23 per cent, while the number in secondary schools increased by 1 per cent. Public sector pupils aged 5 or over are projected to fall by a further 13 per cent by 1991, the number on primary rolls falling by only 1 per cent and the number on secondary rolls falling by 24 per cent.[5]

It should be noted however that the more recent upturn in births will mean an *increase* in primary school populations in the 1990s. As Table 6.1 shows between 1991 and the year 2001, the number of pupils aged 5–9 are projected to increase from under 3.5 to over 3.9 million. Those aged 10–14 will similarly increase in the decade up to 2001.

Table 6.1 Population changes: Great Britain, 1971–2021 (000s)

Age	1971 (no.)	(%)	1986 (no.)	(%)	1991 (no.)	(%)	2001 (no.)	(%)	2021 (no.)	(%)
0–4	4,349	8.1	3,458	6.3	3,740	6.8	3,795	6.8	3,726	6.6
5–9	4,512	8.4	3,311	6.0	3,456	6.3	3,929	7.0	3,583	6.3
10–14	4,069	7.5	3,536	6.4	3,308	6.0	3,737	6.7	3,481	6.1
15–19	3,705	6.9	4,313	7.9	3,530	6.4	3,450	6.2	3,558	6.3
20–64	30,205	56.0	31,777	58.0	32,465	59.0	32,596	58.2	32,469	57.1
65+	7,139	13.1	8,476	15.4	8,688	15.7	8,546	15.2	10,005	17.6
TOTAL	53,979	100.0	54,871	100.0	55,187	100.0	56,049	100.0	56,822	100.0

Sources: Census 1971, Great Britain, HMSO, 1974; Office of Population Censuses and Surveys, *Population Projections, 1983–2023*, HMSO, 1985, Appendix 1, Table A1(b).

Falling rolls are, for the immediate future, mainly a problem for secondary schools and sixth forms. The declining numbers at sixth-form level are every bit as dramatic as the fall in the school population generally. It is estimated that the number of 16-year-old pupils in the United Kingdom will decline from 312,000 in 1983 to 251,000 by 1991.[6] Within this, the decline will affect localities in very different ways.

Household formation

While population changes have particular significance for many areas of social policy, such as social security, health and education, it is household formation that is often of equal significance for other policy fields, like personal social services and housing. Table 6.2 presents some basic facts and allows us to contrast the situation in 1983 against that for 1961. Many of the trends are best interpreted in terms of family patterns, but we should note here the significant rise in the number (and the proportion) of one person households, caused by changes affecting both elderly people and young citizens. Taken together, it can be seen that the proportion of all households comprising just one person has increased from 11 per cent in 1961 to 24 per cent by 1983. In terms of numbers, this represents more than a doubling, from 1.9 million in 1961 to 4.2 million in 1981.[7]

Changing family patterns

The family is probably the most important unit in society that is affected by government policies. In a wide variety of ways, and through many different services and benefits, policies affect families for good or ill throughout their life cycle. So much is obvious, but paradoxically there has been relatively little explicit discussion by government of the assumptions made about family life or the intended impact of policies on families of different kinds.[8] Certainly Britain has never had a visible family policy – a term which is widely recognized in several European countries – and yet there are implicit assumptions about family life

Table 6.2 Households by type

	Percentages		Thousands		
	1961	1983	1961	1971	1981
No family					
One person					
Under retirement age	4	8	726	1,122	1,469
Over retirement age	7	16	1,193	2,198	2,771
Two or more people					
One or more over retirement age	3	1	536	444	387
All under retirement age	2	2	268	304	535
One family					
Married couple only	26	27	4,147	4,890	4,989
Married couple with 1 or 2 dependent children	30	24	4,835	4,723	4,850
Married couple with 3 or more dependent children	8	6	1,282	1,582	1,100
Married couple with independent child(ren) only	10	8	1,673	1,565	1,586
Lone parent with at least 1 dependent child	2	5	367	515	916
Lone parent with independent child(ren) only	4	4	721	712	720
Two or more families	3	1	439	263	170
TOTAL HOUSEHOLDS	100	100	16,189	18,317	19,493

Source: Social Trends, 15, Central Statistical Office, 1985, HMSO, Table 2.5.

underlying various areas of social policy. Sometimes these have been freely stated. When national health insurance was first introduced, for example, government actuaries explained the exclusion of married women in the following way:

Married women living with their husbands need not be included since where the unit is the family, it is the husband's and not the wife's health which it is important to insure. So long as the husband is in good health and able to work adequate provision will be made for the needs of the family, irrespective of the wife's health, whereas when the husband's health fails there is no one to earn wages.[9]

Similarly, Beveridge in his 1942 Report made certain assumptions about family life and argued that:

... all women by marriage acquire a new economic and social status, with risks and rights different from those of the unmarried. On marriage a woman gains a legal right to maintenance by her husband as a first line of defence against risks which fall directly on the solitary woman; she undertakes at the same time to perform vital unpaid service ...[10]

More generally, Abel-Smith has noted the assumptions underlining the Beveridge Plan:

a.) that marriages are for life, even if the parties do not stay together, the legal obligation to maintain persists until death or remarriage;
b.) that sexual activity and child birth takes place or at least should take place only within marriage;
c.) that married women normally do no paid work or negligible paid work;
d.) that women and not men should do housework and rear children;
e.) that couples who live together with regular sexual relationships and shared expenses are always of the opposite sex.[11]

Many contemporary social policies are based on reforms enacted in the 1940s, reforms which often looked back to the needs and problems of the interwar years. It is crucial that future social policy must be based on a firm understanding of contemporary family patterns and the likely future direction of trends. What do we mean by the term 'family' in modern Britain? For many, 'family' conjures up a picture of a man and woman married to each other with two or three of their own children. Implicit also in the conventional picture is the assumption that it is the man who goes out to work and earns money and the woman who stays at home to be housewife and to look after children.

In fact, as Table 6.2 shows, households consisting of a married couple and dependent children comprise just 30 per cent of all households and many such households are dual, rather than single, worker families. Such a 'snapshot' picture of households can be misleading however: it certainly needs to be complemented by figures that show what proportions of *individuals* live in what kind of households. For example, in 1981, almost 49 per cent of all individuals lived in households consisting of a married couple with dependent children. A further 10 per cent lived in households made up of a married couple with independent children.[12] As Kiernan notes: 'Over the last two decades the majority of people, about 80 per cent, lived in households headed by a married couple, and about three out of four of these families contained children.'[13]

A number of important trends have affected the family and many have important implications for policy. Here we review some of the major developments.

Marriage Most families are based around marriage, but marriage itself is undergoing change. In brief (and contrary to much punditry) marriage remains highly popular, but increasing numbers of individuals do not remain married to the same partner 'till death us do part'. For more than a hundred years, marriage rates were on the increase and, compared with mid-Victorian England when some one-third of women remained unmarried owing to an unequal sex ratio and high male emigration,[14] in recent times some nine out of ten individuals were married by the age of 40.[15] Despite some decline in marriage rates in the 1970s (which can be partly explained by changes in the timing of marriages), and despite increasing cohabitation, marriage will remain, at least into the foreseeable future, the relationship around which most families are based. However, the legal and financial advantages of formal marriage are disappearing in such areas as legitimacy and property rights.

Cohabitation Cohabitation is of increasing importance. It has been suggested that 'at no time in our history has it been so easy to obtain the sexual and other comforts of marriage without troubling to enter the institution',[16] and official statistics show that growing proportions of couples live together before marriage. Some 7 per cent of women under the age of 25 who first married between 1970 and 1974 had lived with their husbands before marriage compared with 2 per cent who were married for the first time five years earlier. Evidence from the 1983 *General Household Survey* suggests that this proportion had risen to 21 per cent for those married in 1979–82 and, in addition, about one in ten single women reported currently cohabiting.[17] Some couples will therefore cohabit prior to marriage; others will cohabit, perhaps briefly, as an alternative to marriage; while others may cohabit because one of the couple is unable, at the time, to remarry. Indeed, of those women marrying between 1979 and 1982, where one or both partners were marrying for the second time, two-thirds had cohabited with their husband, prior to the marriage. Altogether, however, only 4 per cent of women aged 18–49 are cohabiting.[18]

In view of these trends it would seem sensible that future social policy is concerned with families, regardless of the form or basis of the relationship between the adults concerned. Future social policy should also be based on a clear recognition that in certain other key areas, family patterns are changing quite significantly, and often rapidly. Particular developments are divorce and the related increase in the number of one parent families.

Divorce Within a relatively short period, divorce has become a major social trend and now affects large proportions of men, women and children. The Divorce Reform Act of 1969, which took effect in 1971 (similar legislation affected Scotland some years later), liberalized the grounds for divorce and led to a sharp upward movement in total numbers. In 1984 there were 158,000 divorces granted in the United Kingdom, against only 27,000 in 1961;[19] today one in three new marriages will end in divorce (and teenage marriages are most at risk with one in two teenage brides divorcing). The Study Commission on the Family has estimated that as many as one in five newborn children in England and Wales will have parents who divorce before the children are 16.[20] In 1981, 159,000 children had parents who divorced in that year, and 40,000 of these children were aged under 5.[21] This is a dramatic trend by any standard and has implications for social services, education, taxation, social security and housing.

Remarriage Related to increasing divorce is an equally significant trend towards *remarriage*. In 1984 some 35 per cent of new marriages involved remarriage for one or both spouses. And some one in six marriages involves a remarriage for *both* partners.[22] On the basis of current trends around one in five men will have been remarried by the year 2000 and a slightly smaller proportion of women will have entered a second or later marriage.[23] The consequence of this is that increasing numbers of children are being brought up in families where one of the adults is not their natural parent and, hence, step-families have become an increasingly significant phenomenon.

One Parent Families Related to increasing divorce is the growing number of one parent families, which has increased from 570,000 in 1971 to 890,000 in 1979–81. The National Council for One Parent Families estimate that there are now about 1 million one parent families in the United Kingdom with 1.6 million children.[24] Today, an estimated one in eight children live in such families, but this 'snapshot' picture underestimates the true proportion of children who will spend at least part of their childhood in a one parent family. The implications of the growing number of one parent families are important because, in general, the adults and children in such families are often severely disadvantaged. The implicit family assumptions which underlie much of our social policy assume the family to be one with two parents, and the consequent failure to adjust policies to the needs of growing numbers of one parent families has severely exacerbated problems. One of the most important of these concerns income.

As a group one parent families in general are less well-off than two parent families. The latest evidence available (for December 1981) shows that some 120,000 children were in one parent families with incomes below the supplementary benefit standard; 630,000 had incomes at the level; and altogether, 940,000 children lived in one parent families with incomes below 140 per cent of this standard.[25] A large proportion of one parent families rely on State benefits, notably supplementary benefits and Family Income Supplement. The risk of poverty among one parent families is high and there is often little to be gained from combining part-time work with receipt of benefit.

Lone parents are therefore often faced with the choice of bringing up their children at the levels of living provided through the benefit system, or are forced to work longer hours than mothers in two parent families to achieve anything approaching a decent standard of living for their children. When supplementary benefits are claimed, new relationships may be hampered by the knowledge that women forfeit benefit in their own right if they begin to cohabit. Moreover, separated and divorced women often face very real difficulties in obtaining the maintenance which they have been awarded by the courts from their ex-husbands. There can be little doubt that social security provisions are failing to cope adequately with increasing marriage breakdown and this produces major strains which are an important feature in the lives of many such families.

Marital breakdown, the growing number of one parent families and remarriage all contribute to an increasing variety of family types in modern Britain. And, consequently, while in 1982 80 per cent of all children aged 0–18 lived with both their natural parents, this is true of only 77 per cent of 10–15-year-olds and only 71 per cent of 16–18-year-olds. Six per cent of all children lived with their natural mother and stepfather and 10 per cent were in families headed only by a mother.[26]

Elderly People A further aspect of changing family patterns, and one with immense significance for social policy, concerns the increasing numbers of elderly people in general and the rapid rise in the numbers of very elderly people in particular. During this century there has been a marked growth in the proportion of elderly people in Britain's population. Table 6.3 presents some basic information. In Britain, between 1901 and 1981 the numbers of elderly people aged 65 and over rose from 1.7 to almost 8 million, and increased as a proportion of the total population from less than 5 to 15 per cent. During that same 80-year period there were also dramatic increases in the numbers of the very elderly population: between 1901 and 1981, the numbers aged 75 and over increased six-fold, from 507,000 to 3,052,000; and the numbers aged 85 and over increased virtually ten-fold, from 57,000 to 552,000.

Table 6.3 The elderly population: past, present and future (ooos)

	1901	1931	1981	2001	2021
65+	1,734	3,316	7,985	8,546	10,005
75+	507	920	3,052	4,006	4,355
85+	57	108	552	1029	1,202
%					
65+	4.7	7.4	15.0	15.2	17.6
75+	1.4	2.1	5.7	7.1	7.7
85+	0.15	0.24	1.03	1.8	2.1

Sources: 1971 and 1981 Censuses, and population projections by the Government Actuary; mid 1983 based principal projections 1983–2023.

These trends will continue over the next two decades into the new century. Between 1981 and 2001 the total number of persons aged 65 and over will increase from almost 8 to almost 8.6 million. However, taking the age-group 75 and over, the numbers here increase by over 1 million, from more than 3 million in 1981 to over 4 million by 2001. Similarly, the numbers aged 85 and over almost double from 552,000 in 1981 to over 1 million by 2001.

Significant proportions of elderly people experience disabilities and levels of dependency. For those aged 65 and above, 5 per cent are estimated to be housebound or bedridden, rising to 21 per cent of the most frail, those aged 85 or over. Similarly, 9 per cent of those 65 and over are unable to bath alone, and the proportion is as high as 34 per cent among those aged 85 and over.

Large proportions of elderly people live alone and the numbers involved are likely to increase in the future. While 34 per cent of all those aged 65 and over live alone, for the frailest the proportions are much higher. The majority (53%) of women aged 85 and over, for example, live alone. Many old people, however, live with others, often family members. Eleven per cent of all elderly people live with a brother or sister, or with a son or daughter, and the proportion is as high as 32 per cent for women aged 85 and over.[27]

A significant factor is that a large number of elderly people either have never had children or now have none surviving. One study showed that 30 per cent of the over-75s had never had children and 7.5 per cent had outlived their children.[28] This has important implications for community care policies.

Housing circumstances, while varying greatly among the retired population, also reveal a number of problems. In general, the housing of the elderly is worse than that of younger groups. For example, of elderly persons aged 75 and over who live alone, 4.5 per cent have no bath and no inside water closet.[29] Central heating is far less common among elderly people: in 1982 49 per cent of households consisting of one adult aged 60 or over had *no* central heating, compared to, for example, only 29 per cent of 'small family' households.[30] Similarly, while the great majority of elderly people are either owner occupiers or council tenants, a higher proportion than for the population as a whole live in privately rented housing which is often associated with poorer conditions. Even those in seemingly good housing may face problems of too much space and have too many rooms to keep warm and maintain and may seek, often unsuccessfully, smaller, warmer and more suitable accommodation.

Lower incomes are also a fact of life for many elderly people. The vast majority of the old face a substantial reduction of income on retirement. In 1985/6 some 1.8 million persons over pensionable age – about 18 per cent of the total – were receiving supplementary benefit.[31] Moreover, the basic rate pension in July 1986 was equivalent to only around 21 per cent of the average national earnings of full-time adult workers for single people, and almost 35 per cent for married couples. Low income pensioners have to spend a large proportion of their income – about two-thirds – on the three basic necessities of housing, food and fuel. At the margins, life for elderly people in Britain can be very bleak indeed, with all too often cruel choices having to be made between heating rooms adequately in winter *or* eating reasonably.

Richard Titmuss once noted that: 'Viewed historically, it is difficult to understand why the gradual emergence in Britain of a more balanced age structure should be regarded as a "problem of ageing" '.[32] Titmuss remarked that this should be regarded rather as a matter for satisfaction. Since Titmuss wrote these words in the early 1960s, the numbers of the very elderly have increased dramatically as we have seen. Certainly in a well-ordered and civilized society, such an ageing of the population would be a cause for satisfaction and we could remark upon the richer variety of communal life afforded by the growth of three- and four-generation families. However, as this brief review of the social and economic characteristics of the elderly has noted, many old people can look forward to retirement years that are often blighted by poor economic circumstances and other deprivations. While some such deprivations, for example those associated with aspects of ill health, are to some extent inevitable, there is nothing 'natural' about an equation between old age and deprivation. Rather this becomes the case because of implicit decisions taken about the distribution of resources within society.

Today, and for the foreseeable future, the increase in the number of very elderly people represents either a crisis or a challenge. If our society cannot respond in appropriate ways to the trends, many elderly people will live out their final years in poverty, squalor, much discomfort and misery. Given the current direction of social policy, this will sadly be the lot for too many of our elder citizens. However, the ageing of Britain's population should be properly regarded as a great social challenge for all of us.

Employment trends

This is not the place to review economic or employment changes comprehensively, but rather to discuss some changes that have greatest importance for social policy.

Since 1951 the total number of employees has not changed dramatically, until the re-emergence of mass unemployment in recent years. Total British employees numbered 21 million in 1951, 22.2 million in 1975 and 20.7 million in 1981. However, within this general picture, there have been some important changes relating to the position of women. Thus, while the total number of male employees declined from 14.2 million in 1951 to 13.3 million in 1975 and 12 million in 1981, the number of female employees rose from 6.6 million in 1951 to 9 million in 1975, and 8.7 million in 1981 (having reached a peak of 9.3 million in 1979). As a proportion of total employees, women represented 40 per cent in 1983 against only 31 per cent in 1951.[33]

There has, moreover, been a dramatic increase in the number and proportion of married women in employment. As Rimmer and Popay have noted: 'In 1921 less than 10 per cent of married women were in the formal labour force, but after the second world war the proportion of married women in paid employment rose rapidly and continuously, and by 1979 nearly half of all married women were economically active.'[34] Whereas married women, non-married women and men were respectively 3.8, 25.7 and 70.5 per cent of the labour force in 1921, the proportions were, by 1979, 25.9, 13.4 and 60.6 per cent. And today, 'two out of every five workers are women, and married women working now outnumber unmarried ones by about two to one. Overall then, one quarter of the labour force are married women.'[35] A clear implication of these trends is that we must rid ourselves of outmoded assumptions about the 'typical' worker, often thought of as a married man, with a wife at home, and two dependent children. How much bargaining around the negotiating table, and how much employment policy, has this family in mind? Yet such a 'typical' worker now represents just *8 per cent* of the labour force.[36]

Associated with the trends towards more female and married women's employment has been the rise of part-time (mainly female) employment. It has been estimated that 20–25 per cent of the female labour force were doing part-time work in 1966, 30 per cent in 1970 and 42 per cent in 1979.[37]

More women at work – and particularly more mothers at work – has led to increasing interest in the relationship between home and work responsibilities, and as argued later, this should be one focus of a future social strategy. How exactly are employment and family responsibilities related?

The *Women and Employment Survey* allows us to answer these questions.[38] In 1980, among women with *no* children under 16, 54 per cent worked full-time and a further 20 per cent part-time. By contrast, among all women with children under 16, only 17 per cent worked full-time, but 35 per cent part-time.[39] The *number* of children under 16 obviously affects employment prospects: for example, while 21 per cent of women with only one dependent child worked full-time, this was true for only 14 per cent of those with two children, 12 per cent of those with three and 11 per cent of those with four.[40]

The *age* of the youngest child is also an important factor. Where their youngest child was under 5, 7 per cent of women worked full-time and 20 per cent part-time. For those whose child was aged 5–10 the respective proportions were 16 and 48 per cent. For women with a child aged 11–15, 31 per cent were working full-time and 45 per cent part-time.[41]

Fatherhood affects employment in very different (indeed converse) ways than motherhood, for its effect is towards *longer* hours at work: the majority of fathers work full-time and those with large families work longer hours on average than those with fewer children. Fathers are also more likely to work overtime.[42] Thus, while parenthood draws women towards the home, it prevents men from spending more time there, because of their need for extra income.

There is a growing recognition of the need to relate work and family responsibilities together if children's welfare is to be enhanced. This concern now needs to be developed, but also to be complemented by a recognition that many employees also have caring responsibilities for elderly relatives. As with children, responsibility for the elderly can affect whether or not someone is able to work outside the home and the hours that can be worked. A survey of elderly people showed in 1976 that among women who gave up work between the ages of 40 and 59, the need to look after people other than husbands comes second only to ill health as a reason for giving up work.[43]

Looking to the future, much will of course depend on policy, both the success of economic policies designed to stimulate the economy and hence tackle unemployment and also the effect of social policies which will help determine the pattern of work and the distribution of resources and tasks between men and women. The question of work therefore looms large and must fundamentally shape any future social strategy.

PART FOUR

Future Strategy

7 Principles for Social Policy: Equality and Liberty

The rank and file of the labour movement ... regard democracy, not as an obstacle to socialism, but as an instrument for attaining it, and socialism, not as the antithesis of democracy, but as the extension of democratic principles into spheres of life which previously escaped their influence.

R. H. Tawney[1]

A major argument of this book is that, not only is this Tory government capable of destroying the Welfare State as we know it, if given the opportunity, but that only a government committed to democratic socialist policies can build the Welfare State that Britain requires. But what is meant by democratic socialism? This is no new question, nor is there a shortage of theoretical literature or practical experience to provide the answer. And the answer could be an exceedingly full one. Here, however, my concern is to put forward a simple and practical statement of democratic socialism, as a benchmark against which to assess the practical social policies that are required.

The choice of the term 'democratic socialism' is, in part, a pragmatic one and it is used to distinguish one philosophy from others. In brief, 'democratic' distinguishes the philosophy from other so-called 'socialisms' that have no respect for democratic systems or for the rights of ordinary men and women, but rather seek to impose on society a set of institutions, policies and beliefs. However ideal the motives behind the concept of a 'dictatorship of the proletariat', the outcomes are invariably grim. This élitist and authoritarian approach to socialism has had its practical manifestation in too many nations and, sadly, there are exponents of such views today on the British Left. At least on the authoritarian axis, their views place them nearer to the extreme Right than the democratic Left. Social policies in this context soon become mere instruments for national objectives and would deny individual freedom and liberties.

These authoritarian versions of socialism are sometimes labelled 'Marxist', but this is very much a perversion of the truth. So-called followers of the teachings of Karl Marx, as with the followers of Christ and other great leaders, have undertaken much evil, but this is not the fault of Marx, a point well made by the late Swedish prime minister, Olaf Palme: 'I have always found it difficult to understand why elitist thinkers and supporters of revolutionary violence should regard themselves as the standard bearers of a Socialist and Marxist tradition which has its roots in Western Europe and in West European humanism.'[2] While the 'democratic' part of our definition distinguishes our beliefs from authoritarian thinkers, 'socialist' distinguishes the philosophy from other radical approaches.

What, however, is *democratic socialism*? This is no easy question, for it is inspired by no one tradition, philosophical school, or set of beliefs. Rather it derives inspiration, ideas and experience from a range of historical strands and, while some come from other parts of the world, it is firmly British in character. Democratic socialism is a practical manifestation of centuries of radical struggle and working-class desire for a better society. Tony Benn is just one of a number of British labour leaders who have noted the rich origins of British socialism when stating that 'the British labour movement draws its inspiration from a history that goes back over many centuries'.[3] Christianity, the Levellers, the Chartist campaign for Parliamentary democracy, trade unionism, feminism, Marxism and other radical and liberal ideas, campaigns and ideals have all influenced socialist thought and action.

Given the mixed origins of democratic socialism, it may lack the theoretical coherence of, say, Marxism or other comprehensive ideologies and is consequently a constant frustration to political analysts. However, drawing as it does on the concerns and beliefs of working-class people, it is practical, robust and enriched by the strengths of many viewpoints. Above all else it is non-sectarian. The description 'broad church' is often used cynically, but it is a truth, and a strength, not a weakness.

Crosland, in his brief review of the traditions of British socialism, concludes in part that there are some fundamental differences between different schools of socialist thought and that the doctrines are often mutually inconsistent:

> Thus Fabian collectivism and Welfare Statism require a view of the State diametrically opposed to the Marxist view. The syndicalist tradition is anti-collectivist. The Marxist tradition is anti-reformist. Owenism differs fundamentally from Marxism and syndicalism on the class war. Morrisite Communes and Socialists Guilds are incompatible with nationalisation: and so on.[4]

Crosland himself, however, notes that 'the single one element common to all the schools of thought has been the basic aspirations, the underlying moral values. It follows that these embody the only logically and historically permissible meaning of the word "socialism".'[5]

Equality

What are the ideals – 'the underlying moral values' – that inspire democratic socialism? A good starting point is the definition provided by William Morris, writing in 1894:

> ... what I mean by Socialism is a condition of society in which there should be neither rich nor poor, neither master nor master's man, neither idle nor overworked, neither brain-sick brainworkers, nor heart-sick handworkers, in a world, in which all men would be living in equality of condition, and would manage their affairs unwastefully, and with the full consciousness that harm to one would mean harm to all – the realization at last of the meaning of the word 'COMMONWEALTH'.[6]

Central to Morris's definition and to democratic socialism is a passionate belief in equality: the belief that all citizens should be born with equal rights, that they should give, and receive, respect to their fellow men and women, that they should contribute their best to society and take on a fair share of responsibility according to their abilities and receive a fair and equal share in the distribution of resources. This belief in equality is substantially different from the view of Conservatives and Liberals – the belief underpinning American capitalism – in equality of *opportunity*. For as Tawney has noted: 'Nothing could be more remote from Socialist ideals than the competitive scramble of a society which pays lip-service to equality, but too often means by it merely equal opportunities of becoming unequal.'[7] Equality of opportunity may well – indeed certainly does – call for social reform, but it is essentially concerned to remove some of the more obvious impediments of capitalism. It is also concerned to maximize the efficiency of capitalism, by providing it with the best talent and enterprise, but it is not what democratic socialism is about. Rather, to quote Tawney again: 'Our aim should be the opposite. It should be to effect a complete divorce between differences of pecuniary income and differences in respect of health, security, amenity of environment, culture, social status and esteem.'[8] To believe in equality is to reject fundamentally the view that access to decent housing, good health services or education should be decided on the accident of birth, inheritance of wealth or current income.

Liberty

But what of liberty? One of the great ironies of modern politics is the ability of the conservatives, of whatever party, to portray themselves as the champions of liberty and, furthermore, to contrast liberty with equality, arguing that the two are incompatible and that equality will inevitably deny liberty and freedom. And what great freedoms does the modern conservative care most about – the freedom to enable babies to live and not to die because of adverse social conditions; the freedom of the young to get jobs, whatever their class or colour; the freedom for old people to live out their lives in decent housing, and not to die from the cold when bitter weather strikes? Of course not. Nothing could be further from their minds: indeed their own actions, when in government, further deny such fundamental freedoms. Rather they define 'liberty' and 'freedom' so narrowly that they become mere labels to justify their own privileges and bloated life styles. Can it be coincidence that such terms are employed by the rich most passionately and consistently to defend their 'rights' to buy privileged education and medical care for themselves and their families, heedless of the consequences for the rest of society?

This has always been the case. Throughout our history, and stretching back at least 200 years, the conservatives and other defenders of the status quo have opposed reform measure after reform measure – be they concerned with factory conditions, taxation, education or health – on the grounds that they somehow infringe liberty and freedom. In the 1945 general election campaign Churchill, in his first radio broadcast, charged that a socialist policy was abhorrent to British ideas of freedom. Attlee replied in the strongest terms:

I entirely agree that people should have the greatest freedom compatible with the freedom of others. There was a time when employers were free to work little children for 16 hours a day. I remember when employers were free to employ sweated women workers on finishing trousers at a halfpenny a pair. There was a time when people were free to neglect sanitation so that thousands died of preventable diseases. For years every attempt to remedy these crying evils were blocked by the same plea of freedom for the individual. It was in fact freedom for the rich and slavery for the poor.[9]

Tawney also warned against the Tory approach to liberty:

It is a doctrine of liberty which is disposed to regard it as involving, not action to enlarge opportunities and raise individual faculty to the highest possible level, but guarantees for the continued enjoyment by fortunate individuals and groups of such powers and advantages as past history and present social order may happen to have conferred on them.[10]

We must expect this time-honoured Tory tradition to continue: the misappropriation of the most inspiring words in the English vocabulary in defence of the most obscene privilege.

Yet, it is not only the Conservatives, and their allies in other parties, who confuse the meaning of freedom and seek to set it against equality. Many of the public see a similar conflict. Indeed when asked to choose between them in a recent survey (a choice which by being so presented biased the response) the majority in Britain, 67 per cent, subscribed to the following statement: 'I find that both freedom and equality are important. But if I were to make up my mind for one or the other, I would consider personal freedom more important, that is, everyone can live in freedom and develop without hindrance.'[11] This was the highest response to this statement among the six nations surveyed. How do we account for this? In part, it is a sign of the successful propaganda for the Conservative Party, backed up by the mass media. However, in large measure it is to do with the experience of so-called 'socialist' regimes in other parts of the world where 'equality', camouflaging privilege to a party élite, *is* in conflict with human liberties. Moreover, the public are further uninspired and discouraged by the pronouncements of some on the Left who describe their socialism in ways which make it sound as liberating as Wormwood Scrubs and as attractive as Victoria Station at midnight – without its charm.

So democratic socialists who care – as we must care – for the battle for hearts and minds as well as for votes have a struggle on their hands to convince the public that, first, the Conservative approach to freedom is severely suspect, to put it mildly, and second, that equality and freedom are not only mutually consistent but that, for the majority of people, liberty and freedom in the full social, economic, and cultural sense depend on a decisive move towards greater equality in Britain.

So much, then, for the Conservatives' approach to liberty. Nevertheless, there remains a possible conflict between equality and freedom. The very nature of government, and the need to govern in the interests of the whole community, involves the restrictions of some 'freedoms', ranging from ones that are non-controversial – murder, robbery and arson – to ones which are the subject of controversy, for example the compulsory wearing of seat belts. In approaching these questions, socialists should be guided not merely by utilitarian principles – the greatest happiness of the greatest number – but also by a strong conviction that equality is not so much a goal in itself – because that might mean merely the equality of drab uniformity – but as the key means to promoting liberty and fraternity. It is only justified to restrict the freedom of the small minority (to get, say, privileged access to education or health care) when it is clear and demonstrable that this will lead to greater freedom for the majority. Action must always be guided by the principles of welfare and justice and never by spite or anger.

Further, democratic socialists should extend their belief in greater liberty by developing democratic control and participation within the social services; and by considering a number of contemporary questions, such as the balance between income maintenance and service provision, and our approach to housing policy, from a libertarian perspective.

Social policy must be concerned to provide a framework of services, benefits and facilities within which all people can exercise the freedoms and the choices which up to now have only been exercised by a privileged minority.

But how much equality? This is a crucial question, though one that is often avoided – not least because it raises some difficult questions. In particular, while it is easy to demonstrate, from a socialist – or indeed any ethical standpoint – that the current distribution of income, wealth, resources and opportunity is based on *no* rational criteria (why should a betting shop manager earn more than a nurse, or a city stockbroker more than a steelworker?) it is harder to determine what an equitable distribution of income should be.

The true egalitarian, of course, would argue for a distribution of resources 'from each according to his or her ability, to each according to his or her need'. This remains a worthy objective, but a programme for five years needs to be based on more humble, albeit still radical, objectives. However, this must be a process that involves the start of a national debate about income. While few would accept today a completely equal distribution of resources, there is a majority constituency to be won in favour of a much fairer distribution.

The Rawlsian principle of justice as fairness is helpful here. This supposes that individuals in a society are able to choose which arrangement for their society would be just, without their knowing where they themselves would be placed within the society. A veil of ignorance operates. From this standpoint Rawls argues that:

... persons in the initial situation would choose two rather different principles: the first requires equality in the assignment of basic rights and duties, while the second holds that social and economic inequalities, for example inequalities of wealth and affluence, are just only if they result in compensating benefits for everyone, and in particular for the least advantaged members of society.[12]

This, of course, is a philosophical construct but it is a helpful one and not without contemporary political relevance. A society based on such principles of justice would certainly be much fairer and more equal than present-day Britain. There is ample evidence, moreover, that most people agree that there is too much inequality today, and that certain egalitarian reforms would gain popular support. In *British Social Attitudes*[13] for example, it was found that the public thinks the gap between high and low incomes is too large by more than a three to one majority. The 1983 survey by Mack and Lansley produced similar findings indicating that the majority think that the poor are entitled to more. Support for the aim of a more equal society was strong: 74 per cent thought the gap between rich and poor too wide; and 76 per cent that the differences between the highly paid and lowly paid are too extreme. Not surprisingly, differences were marked in the attitudes between different income groups, social classes and political affiliations: only 53 per cent of the richest households, for example, thought the gap between rich and poor too wide, compared with 91 per cent of the poorest households.

Support for such principles is matched by a willingness to support more effective policies. Several MORI polls of the 1980s indicated little support for cutting public expenditure, and Mack and Lansley's research indicated 'a surprisingly strong willingness for personal financial sacrifice'[14] to facilitate greater expenditure on the poor. Certainly the evidence 'suggests that the foundations exist in popular attitudes for building wider support for redistributive strategies'.[15]

Moving towards equality

The basic principle of equality, as a means to the end of liberty, has two implications for policy: the establishment of basic rights to meet certain needs, and a decisive move towards redistribution.

While a future government might not be able to ensure equal access to basic rights in the life-time of a single Parliament, it can move towards establishing modern minimum rights to meet basic needs. Now, of course, 'need' can be variously defined – 'felt' need may not always be 'expressed', for example.[16] Yet clearly, at present, provisions in many fields – supplementary benefit, housing, heating and community services – are below what a civilized society should expect. New standards must be set and targets for action determined.

Basic minimum standards, however, must be part and parcel of a strategy for equality. Action across a wide field must tackle such inequalities, and well-informed public debate must be encouraged about the distribution of resources, reward and opportunity in a modern society. What inequalities are justified? This is the question to be asked and each public measure to promote greater fairness, be it a wealth tax, progressive income taxation, health programmes or provisions for children under 5 years old, should be the occasion for debate. True egalitarians will wish to push the argument to its logical conclusion in the long term, but each gain along that road will be important.

8 A Social Strategy

What is national planning but an insistence that human beings shall make
ethical choices on a national scale? . . . The language of priorities is the religion
of socialism.

Aneurin Bevan[1]

Supporters of the Welfare State must enter the next election campaign
with a clear and attractive alternative to Tory social policies. Future
policy needs to be argued at the level of detail, service by service, but
it is essential that the detailed programmes are aspects of a coherent
plan – an alternative social strategy. Such a social strategy should be
integrated with, and be complementary to, the alternative *economic*
strategy.[2]

The aim here is to outline the most important issues, themes and
ideas that should determine such a strategy. They concern fundamental
guiding principles, the nature of social policy and its relationship with
economic policy, two urgent tasks, the social context within which
policy should be developed, and questions of government and implementation.

Equality and social integration

The first focus of the new strategy is its most fundamental guiding
principle. Central to the definition of democratic socialism adopted in
the previous chapter was the goal of equality. Therefore the new strategy
must be, above all else, *a strategy for equality*. This is no new objective
for radicals and socialists. Yet, some eighty-seven years into the century
that has witnessed the coming of the mass franchise, the rise of the
Labour Party, the introduction of progressive taxation, capital taxes
and the Welfare State, the evidence plots the remarkable stubbornness
of inequality.

Radicals must draw on the lessons of the past if policies are to be fashioned to erode significantly the worst inequalities. Further, the concept of class inequalities must be complemented by an understanding of further inequalities. Some of the most important are between men and women. Whether in pay, employment, taxation or many other spheres, the goal of sex equality is still to be achieved and this poses a particular challenge to the labour movement – itself better at representing men than women.

The feminist question – strongly reinforced since the late 1960s – is important, however, not only in the obvious sense in that it focuses on the needs of both men and women, but also in the broader sense that it reminds us that socialism is about the relationships between peoples in a democratic society; and this has implications not only for systems of government and a wide range of policies, but also for individuals within the home and in the community.

Further inequalities relate to age, dependency, race and location, and these need to be understood if the next generation of social policies are to grapple with the complexities involved in developing an egalitarian strategy for the 1980s, 1990s and beyond. Indeed, a comprehensive understanding of inequality is necessary to ensure that in moving towards policy goals in some areas, inequalities of some kinds are not exacerbated (for example, within 'community care'). At least this Conservative administration has demonstrated that a substantial redistribution of resources is possible, given political will.

The major objective of a socialist social policy must therefore be social integration: only through socialism can we build 'One Nation', in the sense of an equal society, rather than a calculated political smoke screen to camouflage privilege.

Future social policies must be concerned not merely with statistical equality as measured by indices of income, education, housing and so on, for equality must become a living reality. This, of course, cannot be legislated for and there are deeply held customs, traditions, fears, prejudices, anxieties and stigmas that bar the road to a true 'commonwealth', to use a term from an earlier generation. But, it is very much within the power of governments and public institutions to develop policies, systems of administration and participation, and attitudes which will help create a more integrated society.

Such policies include, for example, forms of income support that do not specifically isolate the poor. This will involve an emphasis on universal non-means-tested provisions and the focus on integration is a powerful argument in favour of considering seriously the amalgamation of taxation and social security. One system of income and tax assessment should apply to all citizens, as is argued in Chapter 9.

Moreover, the principle of social integration has implications for other areas of social policy. It should be a guiding principle for services and provisions concerned with the care of the sick, the disabled and elderly people within society. It prompts the need for a positive policy of community care and also has implications for housing and planning, for as Bevan observed while minister responsible for housing, it is 'essential for the full life of a citizen to see the living tapestry of a mixed community.'[3]

A total approach to social policy

The pursuit of equality depends, in part, on a broad definition of social policy. A focus merely on the more visible social services and benefits is too narrow and, indeed, seriously misleading. Rather, social policy must encompass all institutions and mechanisms, public or private, which affect and influence, either directly or indirectly, whether through service provision, benefit payments, taxation or other means, the welfare, income, wealth, and status of individuals and families. In particular, as is argued in Chapter 9, future social policy must confront what Richard Titmuss termed 'the social division of welfare', that is fiscal welfare – tax benefits and allowances – and occupational welfare, alongside the more conventional Welfare State. Social policy must include and reform all institutions that affect class and other forms of inequality.

Social policy and economic policy

The third feature of the new social strategy should be a close and positive relationship between social and economic policy. No longer should benefits and services be regarded as side issues – the ones you can get right when the economy picks up – but rather as a key component of an overall strategy.

Too often socialist debates in Britain have emphasized the details of economic and industrial arrangements and neglected – or taken for granted – social aims. This focus on the means of achieving socialism, rather than overall objectives, has been a serious distortion and has ill-equipped socialists to adjust to changing circumstances.

Against this, it is a continuing strength of socialist analysis that it seeks to understand society in relation to the means of production, distribution and exchange and hence is a *class* analysis. A weakness of much social policy thinking in Britain has been its lack of a class dimension. Therefore any socialist social policy has to analyse these two areas of public policy together and to understand that progress towards social policy objectives will depend, in large measure, on parallel developments within the economic sphere.

While some policies must be implemented on social grounds alone (priority to mentally handicapped people, for example), there is a need for an assessment of *both* social and economic objectives together and the measuring of compatibilities and incompatibilities between them. Thus the social policies that are most effective in boosting economic demand might take priority. Similarly, social programmes that provide additional jobs should be introduced early. Housing provides a good example. Unmet housing needs are accumulating at a time when a quarter of all construction workers are unemployed. A major housing investment programme would meet both social and economic policy objectives. So would a national insulation programme, given the need to provide warmer homes for the vulnerable and the importance of energy conservation.

An assessment of both social and economic objectives might require the delay of some cherished reforms. For example, would reducing the retirement age for men to 60 necessarily lead to more employment for younger workers? And might not such a reform lead to increasing poverty and isolation among the old in the first years of a new government? A political movement that is to be taken seriously has not only to argue the first priorities on resources, but also to explain which reforms, however laudable, would *not* be implemented early. Social policies must be aware of other economic objectives. These will concern keeping inflation in check and reducing the flow of imports. A crash programme of insulation, say, might lead to a massive in-flow of imported materials, and hence might not provide as many manufacturing jobs as hoped for and, also, exacerbate the balance of payments – always a danger with economic policies designed to stimulate the economy. The answer, to pursue this example a little further, might be the implementation of a phased programme, involving home manufacturers, with a strong role for a new publicly owned energy conservation industry.

While social programmes might therefore enable economic objectives to be met, it will always be important to keep the social objectives at the forefront. Thus, within housing, the building boom, initiated by the Labour government of the 1960s, provides a cautionary tale. It resulted, in too many areas, in the construction of socially undesirable, damp, ultimately hard-to-let, environmental eyesores which, while not inevitably increasing the welfare of those rehoused, certainly increased the profits of certain giant private building corporations. This must not happen again: social programmes must be monitored and evaluated to ensure that not only the immediate, but also the wider and longer-term effects are socially desirable.

The matching of economic and social objectives requires a level of sophistication beyond an assessment of what overall levels of extra resources can be accomplished within a desirable economic strategy. As Blake and Ormerod have argued: 'the *composition* of public expenditure needs to be planned more carefully from a macro-economic point of view, as well as the actual levels of expenditure'.[4] It follows that there must be clearly defined priorities both within and across policy and departmental boundaries.

The attack on unemployment

The next two objectives of the social strategy concern urgent tasks for a new government. An alternative social strategy would make the attack on unemployment a key target. The inability to find work not only creates poverty, but pollutes the whole of national life. Over forty years on, the words of William Beveridge ring out as a warning that we have ignored for too long.

Idleness is the largest and fiercest of the five giants and the most important to attack. If the giant Idleness can be destroyed, all the other aims of reconstruction come within reach. If not, they are out of reach in any serious sense and their formal achievement is futile.[5]

Present and future studies of urban life, housing, health, education, welfare and crime will provide grim testimony to Beveridge's statement for the 1980s.

The 'future of work' debate will grow in importance throughout the 1980s and beyond, and make an increasingly important impact on the whole arena of social policy debate. Those on the political Right, and even fashionable voices in the centre of politics, will argue that Britain must 'come to terms' with large-scale unemployment. In simple terms this means that large numbers of men and women – but not themselves – will never have jobs. We must be aware that the impact of new technologies *could* lead to increasing inequality within society, as the value of work no longer has to be distributed, in part, to large workforces. It is therefore for socialists to demonstrate that, whatever the assessment about the combined impact of new technologies, changing world markets and other economic factors, there can be no excuse for *unequal* access to the work that is available. Economic and technological trends must be planned to liberate men and women, not to expand the size of the new conscript army of the workless and rejected.

An anti-poverty programme

The fifth objective of the new social strategy must be to eradicate poverty. Together with unemployment, the attack on poverty is fundamental, not just because both are substantial social diseases in their own right, but also because they both exacerbate significantly other social problems and make their alleviation so much harder. Our creaking system of social security must therefore be recast. Social security is not only the most expensive area of public policy, but because of the debilitating effects of poverty on other areas of life such as health, educational attainment and care, the need for reform in this area is fundamental. A coherent reform should involve the integration of social security and taxation, a comprehensive system of benefit provisions for children and other dependants, a recast benefit structure for disabled people, and policies which are in line with changing family patterns and the policy goal of sex equality. Moreover, social security and taxation must be related closely to policies on incomes, which should include both minimum and maximum wage levels, and the overall distribution of rewards and resources in society.

Work and the family

A sixth theme concerns the relationship between work and the family. As argued in Chapter 6 new social policies must be based on a firm understanding of contemporary and future social and economic trends. Quite apart from the impact of unemployment, both family life and work are changing rapidly. The increasing employment of women outside the home, the rise of the dual worker family, more divorce and increasing numbers of one parent families, together with the growing numbers of frail, elderly people within the community who require help and support, all raise important questions. If we continue to regard 'work' and 'family' as separate components of life, we will aggravate the many pressures that social change creates for individuals. Moreover, this would make the goal of sex equality a more difficult one to attain.

The introduction of maternity and paternity leave provisions should be viewed as but first steps towards a realignment of home and work life. The social strategy too must be based on a realistic and broad concept of the nature of 'work', recognizing that much work is done within the home and community. Such work is unpaid, but will grow in importance, given social and demographic trends. For the future, the quest for social justice will be determined in part by a radical evaluation of work: if the traditional concept goes unchallenged a strategy for equality cannot be successful.

All this shows the need for trade unions to become as much involved with 'social' as with 'economic' policy, and their need to consider the wider social requirements of a worker and his or her dependants alongside immediate, and more traditional, questions of pay and conditions.

Democratizing social policy

A seventh emphasis of the social strategy is the need to democratize social policy. Different traditions, and now years of experience, have thrown up a range of ideas about the proper organization and running of society. In the main, the predominant tradition on the Left has involved strong government, at both central and local level. This is an important tradition and, despite defects, is one that can be built on in the future. However, it is important to emphasize a different set of theories and beliefs that involve the organization of both work and social matters through groups of men and women coming together, in co-operatives, to organize and administer their own affairs. In practice, it had been a weaker tradition on the Left, but is one that needs to be developed and expanded in the future as a strong influence on the development of social policy.

This tradition must flourish in the future because the association between equality (and the move towards it) and liberty (and moves to increase it) involves above all else a relationship between the individual and the State.

The need then is to develop more accountable and democratic relationships. This is of fundamental importance after the anti-democratic years of Tory government and their assaults on local government, trade union rights and other aspects of our democracy. Some areas of our Welfare State have grown in size without clear increases in welfare; there has been a growth of complexity; too many council tenants, parents and other welfare consumers have too little power over their own affairs; and too many of our service institutions treat their customers with lack of respect and courtesy. We need therefore to develop those long-held traditions which concern the distribution of power within the community and the need to democratize our institutions.

The new social strategy must therefore be based on a determined, but realistic approach to the question of democratization. It should involve policies that delegate power and responsibility and which also encourage those initiatives which have developed over the last decade in many local communities.

Social planning and implementation

A radical government must consider the machinery of government in the light of its social policy objectives. In part, this is because our heavily departmentalized Whitehall system is ill-equipped to cope with the increasing number of issues – the inner city, social aspects of energy, the care of elderly people, income maintenance – which cut across departmental boundaries. We need a genuine joint approach to social policy that actually works and this requires strong prime ministerial interest in the alternative social strategy and a revamped Cabinet Office to oversee and implement government social policy decisions. The next chapter argues that this will involve a new division of responsibilities within Whitehall; the creation of a Social Policy Development Council and the introduction of social impact statements accompanying new policy measures. Moreover, social policy must be formulated within the context of a more open and democratic approach to government. A Public Information Act should be introduced and full public discussion of policy options encouraged.

Environmental conservation

Social policy is at heart about developing a decent society and therefore the conservation of the environment must be a key objective of any new social strategy. This has a number of features and a number of policy implications. In part, it involves assessing economic objectives against their possible detrimental effect on the environment. It certainly means a rejection of the capitalist values whereby change is justified if it leads to increased economic output and profits. Recent concern about acid rain illustrates the importance of this issue. It is estimated that each year between 60 and 70 million tons of chemical pollutants are released into the skies over Europe. Negative effects of this are dramatic, as research now shows, and the evidence suggests that Britain is 'exporting' the worst of the impact, resulting in an accelerating loss of fish[6] and other organisms from lakes and rivers in southern Scandinavia. Britain is the main culprit. These and other forms of environmental pollution must be prevented in the future.

More generally, a range of policies – housing, planning, architecture and energy programmes – must place environmental concerns in the forefront of policy-making. A specific example, as already noted, is the need for a comprehensive insulation programme.

Similarly, a humane social policy cannot just focus on people. It is a slight to our civilization that so many unnecessary animal experiments are carried out each year. In 1984, for example, almost 3.5 million experiments were performed and, of these, 2.8 million were performed without anaesthetic. Such experimentation in order to develop medical products is difficult territory, but can there be any justification for animal experiments concerned with cosmetics, of which there were over 17,000 in 1984?[7] Such cruelty to animals must be outlawed and, moreover, there must be a determination to reduce substantially other animal experiments, save where it can be demonstrated publicly that medical advance would be severely handicapped if experiments did not take place. The cause of 'animal rights' is rightly gaining prominence and deserves urgent action.

Internationalism

Finally – but certainly not least – it must be emphasized that any comprehensive social strategy must be international in scope and must not restrict itself to the details of domestic policy. The policies of a national government can, perhaps, make their most significant impact on domestic problems, but a socialist concern to eradicate poverty and inequality has to adopt an internationalist stance.

Inequalities between the industrialized countries and low income countries are stark. Figures from the World Health Organization show that food supply as a percentage of requirements is 131 per cent for the industrialist countries, against 94 per cent for low income countries. Moreover, only 29 per cent of the population of low income countries have access to clean water; and while the infant mortality rate in the industrialized world is 11 per 1,000 live births, it is a tragic 130 in the developing world. Health spending for the industrial world represents $277 per head, against just $2.6 per head in low income countries.[8] Furthermore, while Britain has 154 doctors per 100,000 people (in 1980) Sri Lanka has just 14, India 27, and Kenya 9.[9]

The implications of these north-south inequalities are not only that Britain must give greater priority to overseas aid programmes, but that economic and foreign policies must take full account of our obligations to the Third World. For example, no policy of import control, however desirable from a domestic viewpoint, must discriminate against those developing nations that need to export if they are to feed, clothe and house their populations even to a basic minimum in the future.

These are some of the themes which might guide the formation of an alternative social strategy. Most of them need further discussion and other issues need to be raised. But the ideas included represent a commitment to the concept of a Welfare State as a crucial social institution which now needs restructuring and developing in the light of changing demographic, social and economic trends, and to be geared to meeting the objectives of greater equality and social justice.

PART FIVE

Social Policies for the Future

9 Social Policy

Socialist social policies are, in my view, totally different in their purposes, philosophy and attitudes to people from Conservative social policies. They are (or should be) pre-eminently about equality, freedom and social integration.

Richard Titmuss[1]

In the last chapter, the outline of a social strategy was presented. This chapter aims to develop these ideas with reference to some key areas in social policy. It is important to start, however, by raising the question, What is social policy?, not out of academic interest but because it is also a *political* question, as too narrow an answer to it gives a biased view of the Welfare State, and one that fails to confront crucial questions of resource distribution which are essential to an egalitarian strategy. Conversely, a radical view of social policy is necessarily a broad one.

In Chapter 5 it was argued that thoughtful Tory politicians embrace social policy and social reform as an 'effective antidote' to socialism. Therefore, social policy is not necessarily egalitarian and Chapter 4 argued that, all too often, it is *not* egalitarian in practice. But what areas are covered by the term 'social policy'? According to Marshall, social policy is 'the policy of governments with regard to action having a direct impact on the welfare of the citizens by providing them with services or income'.[2] Under this definition would be included health, personal social services, education, housing and social security.

The social division of welfare

The focus on the conventional areas of social policy, however, is too narrow and a key contribution to our understanding of postwar social policy is Richard Titmuss's 'The Social Division of Welfare', a lecture given in 1955.[3] In this he noted the concerns of those troubled by the 'burden' of the Welfare State who felt, in the words of a Conservative Political Centre publication, that 'the social well-being of the nation had been endangered by the redistribution of wealth'.[4] To put these views into perspective, Titmuss argued that, alongside the conventional Welfare State of benefits and services, two other systems operated: fiscal welfare and occupational welfare.

By fiscal welfare, Titmuss meant allowances and reliefs from income tax which 'though providing similar benefits and expressing similar social purpose in the recognition of dependent needs, are not, however, treated as social service expenditure'.[5] Titmuss, rightly, argued that both are 'manifestations of social policies in favour of identified groups in the population and both reflect changes in public opinion in regard to the relationship between the State, the individual and the family'.[6] Moreover, since the introduction of progressive taxation, there had been 'a remarkable development of social policy operating through the medium of the fiscal system'.[7]

Fiscal welfare includes the personal allowances, such as the married man's allowance with an estimated cost in 1985/6 of £12.9 billion, relief for pension schemes of up to £3.6 billion, and tax relief to owner occupiers at £4.7 billion.[8] The example of housing illustrates the grossly unfair nature of much fiscal welfare.

While much public debate about housing benefits focuses on subsidies to local authority tenants – which is a recognized aspect of public expenditure – tax relief on mortgage interest payments made by owner occupiers is also a substantial feature of housing policy. Indeed, between 1978/9 and 1984/5 tax relief grew from £1.1 billion to £4.7 billion.[9]

While both the formal subsidy and the tax relief are designed to help with housing costs, housing benefits favour the poorest, while the amount of tax relief *increases* with income. The Government has not published new evidence on the distribution of mortgage tax relief. However, Institute of Fiscal Studies calculations for 1982 show that those with incomes over £15,000 per annum, despite accounting for just 10 per cent of all households, received some 36 per cent of all mortgage relief – equivalent to £1.3 billion in 1984/5. Over 80 per cent of this group received some relief. By contrast, only 3 per cent of those with incomes below £6,000 received any tax relief.[10] This is the logic of a system where reliefs also operate against tax at the higher rates.

Titmuss also highlighted the importance of 'occupational welfare' which had reached 'formidable and widespread proportions'. How significant is it? One survey of executive salaries and fringe benefits shows that 67 per cent of the executives had full use of a company car, 62 per cent had life assurance, 44 per cent received free medical insurance, and 89 per cent had assistance with house purchase. Such company welfare schemes heighten inequalities and Frank Field has noted its 'two-fold distributional impact' in that it 'helps to spread the tax load of high income earners over what can sometimes be decades, while appreciably increasing the difference in living standards between high and low income earners'.[11]

Titmuss argued that in the light of these three separate systems of welfare – the social division of welfare – the criticisms of the early postwar Welfare State were 'narrowly conceived and unbalanced'. He drew out the lessons for egalitarians:

Within this theoretical framework it becomes possible to interpret the development of these three systems of social service as separate and distinctive attempts to counter and to compensate for the growth of dependency in modern society. Yet, as at present organized, they are simultaneously enlarging and consolidating the area of social inequality. That is the paradox: the new division of equity which is arising from these separate responses to social change.[12]

In addition to Richard Titmuss's three systems of welfare, *State* services and benefits, *fiscal* welfare and *occupational* welfare, we should note further institutions that allocate welfare, formally or informally. Of growing importance is the private market, always, of course, the major distributor of resources in the broadest sense, but now rapidly expanding, within the social arena. Certain sectors of private market welfare, for example education and medicine, are also heavily supported and subsidized by the State, not least through the training of staff.

A further aspect of welfare is that provided by voluntary organizations which operate at both national and local levels. In some fields, a prime example being meals on wheels, such voluntary services act as a substitute for local authority provision and are substantially grant-aided. Voluntary organizations range in their work from traditional service-giving to the elderly, the blind and the disabled, through to the provision of services at the frontiers of welfare, for example family planning and abortion services. Much of this work focuses on health and welfare, but voluntary bodies act in many other areas as well, from housing associations to law centres to unemployment centres. The development of new 'self-help', and many campaigning and action groups, are also important.

Finally, it is important to note the immense amount of care that is provided by the 'community' in general and the family in particular. While it is not easy to distinguish much informal community care from general good neighbourliness, many of those in need, particularly the very frail elderly, receive practical assistance with a range of day-to-day tasks from friends and neighbours. Even more significantly, the family (in practice its female members in the main) provide substantial amounts of care, and is a significantly more important provider of services and help than either statutory or voluntary social services. Many of the most vulnerable, the very elderly, live with relatives. For example, among women aged 85 or over, for 1980/81, some 19 per cent lived with their own children, 8 per cent lived with sons- or daughters-in-law, 5 per cent with siblings, and 4 per cent with other relatives.[13] And, among those living alone, help with day-to-day tasks is often provided by family members: of those unable to shop by themselves, over half were helped by relatives, for instance.[14] It is likely that there are at least 1.3 million carers throughout the country. More generally the role of the family in social policy areas like education and health are of immense importance and will need to be better recognized within the framework of an egalitarian strategy.

To grasp the meaning of 'social policy' then requires an understanding of the different systems of welfare which operate and which affect the nature, scope, quality and distribution of income, benefits, services, facilities and opportunities. The goals of the social strategy will only be achieved if these systems are understood and the inter-connections between them comprehended. Thus, a redistribution of income in favour of low income groups will only be achieved if tax systems and allowances, as well as social security benefits, become a feature of social policy arithmetic. Inequality will only be eradicated if the role of occupational welfare and the private market are understood and re-formed, while the provision of adequate health and care to the frailest members within the community and the building of positive policies of community care necessitate a new partnership between the family and the State.

Social policy therefore needs to be defined widely and is not suscept-ible to any quick and neat definition for, as Donnison has remarked, 'we are concerned with an ill-defined but recognisable territory'[15] and the territory is expanding. For example, public transport might make a bigger impact on the welfare of a rural community than some more conventional social services. And new issues keep coming to the fore. In the late 1960s there was renewed concern about the access of the poor to the legal system and this led to an expansion of legal services. And in the 1970s anxiety about the effects of cold on elderly people during the winter, and the rapid increase in energy prices, led to interest in the social aspects of energy and a new range of policy questions.[16] Moreover, there are some areas of public policy, such as 'law and order', which while not traditionally a concern of those engaged with social welfare could be usefully analysed as an area of social policy.[17]

Employment policy

Finally, it is important to underline the point made earlier that any future social strategy will need to link together social policy and economic policy objectives. Nowhere is this more important than in the field of employment. Indeed, it is unemployment that has forced upon society a need to consider the boundaries between 'social' and 'economic' issues in the field of public policy. Not only do social policy objectives become immeasurably easier to attain if unemployment is tackled and equal access to work successfully achieved but, more specifically, other aspects of social policy are intrinsically linked to employment questions.

Increasingly, for example, we will need to relate as part of a total package, questions of employment, education and training, throughout the working life cycle but particularly, and pressingly, among those aged 16–19. And, if we are to develop successfully the right network of child care arrangements to suit the needs of parents and children in the last years of this century and beyond – in an age when more and more families will be headed by dual workers – much will depend on employment policies as well as child care services.

The rest of the chapter examines three important social policy areas to illustrate how the objectives of the social strategy can be implemented. Clearly, many policy areas relate to the strategy – health, education, transport, law and order and energy are some further examples – but here we consider just three: social security, housing and community care.

Social security and income support

Social security occupies a key place within social policy: not only is income support crucial in its own right, but failings here can prevent other services – education, health and welfare, for example – from achieving their objectives. Moreover, expenditure on social security at an estimated £43 billion in 1986/7 is, by far, the largest element within public spending as a whole: indeed, it is almost two-and-a-half times higher than spending on health and personal social services and accounts for 31 per cent of all public expenditure.[18] Social security affects a large proportion of the community and the numbers dependent on, and supported by, social security provisions are generally increasing in the wake of demographic trends, the growing number of one parent families brought about by the rising divorce rate, unemployment and an increased recognition of disability.

Future policy

Future social security provision must be designed to further several crucial objectives. These are the attack on poverty, through the establishment of a right to a non-means-tested guaranteed minimum; adequate support for those who care for children or others, such as elderly relatives; taxation policies that relate equitably to current work patterns; and systems of benefits that are easily understood and simple to administer. Moreover, social security should aim to spread resources more equitably over the life cycle, and also, in other ways, to help the key aim of greater equality.

By any measure, this is an ambitious agenda and it has both long-term and short-term policy implications. In the long term, the possibilities of integrating the social security and taxation systems into one single income transfer programme should be investigated. In the short term, a few key and critical policies should be identified for implementation in the early years of government.

Long-term objectives: a social security and income transfer programme

A major cause of complexity is the lack of co-ordination between social security policies and the assessment for income taxation. For this reason alone the integration of social security and income tax into one unified system has obvious attractions. It is no new idea.[19] In 1972 the Heath administration published a Green Paper on tax credits,[20] a proposal that was open to important criticism. The Institute of Fiscal Studies has also advocated the introduction of tax and benefit credits.[21]

What is the right approach for the future? In principle, a complete integration of tax assessment and benefit provision (including housing support ultimately) is the goal to aim for. This may be difficult for some on the Left who have been hostile to such ideas, not least because many such schemes have been advocated by those on the Right who see such mechanisms as 'negative income tax' as part of a strategy to scale down the Welfare State. However, such an approach can also service socialist objectives. Indeed, by involving all the community, including all taxpayers, such a scheme is potentially an important means of achieving a radical distribution of income in favour of low income groups and those with caring responsibilities. By treating every citizen through the same scheme, stigma could be avoided.

How would such a scheme work? First, each individual or family unit would be awarded a basic benefit entitlement or 'credit' depending on circumstances. This would involve an adequate minimum income, which would vary depending on the number (and possibly the ages) of children and could include a home responsibility payment for those who provide care within the household (for children under 5, say, or mentally ill or disabled people or elderly persons). Ultimately the scheme would also include housing payment. Second, each household would have this basic minimum assessment offset against earnings. The result would be that some groups, including the elderly, the unemployed, some of the disabled and the low paid, would receive a benefit or credit, while others would pay tax in the normal way on their earnings.

Such an approach is clearly attractive, in principle, and would involve the abolition of a host of separately assessed means tested benefits, existing tax reliefs and allowances, much of the supplementary benefits system and, ideally, housing benefits.

It does, of course, incur a number of major problems. For example, what about those whose earnings fluctuate regularly – sometimes week to week – and who consequently need immediate financial help, which is unlikely to be forthcoming from a comprehensive tax–benefit scheme? What 'needs' should be allowed for, including those which currently are allowable under the income tax system? Who should qualify for a home responsibility payment? And how can provisions be so designed as to provide greater equality between men and women, rather than assume – or even solidify – existing sex roles? What should be the unit of assessment – the 'family' or the individual adult?[22] How would housing costs be met?

The above are just a few of the questions that are raised when tax–benefit reforms are proposed. They are crucial and yet are often ignored by many advocates of integration. However, in the past many radicals have appeared to be better at raising questions – and suggesting why proposals are imperfect – than themselves working on the details, in order to make idealistic proposals workable. Indeed, sometimes, the attention of radicals to the minutiae of administrative detail has made them ill-equipped to develop the ideas which are needed as we approach the next century and which might capture again the public's imagination for social reform. Instead of merely fighting over the details of an antiquated social security system which has dwindling public support, it is essential to develop new proposals around which support can be won.

At present, no new integrated tax–benefit package has been adopted by the Left but, fortunately, time is on the side of reform for the computerization of Britain's income tax system will not be complete until the late 1980s. It will therefore be then and in the early 1990s that any major new reform could be implemented. There is therefore time to develop the ideas, and work out the details, of a new social security and income transfer programme.

Short-term social security priorities

The above represents one approach to the long-term planning of income support. But what of the intervening years? What should be the immediate priorities? Much will depend on the strength of rival bids for public spending and on economic growth. However, future improvements do not just depend on extra spending for within the tax and social security budget *savings* can be made, and money so saved can help fund short-term improvements.

As is argued in the next chapter on resources, money could become available to fund desirable reform through the reduction of unemployment (and hence expenditure on benefits), the reform of the married man's tax allowance and other tax reliefs together with the restriction of all tax allowances and reliefs to the standard rate.

A programme for action

The following illustrates the kind of immediate programme for action that a radical government must implement in the field of social security and taxation. Some of the proposals concern anomalies that cause inequity, while others are designed to bring extra support immediately to hard-pressed groups in the community. Several of the proposals are linked to the longer-term strategy that has been advocated.

Reductions in tax for the low paid While the Tory government's priority in fiscal matters has been to reward the rich with tax cuts, an alternative strategy must involve a radical redistribution from the rich to Britain's low paid workers. In part, this can be done through tax changes and the introduction of a new low tax band.

A guaranteed minimum For those not working, a guaranteed non-means-tested minimum income should be introduced. There are a number of groups deserving more support and balancing priorities will be no easy question. On the agenda must be a quick move back to a State pension index-linked to earnings. The restoration of this cut imposed by the Conservative government must be an immediate priority. Second, and within the context of a move back towards full employment, unemployed workers must receive the long-term rate of benefit. Third, there must be a new package of benefits for Britain's disabled people.

A minimum wage Proposals for a minimum wage have been much debated. It is no easy option and is not without difficulties, in terms of differentials, regulation, and wider impacts on job creation. However, within the context of an expanding economy, it can be implemented.

In the first instance, it might be at the level of £100 per week, as was proposed by the Low Pay Unit in 1983/4.[23]

Child support An enhanced child benefit scheme must be at the forefront of the new social security programme. Precise proposals cannot usefully be put forward but, for example, an immediate £1 increase in child benefit would cost some £550 million. Again, within the context of the abolition of the married man's tax allowance, this proposal could be funded through a redistribution of resources within the tax–expenditure budget.

Home care allowances Fundamental proposals in this area belong more to the long-term strategy, but, under pressure from the European Court, the Invalid Care Allowance has now been extended to those married (and cohabiting) women who care for their dependants. The cost of this is small at £85 million. A radical government must build on this modest step to develop, probably, a range of care allowances, to meet the needs of different people who are dependent throughout the life cycle. Early attention might, for example, be given to those who have caring responsibility for very young children within the home, and thus are denied employment opportunities.

In parallel with these developments, a phased withdrawal of means-test provisions must be accomplished. Early contenders for abolition would be those means tests that relate to health charges, in association with the withdrawal of such charges; the diminution (and eventual end) of Family Income Supplement (family credit); and a reduction in the role of supplementary pensions, in line with real increases in the non-means-tested State pension.

It cannot be done immediately, but the aim, even in the first years, must be to move towards a social security system with clearly understood rights and responsibilities. To aid this, there must be greater customer access to information, and computerization should be seen as a welcome development here. It could allow the customer immediate access to entitlement information and thus free staff to have more face-to-face contact with those customers with particular difficulties.

Housing

While it is questions of income and wealth that often feature most prominently in discussions about equality and social policy, it is within housing policy that much of the key to building a true egalitarian society lies. For it is only if we can learn to live together in the most literal sense, that we can hope to achieve a true fraternal equality and a socially integrated society. At present there could be no more accurate testimony to our divided Britain than the large and isolated council housing estates, which surround too many of our cities, or the private sector developments, the former divided from the latter not only by distance, but also by tenure. Moreover an adequate 'community' care policy for our old people depends very much on housing policy. Accommodation must be built which is not only technically equipped with the best amenities, adequate heating and easily negotiated facilities, but which is also a part of a living and total community.

A future government will face some immediate and urgent housing problems which will demand attention, as a consequence of the Conservatives' quite shameful neglect of housing. But it is essential to devise a clear and long-term housing strategy and not just a package of *ad hoc* and immediate measures.

Yet the immediate housing problems facing the next government will be formidable. As described in Chapter 4, the public sector housebuilding programme has declined to only 38 per cent (in 1982) of its level in 1976, the condition of the housing stock has deteriorated, waiting lists are growing, rents have increased significantly ahead of inflation, while subsidies to owner occupiers have risen.

What should be the key objectives for housing policy? In brief, the aim should be to both raise absolute standards for the worst-off and to move towards social equality, and this raises important questions about both tenure and finance.

If current policies continue, British society will be dominated increasingly by two tenure groups, owner occupation and council housing, rigorously divided on class lines. This is not only a recipe for increased social division, but also makes no sense at all from the viewpoint of housing needs. Indeed, the challenge during the remaining years of this century and beyond is to develop policies which increasingly break the link between tenure and class and, indeed, relate housing provisions in the future to the varied needs of individuals and families over the life cycle. This involves both enabling more of those from low income groups to become owner occupiers and allowing those who have traditionally looked to the private sector to obtain good quality local authority housing when this can best meet needs. This occurs, for example, early on in the housing cycle when single people or couples (or small groups of young people) require rented accommodation and also at the end of the life cycle when local authorities will often be in the best position to provide the range of housing types – sheltered housing and other smaller units of accommodation – which best suit the needs of many retired people, particularly the very frail.

One particular challenge for the Left is to come to terms with owner occupation and to develop those policies which will enable a socialist strategy towards ownership to become part of an overall egalitarian housing policy. This will not always be easy and there are psychological barriers to be overcome: the rise of the Labour Party closely parallels the development of local authority housing, and is associated with it. In 1906, when the Labour Party was formed, most of the population were private tenants. Given this, and Labour's collective approach to social problems, it was right and understandable that Labour pinned its housing aspirations to the building of council housing, particularly as Labour was to win control of many large municipal authorities which had the power to build council houses. Thus in 1910, 1930 or even 1945 (when still only about one-quarter of all households lived in owner occupied housing) it was justifiable to place emphasis on local authority housing and, by implication, to assume that a socialist society would be one where the people lived together in houses provided by the State. But it was an essentially statist approach. As David Griffiths and Chris Holmes have noted: 'Labour's management of public housing has developed within a framework of centralized bureaucracy and a tradition of Victorian paternalism.'[24]

A new vision is now required: changed circumstances and aspirations demand this. In 1984 around 61 per cent of all United Kingdom housing was owner occupied and, notwithstanding the close links between tenure and class described in Chapter 5, in 1983 a majority (62 per cent) of skilled manual workers were owner occupiers, as were 42 per cent of semi-skilled manual workers, and 28 per cent of unskilled workers. Moreover, we know that many of those who are not owner occupiers would dearly wish to become so. While the popularity of owner occupation can be partly explained by its financial advantages, this is by no means the whole explanation. The human scale of much owner occupied housing, compared with some – but by no means all – council accommodation, and the greater power and responsibility which owners have over their accommodation are also important. If the Labour Party wishes to remain (or become again) a mass party, its housing strategy must involve, fully, owner occupation.

Nor need true acceptance of owner occupation, within a comprehensive housing strategy, be purely for practical grounds, for there is nothing incompatible between a democratic socialist philosophy and ownership of one's own home. Indeed, an emphasis on equality as a means of achieving greater freedom should welcome owner occupation. A socialist society would be one where all the people enjoy those rights, historically the preserve of the privileged minority, which allow them to extend their own choices about their immediate environment. A useful distinction, made by Hobhouse, is between property involving 'control over things which gives freedom and security and the control over persons through things, which gives power to the owner'.[25] Historically, housing has often fallen into the last category but the challenge for democratic socialists is to move towards the former, that is housing which gives freedom and security.[26]

As noted earlier, the aim of housing policy must be to break the link between class and housing tenure and to move instead towards a position where varying housing needs over the life cycle are met, sometimes through owner occupation, and sometimes through the public sector. This strategy has implications for housing finances, subsidies, house-building and improvement policy, as well as for design, architecture and planning.

Since the 1950s, there has been a move towards the building of smaller housing units and this should be maintained in the future, subject to one proviso. It should not be assumed that two or one person households necessarily need small accommodation: for some a bedsitter or a one bedroom flat might be desired, but others may need more space. Indeed, expanding leisure in the future may require more housing space, as will increasing household appliances and domestic gadgetry. Receiving visitors also requires more space. Nevertheless, the trend towards smaller households – the proportion of one person households increased from 11 per cent in 1961 to 24 per cent in 1983[27] – has obvious implications for policy.

Smaller units are needed for the increasing number of younger people who live away from their parents, for educational, employment or other reasons. Within the context of other priorities, provision should be made by the public sector for such young people: in some cases, tower blocks may be appropriate for such housing requirements. For young couples, it is imperative that separate housing is provided; inadequate housing in general and sharing accommodation with parents in particular is no way of starting married life, and the particularly high divorce rates among those marrying in their teens is probably associated with inadequate housing.

Policy must aim to ensure suitable housing within the reach of all families with children. (In 1977, some 12 per cent of all children lived in flats and 3 per cent lived in flats on the second floor or above.[28]) A target for the future must be to offer all families with children the option of living in a house with a garden.

Towards the end of the life cycle, the aim of housing policy must be to ensure suitable accommodation for the elderly. This will involve a flexible and varied strategy. It will include policies to enable the elderly to 'unlock' the capital value of their homes in order to finance adaptations and improvements, the option of moving to smaller accommodation, much of which will have to be provided by local authorities, and more sheltered housing.[29]

The pursuit of a strategy to meet the varying housing needs which arise during an individual's lifetime will involve imaginative policies from the public sector. In some areas, it will be appropriate to sell council accommodation – when there is no shortage of housing or unmet demand for local authority housing. In other areas, house sales must be accompanied by new building, and local authorities should also buy private housing in order to meet existing needs. Indeed, given the state of much of the privately rented housing sector, a programme of social ownership would be desirable.[30] Moreover, given the importance of housing in achieving social integration, it is sensible for some public housing to be in the midst of private housing. Certainly, no massive new housing estates should be built. New accommodation should, in the main, be on smaller sites – sometimes just one or two dwellings.

A priority for a new government will be the provision of rented housing for those in the severest need. This will involve new building and the purchasing of accommodation within the private sector. A related priority must be the up-grading of the public housing stock, much of which is now in an appallingly rundown state. This strategy must involve the demolition of certain existing dwellings, often high rise. Much of this accommodation is relatively new, but the financial implications of this will have to be faced. Some local authorities, for example Liverpool, are now pursuing such a programme.

The 'democratization' of public housing must also be a key objective. There must be a decisive move away from the paternalism of old. There is experience to be drawn on[31] and it should not be imagined that the translation of participatory aspirations into practical reality is an easy task. Moreover, the danger of off-loading on to tenants responsibility for problems which only local authorities have the resources to tackle (and which public policy decisions created in the first place) should be recognized. Nevertheless, in a number of fields – the management of caretaking services, decisions about car parking, play space, external decoration and maintenance, for instance – more properly funded control by tenants is important. Similarly in other areas of housing, not least maintenance and repair, a less bureaucratic approach is required. Co-operatives of building and maintenance workers should be encouraged and should compete for contracts, which tenant co-operatives would allocate.

For private housing, policies must be introduced to help owner occupiers overcome the restrictive and expensive practices of lawyers, estate agents and surveyors. Housing authorities should be encouraged to establish 'shop front' facilities to offer buyers and sellers alike a comprehensive, inexpensive, yet unsubsidized, service. A national computer network could be established. A surveyor's report on a house should be made readily available to all with a bona fide interest, and legal services should be provided. The solicitors' restrictive and extortionate hold on this territory should be thoroughly attacked.

It should also be recognized that the privately rented housing sector has no lasting place. Indeed private tenants should have the 'right to buy'. This would, incidentally, quickly expose the Tory's partisan approach to this principle.

In the crucial area of housing finance, the aim should be to integrate housing subsidies into the new Income Transfer Programme that has been outlined. This would involve the abolition of both means-tested rent rebates and allowances and mortgage tax relief. However, prior to computerization of taxation in the late 1980s, this cannot be introduced easily.

Immediate priorities

In the short term therefore we require a more pragmatic strategy, but still an egalitarian one. This would include (a) maintaining the £30,000 limit on mortgage payments eligible for tax relief (inflation in this context becomes a useful egalitarian tool); (b) restricting tax relief to the standard rate of tax; and (c) restricting rent increases to levels compatible with inflation.

On assuming office, the next radical government will find itself faced with a major deterioration of the housing stock. The response should be the launch of a national programme of housebuilding and improvement. This should focus on those regions, localities and groups of people, suffering the worst conditions and should be concerned as much with quality as with the quantity of dwellings built or improved. The aim should be to upgrade the minimum conditions of the poorest and to produce greater housing equality. The policy must not become a means of subsidizing well-off owners to carry out unnecessary improvements or to pour money into the bank accounts of speculative building companies.

Some important targets should be set for housing, for example the provision of basic amenities to all over, say, five years, a house with a garden for all families with children, and warm and adequate homes for the most vulnerable elderly people.

The principles and policies outlined above would be the basis for an attractive socialist housing programme. It avoids the negativism that has been apparent in the past. As Griffiths and Holmes argue: 'if, come the next Election, the central housing issue is still whether council tenants should have the right to buy on current terms, the Left will have failed.'[32] It is also a programme that puts housing at the heart of the overall social strategy and that is where it must be if the goals of equality and social integration are to be achieved.

Community Care

A key test for a civilized society is how it cares for its most vulnerable citizens and, as noted in Chapter 8, demographic trends have made this an issue of growing importance in the late twentieth century. The growing numbers of very elderly people in the community pose a major challenge for social policy, particularly as advanced age is associated not just with ill health and increasing disability, but also with poverty, poor housing and other deprivations.

Moreover, there are other groups in the population who require adequate care in the community. It is estimated that some 15,000 mentally handicapped people at present in hospital – a third of the total number – could be discharged immediately if adequate community care were available. And, among mentally ill people, it is thought that there may be 'up to 5,000 people now in hospital who ... may be capable of leading more independent lives'.[33]

Richard Titmuss's question of twenty years ago 'Community care:

fact or fiction?' is now, therefore, a more important one than when he
originally asked it. Titmuss had noted that 'community care' was an
example of a characteristic of the English 'to employ idealistic terms to
describe certain branches of public policy' and he went on:

The motives are no doubt well intentioned; the terms so used express, in
civilised phrases, the collective aspirations of those who aim to better the
human condition. It is necessary to remember, however, that this practice can
have unfortunate consequences. Public opinion – in which I include political
opinion – may be misled or confused. If English social history is any guide,
confusion has often been the mother of complacency. In the public mind, the
aspirations of reformers are transmuted, by the touch of a phrase, into hard-
won reality. What some hope will one day exist is suddenly thought by many
to exist already.[34]

Titmuss's perceptive questioning of fashionable terms shows the need
to consider the meaning of 'community care' carefully, not least when
in the hands of the Conservative government it has become little more
than an assertion that the Government will do less and so others,
voluntary bodies, friends, neighbours and the family, must do more.

Given the scale of need, a positive and energetic policy of community
care must be one major priority for the next Labour government, not
least because those in most desperate need – the frail 86-year-old widow,
the mentally handicapped child or the disabled 40-year-old man – will
not be able to campaign for their own share of resources, nor do they
have powerful interest groups to represent their needs effectively.
Community care thus provides a key test of Bevan's 'religion of
socialism' – our ability as a society to make priorities, according to
ethical choices, and regardless of either individual financial means or
the ability of some to elbow a place near to the source of public finance.

A starting point for a socialist community care programme must be
a recognition of who it is that currently provides the bulk of such care.
And, as noted earlier, despite the fashionable view that the 'family no
longer cares', it is in fact the family, and particularly its female members,
who provide the majority of care in the community.

The fact of family care should be a major building block for social policy, but there should be emphasis on *quality*, both the quality of care received by those in need *and* the quality of life of the carers. Both are important.[35] Both interact with each other. To make the point bluntly, an elderly woman living with her married daughter may swell the statistics which measure 'care in the community' but it might involve the daughter having to give up work, resulting in a lower standard of living for her family, more crowded housing, an intolerable burden for the carer, poor relations between elderly mother and daughter, marital stress, and much else besides. The evidence about the burdens of caring may be matched in the future by increasing evidence and scandals about the treatment of old people within their families.

What would a positive community care policy towards the elderly involve? First and foremost, it requires a strong role for government, both at the level of provision and planning, but this does *not* mean that government itself should provide most day-to-day support and care.

There is no evidence to suggest that a professionalization of care in this area, by definition personal and intimate, is what is required. However, the encouragement of true community care would involve a broad approach and genuine joint strategies in social policy. We must be concerned not only with the immediate needs of the elderly, but also with the wider social environment which affects such needs and the possibilities of tackling them. This involves not just community care services, but also a community care *perspective* within social policy. Some of the implications of this for housing policy were discussed earlier in this chapter.

A key aspect of social policy towards the elderly must be a positive partnership between the family and the State. At present, scarce domiciliary services are concentrated on elderly people or couples living alone, and not provided to families who care. Some local authorities will not, for example, provide a home help to an elderly person living with a daughter – even if the daughter works full-time outside the home. Given the scarcity of resources and the need to ration home helps, district nurses, and other services carefully, the reasons for this failure to support the supporters are clear, but the consequences are dismal.

The decision as to whether or not a family can provide care within their own home to an elderly relative – with all the associated burdens that might be involved – or the decision whether such care can be maintained, in the wake of increasing difficulties, might often turn on seemingly small factors such as difficulties with bathing, laundry or cleaning. The availability or not of State support might often be of critical importance. Of course, such services cost money and the total cost is substantial: for England in 1982/3 the cost of personal social services for each person over 75 was £305.[36] But the financial costs of more and more institutional care are significantly more substantial. Indeed, we have estimated that if by 1991 just one-tenth of the elderly over 75 who might be expected to live with their families did not, in fact, do so and had to live in old people's homes instead, the extra 70,000 places would cost £389 million in current expenditure alone.[37] Moreover, the economic value of family care is substantial and we calculate the annual amount to lie in the region of £3.7 – £5.3 billion.[38]

The family is the first refuge for those most in need, but some one-third of the elderly do not have living children, and it has been shown that 30 per cent of the over-75s never had children.[39] For many of the frailest in this group, personal social services have a vital role to play. While conventional services, such as home helps and meals on wheels, need to be critically assessed in terms of their impact and social and economic cost-effectiveness, it is clear that mainstream services of these kinds have a crucial role to play in the future for the most vulnerable. This is indicated by the fact, for example, that over half of all women over 75 live alone, and the evidence that a significant minority of the very elderly need help with ordinary day-to-day tasks but do not receive any.

The care of elderly people, and other dependent groups too, raises important questions about sex equality. Most family care is provided by women, often the daughters or daughters-in-law of those being cared for. It remains the case that many women have to leave employment in order to provide such care. While the historic trend towards smaller families has been a liberating one for women, enabling them to spend relatively less of their lives providing care to children, the ageing of the population now threatens this freedom, bringing as it does huge demands for care at the other end of the life cycle. How can these increasing needs be tackled without this affecting women adversely, as is the case today? This is one of the most vital – and difficult – questions in contemporary social policy. And, while changes in attitudes are crucial if men and women are to share care in the future, the right kind of social policy infrastructure is also essential.

A better understanding of family needs, a joint approach to social policy, a knowledge of good practice, and a firm lead by central government will all be necessary if families are to be able to meet adequately the social challenge of Britain's ageing population. If we fail, as a society, to mobilize the resources necessary to meet the varied needs of our old people, too many of them will live out their days in discomfort, misery and, sometimes, squalor. However, we have it in our collective power to build a caring community. The ageing of the British population should represent, therefore, not a crisis but a challenge.

In this chapter, a number of proposals have been put forward for reform and there is no getting away from the fact that many are expensive. Are they therefore realistic? Can a worthwhile social strategy be implemented, not least at a time of economic constraint and mass unemployment? These questions are discussed in the next chapter.

10 Redistributing Resources and Raising the Revenue

The present government has proved that it is perfectly feasible to transfer resources on a scale that would put an end to most kinds of poverty.

David Donnison[1]

How can an alternative social strategy, including the kinds of policies outlined in the last chapter, be funded? While a socialist strategy for social policy does not depend entirely on increasing public expenditure, there is no getting away from the fact that increased public spending will be necessary, and on a substantial scale. In this respect, the social strategy is at one with the requirements of the alternative economic strategy: social need can be tackled in part by increasing economic demand, services can be expanded and useful jobs created. In addition, there will be a need to redistribute public resources, including tax expenditure.

This chapter therefore considers revenue and resources. Getting priorities right will be crucial in the future. This has major implications for the Labour Party's own policy-making process. The debates about internal democracy over the last few years have resulted – rightly – in the Labour Party Annual Conference having more say and influence over policy. But Conference now needs to reform its own procedure if it is to be able to carry out its own responsibilities effectively. Curiously, the Party, while critical of the methods of other institutions, still seems to regard a week-long mass plenary of some 1,000 delegates as an effective means of doing business. As Tessa Blackstone has observed:

The Party Conference can hardly be said to embody a carefully thought out method for determining priorities. What gets on to the agenda is fairly arbitrary. It is largely based on the number of resolutions on different issues received from constituency parties. The debate takes place in an atmosphere unconstrained by reference to the likely cost of new policies or how they will be paid for, or to the problems or consequences of implementing them. As a consequence, a whole range of highly laudable goals are adopted with little reference to the realities of financial constraints, and with no attempt to attach priorities to them.[2]

Moreover, if the Party seeks to initiate comprehensive planning in government, it must ensure that this also happens in Opposition. To quote Blackstone again: 'There is some effort by political parties whilst in opposition to work out their priorities *within* particular parts of their programme ... However, there is little or no attempt to draw up a list of priorities around the whole range of social policies.'[3]

Raising the revenue

A government that is serious about attacking inequality must be bold and must not be afraid to think on a substantial scale. Compared to a Labour government's past readiness to impose prescription charges to raise a few millions to impress the International Monetary Fund that it was getting tough, the Conservative government under Mrs Thatcher is an object lesson in firm government and the ability to have the courage of political convictions: it has not hesitated to slash billions from future spending plans for health, housing and education while at the same time redistributing substantial resources to the rich.

What follows is not an attempt to draw a carefully balanced budget – that would not be a realistic exercise here – but rather to illustrate methods of raising revenue, and the sums that can be so raised.

The Welfare State which might be a new government's inheritance in 1987 or 1988 will be seriously undermined, underfinanced and undercapitalized. Furthermore, mass unemployment will add to the serious pressures on all areas of social policy. Moreover, of the money being spent by the Conservatives, a significant proportion of it is spent on propping up the nationalized industries, on unemployment benefits and related schemes, and increased spending on defence and law and order.

Against this gloomy background, a new government will come in with a magnitude of cuts to be restored, damage to be made good, a legion of pent-up pledges from the Party manifesto and a range of demands from the pressure groups. Furthermore, there will be a massive task on hand to save the British economy and to invest public money in British industry: social policy will certainly not have the only call on public resources. Even if public expenditure is increased substantially – as it must be (Peter Shore before the 1983 election advocated an expansion programme of around £9 billion) – much of the extra expenditure will not be on social programmes and there will still be a need for priorities – a word unpopular among some of the unworldly but to that practical revolutionary, Aneurin Bevan, 'the religion of socialism'.

Economic growth

Crucial to tackling social need in the future is economic growth and again the goals of the social strategy are in accord with the alternative economic strategy. Since the war Britain has performed worse in terms of economic growth than its industrial competitors. Between 1973 and 1982 GDP per capita increased at an annual average of 0.8 per cent which was very much lower than France (1.9 per cent), West Germany (1.7 per cent), Italy (1.7 per cent) and, most noticeably, Japan (2.8 per cent).[4]

While in some fashionable quarters, economic growth is down-graded and an emphasis is placed on environmental protection, those concerned with major social problems, often affecting those without decent environments to protect in the first place, look to growth as a major means of producing resources in the future. Nevertheless, a key aim of any social strategy has to be a balance between economic objectives and environmental concerns.

What can we expect? Given the goals of the economic strategy, plus the capacity for growth through unleashing the potential productivity of the unemployed, a significantly improved growth rate can be anticipated. In a recent analysis Davies and Piachaud have calculated the extra resources that would be made available from a growth rate of 2.5 per cent per annum – much lower than some would hope for.[5] Their analysis showed the scope open to a Labour government elected in 1983. However, their estimates illustrate the potential for the future. This calculation shows that by 1988 extra resources of approximately £31.5 billion would be produced. However, not all of this would be available for increased public expenditure and they argue, realistically, that some of this would be needed for increased consumer spending, much of it by the unemployed returning to work, and for other purposes. However, £11.9 billion could be devoted to public consumption, although some of this would be required for aspects of public policy, other than social policies, such as industrial investment. The assessment of Davies and Piachaud is shown in Table 10.1. The importance of increased, and sustained, economic growth is illustrated by the fact that a 1 per cent growth rate – the recent average – would yield only £5.5 billion extra for public consumption.[6]

Would economic growth at the level of 2.5 per cent per annum be enough to fund an enhanced social programme? Davies and Piachaud considered this point and estimated the cost of Labour's commitments prior to the 1983 election. For the NHS there was a pledged increase in real expenditure of 3 per cent per annum. If this had been the aim in the five years up to 1988, extra annual costs would be approximately £2.5 billion (including personal social services expenditure). For education, the restoration of Conservative cuts and the 3 per cent growth rate (to allow more expenditure on the under-5s and those aged 16–19) would add up, by the end of five years, to £1.9 billion. For housing, the pledge to restore Tory cuts would add up to a substantial £4 billion extra per annum. Thus, these pledges total something approaching £8.5 billion per year by the end of the five-year Conservative term.[7] It is clear that, given that some of the enhanced public resources from growth should be directed towards industrial investment, overseas aid and other purposes, and that moreover the above estimates do not include the most expensive programme of all, namely social security, further means of obtaining the resources for social purposes will be

Table 10.1 Resources available for public consumption, 1983–8 (at 1982 prices)

	1983*	1988‡	Extra resources	Comment
GDP (exp. based)	240.6	272.1	31.5	2.5% p.a. growth
Consumers' expenditure	169.6	187.3	17.7	2% p.a. growth
Gross domestic fixed capital formulation	46.6	52.7	6.1	Maintains GDP share
Stockbuilding	4.9	3.5	−1.4	Trend level
Net exports	−7.9	−9.3	−1.4	Current a/c balance maintained
Less factor cost adjustment	29.7	31.1	1.4	In line with consumers' expenditure
AVAILABLE FOR PUBLIC CONSUMPTION	57.1	69.0	11.9	4% p.a. growth

Notes: *Forecasts. ‡ Illustration.
Source: Gavyn Davies and David Piachaud, in H. Glennerster (ed.), Future of the Welfare State, Heinemann Educational Books, 1983, Table 4.8.

necessary. Whatever the precise situation prevailing after the next election this is likely to be the case. How can resources be raised?

There are different possibilities. The first is restructuring and enhancing tax revenue. The second is through *reducing* certain aspects of public expenditure. The third is the quest for efficiency.

Taxation

A progressive and a bold approach to taxation policy is critical to the implementation of the social strategy. While the Conservatives have defined the problem as simply 'too much' taxation (particularly for the rich) from a radical standpoint the problem is the lack of progressiveness. At present, 95 per cent of all taxpayers pay tax at the standard rate. Indeed, it is a myth to suggest that Britain is a heavily taxed nation. In fact Britain, compared with other European nations, is not over-taxed. In 1983 taxes and social security contributions, as a percentage of GDP, were 37.8 per cent compared to, for example, 47 per cent in the Netherlands and 44.1 per cent in France.[8] The need is to develop a progressive system of taxation, so reducing the tax burden on the poor and those with caring responsibilities, while producing enhanced resources for social priorities.

Raising more revenue This would be achieved by, for example, restoring the tax cuts made since 1979 to the very well-off. From the budgets since 1979 (as Table 4.2 showed) those with incomes above £20,000 gained some £1.8 billion overall. Also there could be a restriction on tax reliefs and allowances to the standard tax rate which would have saved an estimated £600 million in 1983/4.[9] Most of the revenue so raised should be redistributed to those at the lower end of the earnings scale, by relieving their tax burdens, and by similar help to those with dependants.

These, however, are piecemeal measures – the sort that could be introduced in the short term. In the longer term a more radical move towards progressive taxation is required, as an essential complement to a universalist social security system. Michael Meacher's proposals for an income tax system with four or five separate rates starting at 15 per cent and rising to 60 or 75 per cent is a pointer here.[10]

Wealth tax and company taxation   In Chapter 5 the massive inequalities in wealth in Britain were described. These are an affront to a civilized society, but tackling them is a means of developing social policy. The last Labour government bungled its attempt to introduce a wealth tax. Although a Green Paper was published in 1974[11] the select committee which considered this was divided and produced rival proposals. It was a recipe for inaction. However, even the modest proposals floated in the Green Paper showed the scope for raising extra resources through a wealth tax. One option, for example, showed that, for the year 1972, a wealth tax could raise in the region of £350–£425 million. After translating these figures into the cash figures applicable in the 1980s, and given the scope for more radical options than those considered in the Green Paper, substantial amounts of money could be raised.

Similarly, there is great scope to raise extra resources through an effective policy of company taxation. In the recent past, the yield from companies has decreased.[12] It will be one of the challenges for a new Labour government to reverse this trend, but the complexities of this should not be underestimated in the age of the multi-national company.

Attacking tax evasion   The attack on tax evasion must be a priority. There is not only a case for this on the grounds of simple justice, but also the extra revenue so raised could boost considerably the resources available to a reforming administration. It was estimated for 1981 that the tax *loss* could be as much as £4 billion or about one-fifth of the entire income tax yield. A tough-minded approach to tax havens must be part of this strategy.

Reforming fiscal welfare

As argued in Chapter 9, the feasibility of introducing in the late 1980s an integrated tax–benefit Income Transfer Programme should be pursued, and this will involve a systematic appraisal of the worth and cost-effectiveness of all reliefs and allowances in due course. Meanwhile, there are some obvious anomalies and inequities to be tackled. The married man's allowance, as argued earlier, is an obvious candidate for reform. After allowing for a new 'single person's' allowance for married men at an estimated cost of £6.5 billion, this still leaves some £3.5 billion for redistribution, and there is now debate as to how this substantial sum should be distributed in future. The most progressive way of using this sum of money would be to support those families with caring responsibilities, both those with children and those with responsibility for caring for elderly relatives and others who are disabled. The residual amount left over from reform of the married man's tax allowance should therefore be spent on increasing child benefits and on developing home responsibility payments.

Tax relief on mortgage interest payments is a further candidate for reform, but this needs to be done within the context of a far-reaching housing subsidy strategy which will not be easily accomplished early in the life of a new government. However, by reducing this to its former level of £25,000, this tax expenditure can be immediately constrained.

Public expenditure reduction

It will also be possible to *reduce* public expenditure in two critical areas: defence and unemployment. Defence expenditure has increased substantially in real terms under the Tories, so there is substantial scope for a redistribution of public resources. Much would depend here, of course, on future defence strategy: the implementation of a non-nuclear policy and the implications of this for conventional weapons expenditure. However, the scope for substantial reductions is apparent. Even if British defence expenditure was reduced to the level of expenditure in West Germany and France, for example, which are themselves relatively high spenders on defence in the NATO league, considerable resources could be freed. In 1983, United Kingdom defence spending was 5.4 per cent of GDP, against 4.2 per cent for France and 3.4 per cent for West Germany.[13] If United Kingdom expenditure as a percentage of GDP was at the German level, this would free some £6 billion. If it was down to the French level, over £2 billion would become available. This approach would be in line with Labour policy before the last election: 'Labour will reduce the proportion of the nation's resources devoted to defence so that the burden we bear will be brought into line with that of the other major European NATO countries.'[14]

Unemployment Costs The current annual cost of benefits for the unemployed is in the region of £6.8 billion and this is only the tip of the iceberg concerning public expenditure costs relating to unemployment. Given that the objective of the alternative economic strategy is to reduce unemployment, there is obviously considerable scope for savings here.

Value for money

The search for efficiency and cost-effectiveness must be a key aim of future social policy, but it will be pursued in a different context – for different reasons – than the Conservatives' quest for 'efficiency savings' which are simply part and parcel of a crude cost-cutting exercise. A government that is committed to increasing public expenditure in order to pursue social objectives should be particularly concerned with value for money, not only to ensure that scarce resources are spent effectively, but as a means of developing public confidence in social expenditure. As Jack Straw has argued '... those of us who believe in the sustained use of public money should have a far greater interest in the efficiency of the public sector: far more to gain from efficiency, than ever the welfare state's detractors'.[15] Moreover, if this is done in the context of general expansion, jobs can be safeguarded and, hence, trade unions and professional associations can be reassured.

The search for effectiveness is particularly important in those areas where the benefits of expenditure, in the past, have been less apparent to consumers than to the industries or professions who should be serving them. Moreover, there are some particular areas where public resources are not being deployed effectively. The NHS drugs bill is a classic example and substantial savings can clearly be made from a general switch from branded drugs to equally effective generic equivalents. Recently revealed abuses of the remuneration system by dentists is a further area requiring urgent attention.

The importance of cost-effectiveness has a number of implications. One is that we need to develop good measures of *output*, so as to be able to judge the effectiveness of social policy. Certainly, public expenditure is a very poor guide to output. Socialists must stop suggesting that increasing public expenditure, which might be caused by, say, more senior officials or more highly expensive medical technology – or simply higher interest rates – is inevitably 'good' and less public expenditure necessarily 'bad'. If, in future, public support for extensive programmes of public expenditure is to be forthcoming it must be demonstrated that money is spent wisely and that there is a demonstrable link between spending programmes and a reduction of housing stress, educational disadvantages, poverty and so on.

Conclusion

This brief analysis demonstrates three things. Firstly, it will be possible during the lifetime of a government to find the resources available to fulfil social objectives and therefore to meet pressing needs. Priorities, of course, will be necessary but many desirable policies can be implemented. Second, this will only be possible if economic policy works, both in terms of achieving growth and in doing so without creating adverse economic consequences. Third, it will nevertheless not be possible to rely solely on growth – and not at all in the early days – and, therefore, a willingness and a determination to redistribute both income and wealth is crucial.

This is not to argue that a radical social strategy can be easily funded and that consequently there is little to worry about. Far from it, because the implementation of policies of this kind will bring any future government into direct confrontation with some of the country's most powerful and sophisticated vested interests. Foreign interests will also be mobilized against reform. It will be the crucial test of a reforming government to see whether it has the political authority to raise the resources to implement a radical social strategy.

11 Democratic Social Planning

... I feel sure that a Socialist Society that is to be true to its equalitarian principles of humanitarian brotherhood must rest on the widest possible diffusion of power and responsibility, so as to enlist the active participation of as many as possible of its citizens in the tasks of democratic self-government.
G. D. H. Cole[1]

The outlines of a social strategy were drawn in Chapter 8 and in Chapter 9 some specific social policies were discussed. However, questions of policy implementation are crucial, for in the past there has all too often been a fundamental failure actually to carry out many aspects of Labour policy. In part this was due to a lack of commitment to socialist policies within Cabinet, but also to some inherent defects within our system of government. Yet concerns about social planning and rational policy-making also need to be integrated with the fundamental concern to promote a more democratic social policy.

This chapter therefore opens by discussing how social policy can be made more democratic and more accessible to those who depend most on good social policies. It then considers (a) establishing political control; (b) promoting democratic accountability; and (c) developing social planning, both within and across departments. The focus here is on central government, but many of the arguments relate with equal force to local authorities and other bodies.

Democratizing social policy

In Chapter 2 it was argued that one reason for increasing anxiety about State welfare was its undemocratic nature. In brief there was perceived to be a growing gap between citizen and State. This critique was explored in Chapter 5 and the need to 'democratize' social policy was advocated as one key objective of any new social strategy.

But what would a 'democratic' Welfare State look like? This is not such an easy question to pursue as some of the rhetoric of 'participation' and 'decentralization' might suggest. It involves fundamental questions of power and, in the past, some theorists have too readily assumed that solutions would be easily found. Lenin in *The State and Revolution* pronounced that: 'under socialism all will govern in turn and will soon become accustomed to no one governing'.[2] As Anthony Wright, who quotes this passage notes: 'we know the rest of that particular story'.[3] Today, 'the generation of 1968 has completed the long march through institutions'.[4] For them, perhaps, Lennon, rather than Lenin, catches the mood, yet 'power to the people' is easy to sing along to – more difficult to achieve.

We must not, for instance, adopt too readily solutions which depend on – or assume – that ordinary people want participatory systems that eat too much into their leisure time. As George Bernard Shaw noted, the trouble with socialism is that it requires too many meetings. Political activists may find fulfilment through a seemingly endless series of meetings in draughty halls, but that is their problem. Moreover, it should not be taken for granted that voluntary action is necessarily superior to statutory action – sometimes it may be, but it can be equally (or more) remote, less reliable and is certainly less accountable. A realistic and constructive strategy can be developed, however, and would be built on approaches that included the following.

Local government

Just as local government has been seen as an obstacle by a centralizing Conservative administration, so it must be recognized as a major foundation in the development of democratic policies. Many of the key components of social policy – education, social services, planning, transport and housing – are first and foremost local, rather than central government responsibilities. Moreover, issues relating to the local economy are also influenced by local policies. Local government must be enabled to undertake its role effectively – fully accountable to its local electorates.

The importance of local democracy suggests the need to think carefully about the kind of governmental units that should be introduced to restore effective government to Greater London and the other major metropolitan areas. Some forget, in all the excitement of recent years, that the GLC was constituted, both in terms of its geography and its powers, as essentially a means of abolishing the progressive London County Council. It is not obvious that exact duplicates of the GLC and the metropolitan county councils should be established.

One radical option to consider would be the integration of the NHS into the local authority system. Why should one of Britain's key services – and its major employer – be outside the local democratic system? Powerful medical interests would, of course, oppose such a move to democracy, but there are fundamental arguments in its favour, not least the need to develop effective community services, involving a comprehensive health and welfare package. Water authorities, too, should be part of local government. A new regional tier of government is necessary.

Decentralization

Much of the Welfare State has become too remote and over-centralized. Means of locating services as locally as is compatible with effectiveness are therefore important. However, a note of caution may be sounded by the 'flavour of the month' aspect which currently attaches to much of the decentralization fervour – and reminiscent of earlier 'community' and 'neighbourhood' flavoured enthusiasms.[5] Nonetheless, for the personal social services, for example, a number of experiments have taken place in the wake of the Barclay Report's advocacy of patch-based social work,[6] and the announcement that services are 'going local' is increasingly common. The arguments for rooting services in the communities they serve, if needs are to be effectively met, are clear,[7] and are of relevance to a wide range of policies – not least housing and education, while acknowledging that certain functions will always be best administered centrally. The decentralization issue indeed underlines the importance of good centre–local relations both between central and local government and between local authorities and neighbourhood.

Participation

Opportunities for people to participate in local services are sometimes appropriate, sometimes not. Most people would not wish to sit on street committees to administer the sewage system, but many parents are interested closely in their children's schools. We need more initiatives to involve parents, and older pupils too, in the running of their own education. Moreover, the extension of services for the under-5s should involve parents wherever possible. These services must be in tune with actual family circumstances and needs, and not simply the traditions and convenience of professionals and bureaucrats in this area. As David Donnison has remarked:

... when the education authorities decided to provide nursery schooling they laboured for years to create an inadequate and very expensive all-professional system, operating at times of the day and for periods of the year which were devised to suit teachers, not children or their parents. The children of working mothers, who needed this service most of all, were left to the voluntary play groups – if the mothers were lucky enough to find one – and to private childminders.[8]

In other areas, services for the mentally handicapped, and mentally ill, for example, or in aspects of health care or social security, it is not too easy to see how democratization can be encouraged, although the debate is under way in many services.

For those living in, for example, old people's accommodation, it is appropriate that they should help organize and run *their* homes. And council tenants should have much more say about their homes and the administration of estates, and control of funds to enable them to do so effectively.

Complexity

One means of gaining public confidence is by waging a war on unnecessary complexity, not least in the areas of income maintenance. That is one argument in favour of moving towards the integration of social security and taxation. Sound social policy must be based on a foundation of clearly understood rights and responsibilities, rather than involve a motley mixture of discretionary payments, means-tested provisions, form-filling and rumour. 'Simplicity', however, can be as dangerous as complexity, if social policies fail to meet sensitively the variety of needs that are present in a complex society. The attack on complexity is therefore a means, not an end in itself. The guiding principle must be the needs of the citizen, not those of the bureaucracy.

Voluntary organizations

The spreading of power and responsibility within the social policy field can also be achieved through voluntary organizations, not simply large national organizations, but also through the encouragement of local grassroots bodies, often self-help groups, which in the past – and in the future – have so much to offer in terms of energy, commitment, compassion and innovation. Voluntary organizations are not the appropriate vehicles to provide mainstream services, although there can be successful exceptions to this.

These groups too are often the most articulate representatives of social services customers and are crucial thorns in the flesh of government and public and private sector institutions. Self-help groups, often with a membership comprising those suffering from specific medical conditions, are particularly important. Not the least significant of all the tests for a mature democracy in Britain is the need for government, central and local, both to fund such organizations (for the money will often not be available from elsewhere) and yet, while properly safeguarding public money, to administer grants in a way which does not inhibit independence, enterprise and criticism. The evidence to date suggests that we are finding this a difficult democratic balance to strike.

Rights and access

A key indicator of any democratic social policy must be the extent to which it allows for both a full, yet clear, account of citizens' rights, and swift and widely known remedies for grievances. Several parts of the Welfare State do have appeals and grievance procedures, but too many have no well-recognized means of expressing dissatisfaction: the NHS is a particular example here. Very often, however, the problem is not so much a lack of processes, but rather that the systems designed to sensitize bureaucracy are themselves shrouded in a cobweb of obscurity. Perhaps the time has come for a new approach. Do we, perhaps, need to establish in each borough or district a Complaints Office where all cases, be they about health, housing, social security or the entry to schools, could be initially dealt with by specialists who would then guide (and represent where necessary) citizens through the appropriate channels?

Democratic rights and responsibilities

Social policy, concerned as it should be with equality and liberty, must involve a spreading of power and the decentralization and democratization – where possible – of services and systems of administration. As the Australian sociologist Bob Connell has argued: 'A socialist programme ... while arguing for public enterprise as a basic good and as an immediate need, must combine it organically with the idea of democratizing the state itself.'[9] We must rethink the relationship between the citizen and State, be wary of providing benefits without also conferring clearly understood rights, and be suspicious of developing services that are not run by democratically elected or accountable bodies. Above all else we must measure progress not by the growth of bureaucracies or the increasing strength of professionals or paraprofessionals, but by *output*, both the number and quality of services provided to those requiring them, and by the increase in the standards, self-esteem, dignity, power and liberty of ordinary people. If these goals can be obtained by conventional social policies – as they often will be – so be it. But if they cannot (or if these goals are inhibited by such approaches – and sometimes they might be) new strategies must be developed and we must be prepared to overcome the opposition and prejudices of vested interests who will feel threatened.

This emphasis on the need to bring greater democracy into social policy is important, not least because it raises questions about both the rights *and* responsibilities of individuals. Spreading power, whether through the encouragement of voluntary, self-help and co-operative groups, tenant participation and control over housing management questions, or by encouraging a more effective partnership between individuals and the State in areas like health and education, is no easy option. Indeed, to some extent, it poses challenges for the comfortable critics of Britain's Welfare State. Such a strategy for democracy also undermines the ignorant, yet often-voiced, cry from the enemies of the Welfare State, that its exponents simply focus on the rights and needs of people and not on their responsibilities – as wealth producers, taxpayers and citizens. 'Power-sharing' is not a 'soft' solution, for its challenge is that it offers to people in general, rather than a small élite (however beneficent) the opportunity of building a compassionate society which is the overriding goal of a new social strategy. The rest of this chapter now considers questions about the machinery of government, themselves closely related to the theme of democracy.

Political control

The textbooks tell us that once elected a new government will be dutifully and democratically served by its Civil Service and new policies will be carried out. Furthermore, a vigilant Parliament will keep a determined check on the Executive. It is a good story, but like many such is largely fictional. In practice the Whitehall machine ticks on, from minister to minister, administration to administration, and all too often is seldom interrupted by anything so vulgar as political change. That this is often the case, we are assured by some worldly-wise political commentators, is largely due to the low calibre of politicians. At best, we are told, ministers – even the best ones – can get to grips with only two or three issues during their term of office and, inevitably, officials will have to cope with the rest.

A key test for a radical government, particularly one committed to a strategy of equality, will be to break with this conservative tradition and take authoritative and democratic control of the machinery of government. How can this be done? First, it must take decisive steps along the road to a more representative and non-élite Civil Service. In practice the higher echelons of the British Civil Service can often form a huge barrier to the implementation of radical policies. The recruitment into the senior ranks of the Civil Service effectively provides a bulwark against radical change. The testimonies of former Labour ministers Richard Crossman and Barbara Castle provide authoritative evidence of this.[10] Moreover, the scheming of senior Civil Servants against Tony Benn, while he was Secretary of State for Industry, is an important example of the determination of the political Establishment to block radical change.[11]

Michael Meacher, a junior minister in the last Labour administration, has described how the Civil Service can effectively put the brakes on radical policy.[12] He describes three ways in which the Service 'subverts the effect of the democratic vote'. First, there is the manipulation of individual ministers – 'an exercise in man-management which is skilfully orchestrated and on which a great deal of time and care is spent'. Devices include the filtering of information by officials whereby papers are progressively screened until only one departmental 'line' is presented to the minister – rival views from officials will not be heard by the minister, the simple withholding of information, the timing of information whereby important papers are presented late in order to discourage thorough reading and argument, and the Whitehall briefings to the Press whereby compliant ministers get good reports while others – those giving trouble – get bad ones.

A second means of preventing radical policies is to exploit a minister's isolation within the policy machine. The former head of the Civil Service, Lord Armstrong, explained how this worked: 'The biggest and most pervasive influence is in setting the framework within which questions of policy are raised ... It would have been enormously difficult for any Minister to change the framework, and to that extent we had great power.'[13]

In practice, isolated from party members and Parliamentary colleagues a minister becomes – and this is the role welcomed by Civil Servants – a spokesman for the Department. Consequently, as Meacher notes, 'So far from being seen as the political guardians of their party manifesto, they are ranked in Whitehall and the media according to how well they do for their departments.'[14]

The third approach lies in the network of inter-departmental committees and contacts. Thus a departmental Civil Servant having difficulty with a minister who will not accept the departmental line will not hesitate to brief his colleagues in other departments to brief their ministers against the minister's policy in the inter-departmental committee discussing the issue. Based on his experience in government, Crossman has given an example of how this can work:

When I was Minister of Housing I was very keen to substitute local income tax for local rates as the main basis of our local taxation. So I made a speech or two about this before I squared my officials. What happened? An official committee was established which did a tremendous lot of work in order to prove that rates were the only practical form of local taxation. And so before I could get to my colleagues and argue the case for the local income tax, every one of my colleagues had been briefed by his officials that there was no alternative to the rates. So that was that! If Whitehall gangs up on you it is very difficult to get your policy through, or even to get a fair hearing for a new idea.[15]

In practice, some radicals exaggerated the power of the Civil Service (while many more have certainly underestimated it). It is not impossible to control the Civil Service and to use what can be a very efficient and professional machine to implement socialist policies. However, at present, it is hard to argue with Meacher's conclusions or the emphasis he gives to this aspect of Labour's task:

In short, the power system in Whitehall is in no sense a democracy, but rather a mandarin-dominated bureaucracy with only limited ministerial control. If democracy is seriously intended, in the sense of electing government with the effective power of enforcing its electoral pledge on the state officialdom, then this present power system requires a very radical overhaul.

That task has now perhaps become more important than the preparation of any specific new policy departure since only if the former is tackled can the latter be expected to be achieved. That is the measure of what now needs to be done at the centre of government.[16]

Quite apart from the specific ways in which Civil Servants can develop methods of blocking radical initiatives, there is a more pervasive ethos, a definite culture, that must be overcome if radical change is to be implemented. It is an ethos which positively distrusts conviction, compassion and commitment, the qualities that will help bring about social reform. It is exceedingly unlikely that bright young graduates with an idealistic wish to make the world a better place will find their way into the ranks of the Whitehall senior Civil Service. Rather the dominant culture favours public administration as some kind of sophisticated game, albeit one played with immense skill and professional rigour.

Restructuring and re-invigorating the administrative class of the Civil Service will, however, take time although a determined socialist government can set the pattern for the future. More immediately, taking political control of the government machine can be furthered by the appointment of political advisers. This process has already started and has been given treatment little short of contempt within part of the Civil Service – within the Home Office the memorandum circulated describing the 'expertise' of the new recruits to the prime minister's Policy Unit in 1974 was drafted with much irony. However, so far we have done little more than play with the idea, for the recruitment of one recently graduated 'adviser' to a huge Whitehall department will barely vibrate the conservative walls.

There is an urgent need to implement the proposal to appoint 'political cabinets' to advise Cabinet ministers.

Ministers need more support in the running of departments from outside the conventional Civil Service, not least because of all the tasks which ministers undertake: 'running the department is the one for which most ministers are, by training and background, least well equipped to fulfil. Few senior politicians have previous top level experience, outside government, of working in, let alone running, large organisations.'[17] That was the view of a Fabian Society study group established after the last election. And they put forward a number of useful proposals. Arguing for the 'politicization' of key departmental posts, they recommended 'the appointment of more *political* advisers to act as the eyes, ears, consciences, and channels of communications' for ministers. Also the appointment of more *policy* advisers 'to act as sources of expert advice independent of career professionals in departments'. Furthermore, the study group recommended that both these groups should be integrated closely into ministers' private offices 'where they would be best placed to achieve a strategic position in progress chasing, as heads of *ad hoc* task forces, in generating new policy thinking and, generally, in enhancing effective ministerial control'.

Democratic accountability

The second major requirement is to make the social policy process more democratically accountable to both Parliament and people. Parliamentary control of the Executive is ineffective and all too often does not take place. Indeed, a House of Commons committee reported that 'the history books say that Parliament controls the Executive, but in practice it can virtually never debate or vote on particular items of expenditure'.[18] The failure to control the Executive is in large measure due to the antiquated procedures of Parliament and the system of patronage that petrifies many back-benchers into loyal obedience, on the supposition that an inquiring mind is the enemy of career advancement. However, it has much to do also with the obsessive secrecy of our government machine. While examples of this secrecy are often given from more exotic fields of government, the implications for social policy are particularly important. Three examples illustrate the effect of making policy behind closed doors.

Urban deprivation

The first example concerns policies to attack urban deprivation, an issue which grew in importance during the 1970s and exploded on to the streets of the inner cities in the summer of 1981. In 1974, shortly after the return of the Labour government, Roy Jenkins, Labour Home Secretary, announced to the House of Commons 'a new strategy for tackling urban deprivation', Comprehensive Community Programmes. It was a potentially important initiative, for decisive action in the mid 1970s could have prevented the violent and divisive events of the early 1980s. The aim of Comprehensive Community Programmes was to establish, initially on a trial-run basis, a number of projects to test out effective means of tackling urban deprivation. It was a modest enough proposal, but soon ran into difficulties. Indeed, some two years after its announcement in Parliament, which earned for the minister Press headlines such as 'Labour to Give from Urban Rich to Poor' and 'Jenkins Plans New Deal for the Poor', no Comprehensive Community Programmes had been initiated and not one deprived person had been helped by this 'new initiative'. The story of the failure of Comprehensive Community Programmes has been told elsewhere,[19] but its relevance here is that for at least two years while the policy was foundering, Parliament had no inkling at all that things were going wrong. Even concerned MPs stood little chance of successfully questioning the Executive about the development. Parliamentary questions were taken seriously, but often answered misleadingly, being drafted with more regard to the needs of the Department than the rights of the House of Commons.

More generally, urban deprivation policy during the period 1974–9 provides a good example of secret government at work. During this time there were *three* major reviews of urban deprivation or inner-city policy, none was published and only one was even publicly announced. Major problems were discussed behind closed doors and yet there were many outside Whitehall who could have usefully contributed to such discussions.

Hypothermia

A further illustration of both Parliament's inability to question effectively the Executive, and the power of Civil Servants and their commitment to secrecy, is provided by the problem of hypothermia among
elderly people. In January 1976 a Labour back-bencher, Mr John
Golding, put down the following Parliamentary Question: 'To ask the
Secretary of State for Social Services, what is the estimate of the
incidence of hypothermia in the years since 1970'. Michael Meacher
had the responsibility of answering and the Department provided the
following answer for him: 'I am unable to make such an estimate, but
since 1970 the number of deaths each year in England and Wales
attributable solely or mainly to hypothermia are as follows: 1970, 16;
1971, 15; 1972, 21; 1973, 22; 1974, 17.' This answer followed the usual
DHSS formula of relying on death certificate figures.

At this point it should be noted that no authority in the field would
accept that this is a reliable basis for estimating deaths from this
condition. We do not, in fact, know how many deaths are caused
by hypothermia, but certainly the DHSS figures represent a gross
underestimate. As far back as 1964 a special committee of the British
Medical Association noted that: 'most cases of hypothermia are missed
because ordinary clinical thermometers do not record the condition'
and they also observed that 'many elderly bedridden patients may die
in their homes without the condition being diagnosed. We therefore
suspect that the incidence is very much higher than is commonly
supposed.'[20]

Other studies also showed the importance and extent of hypothermia,
including one by the Royal College of Physicians.[21] And in 1972, a
multi-disciplinary team, including this writer, found that 0.58 per cent
of a sample of 1,020 elderly people throughout the United Kingdom
had inner body temperatures below 35°C (95°F) when these were
measured in the morning. The survey also estimated those who were
at risk of becoming hypothermic and for this purpose a cut-off point of
35.5°C (95.9°F) was taken; 9.6 per cent of the sample had inner body
temperatures below this level and this group, regarded as 'at risk'

because of their low reserves of body heat, represented approximately 700,000 elderly people.[22]

The purpose of this brief discussion of available evidence is to show that the research results that exist give a very different, and more alarming, picture than that presented by the DHSS. Clearly, the public and Parliamentary reaction to the problem of hypothermia depends to a large extent on the information they receive about the incidence of the problem. Ideally any 'Department of *Health*' would be committed to improving the health of the nation and mobilizing public support for policies to tackle evils such as hypothermia. In such a world the DHSS would wish to conduct itself in a responsible manner and set before Parliament the reliable evidence that is available. In the less satisfactory real world things are very different as the response to Mr Golding's Parliamentary Question shows.

Michael Meacher was not happy with the suggested reply that was provided by his officials. The junior minister, himself the author of a book on the confused elderly, was aware of the existence of independent evidence and asked his Civil Servants to incorporate some of this in the Parliamentary Answer. At this stage Civil Servants pulled out all the stops to cast doubt on the independent research. A major point raised, for example, was the fact that part of the 1972 survey occurred during the period of the miners' strike which disrupted fuel supplies and it was argued that this cast 'doubt' on the results. This was a potentially serious point, but the DHSS did not consult the researchers about it. In fact, we had inquired about the effects of the strike and found that these were negligible. But the DHSS were not interested in these facts, only in casting doubt on the evidence.

Department of Health officials also raised some more valid questions about the exact significance of evidence about the incidence of hypothermia. The definition of hypothermia *is* inevitably an arbitrary one and the precise medical significance of body temperature just below 95°F is not always clear, although we know that at temperatures several degrees below this level there is a high chance of mortality. Certainly doctors regard low body temperature as a sign that all is not well and regard the condition seriously. A Parliamentary Answer, responsibly drafted, would have noted the arbitrariness of the definition and perhaps made other qualifications, but would also include the research findings which show the large-scale nature of the problem. It is noteworthy that the answer presented to the minister not only quoted nothing of the independent research, but included *no* qualification to the figures derived from death certificates. The concern was not to present the facts, but to camouflage them.

There followed a to-ing and fro-ing of minutes between minister and officials, the former asking for the evidence (and any qualification to it that should be made) and the latter arguing that it should not be given.

The following section from one of the memoranda produced at the time of the Parliamentary Question saga makes the point clear:

We felt that in this politically sensitive area it was of great importance not to be issuing information which may be misleading and which could certainly be used against the government. It is almost certain that any reply which suggested that large numbers of old people might be suffering from hypothermia would be used to bring pressure on the Government to improve heating provision for old people in some way.

The determined rearguard action by the DHSS officials was a success and the only data given in the answer presented to Parliament on 12 February was that derived from death certificates. As Meacher has noted: 'yet another anodyne answer reached the pages of Hansard'.[23]

Child benefits

The third example of excessive secrecy within social policy-making concerns the introduction of child benefits. In 1975 the Labour government introduced legislation to create a unified child benefit to take the place of family allowances and child tax allowances. It was a reform which was widely welcomed by those concerned with social security and poverty. But after the Bill was passed and the reform seemingly in the bag, things started to go wrong. During the first half of 1976 a not unfamiliar battle raged in Whitehall between the DHSS and the Treasury about the level of the new child benefit. This was only to be expected but, in the Cabinet discussions of this question a new issue was introduced, which rapidly gained in importance. This concerned the effect of withdrawing child tax allowance (therefore reducing fathers' net pay) on the negotiations that were taking place for a phase three of incomes policy. Mr Callaghan, the prime minister, started to have strong doubts about the child benefit scheme.

Despite the fact that the TUC had always supported the switch from 'wallet to purse' – a switch that was fundamental to the policy – one factor which strongly influenced the Cabinet was the reported view of certain TUC leaders. As the Cabinet minutes of the time recalled: 'on being informed of the reduction of take-home pay, which the child benefit scheme would involve, the TUC representatives had reacted immediately and violently against its implementation, irrespective of the level of benefits which would accompany the reduction in take-home pay'. In fact, as was revealed later, the situation was more complex than this. Congress leaders were apparently told by Mr Healey that a majority of the Cabinet and back-bench opinion was against the scheme. This influenced the TUC and its reported reaction was then used to secure the Cabinet rejection of child benefits.

These anxieties led to the abandonment of the scheme. As a *Sunday Times* story at the time pointed out: 'Those most strongly in favour of the child benefit scheme found themselves not only up against the Treasury in its most penny-pinching mood; they thought they were up against the trade unions too. There seemed little choice but to kill the scheme as quickly as possible.'[24]

It took a dramatic article in *New Society*, based very heavily on, and quoting verbatim, secret Cabinet minutes to bring home the full extent of the about-turn on child benefits and the manoeuvrings in Cabinet that led up to it.[25] The article, by Child Poverty Action Group's Frank Field, became front-page news and the pageant that followed included hunts to catch the source of the Cabinet leak (with policemen roaming the corridors of power), threatened back-bench revolts, the setting-up of a special TUC–Labour Party Committee to save the scheme and the mobilization of a formidable alliance of family groups to campaign for the implementation of child benefit.

This story illustrates the secrecy in which major decisions about social policy are made. An important debate about the effects of switching benefit from father to mother was addressed only by small groups and was never aired in public. Moreover, excessive secrecy meant that trade union leaders could be seriously misled about back-bench opinion and, furthermore, once trade union leaders had been scared by this, their anxieties could be put to Cabinet as a reason for abandoning the scheme. In this instance, but it was a rare one, a leak of Cabinet papers enabled the public, the Parliamentary Labour Party and pressure groups to get in on the debate and the effect was to save the scheme.[26]

Secrecy is an endemic feature of British government and it would be no easy task to open up the policy-making process to the public. An example from David Donnison's time as Chairman of the Supplementary Benefits Commission, illustrates the variety of arguments employed to prevent the glare of the torch penetrating the gloomy corridors of power. In his book, *The Politics of Poverty*, Donnison quotes from a Treasury memorandum to the DHSS concerning the Supplementary Benefits Commission's response to the review of the supplementary benefit scheme. Having noted that there was 'clearly room for improvement', in a manner which would suggest she was marking an undergraduate essay, the DHSS official went on to voice her disapproval of the Supplementary Benefit Commission's views before noting:

I understand that there is a suggestion that this document should be published. There are serious problems about the provision of paper and HMSO are likely to be exhorting Departments to economise in the use of paper, particularly during 1979–80. It is, therefore, for consideration whether this document of 60 pages – which reproduces in shriller tone what has already been incorporated in the Commission's annual reports for 1975, 1976 and 1977 – should be published at the taxpayers' expense. In particular, I would have thought that your Ministers would wish to consider whether the attack on this Government's social policies, as expressed in the comments on the level of social security benefits, housing policy, and employment measures, should be published in this form.[27]

This illustrates the lengths – the absurd lengths – to which the

Establishment will go to prevent the publication of information and the promotion of public debate about vital social policy issues. However, the record of David Donnison's Supplementary Benefit Commission for a few years in the late 1970s shows the possibilities of turning even the most conservative and cautious public agencies into promoters of public participation in policy discussions.

A further indicator of the extent to which government will go to control information comes from the attempt by outsiders to get access to the contents of Programme Analysis and Reviews which were undertaken by government in the late 1970s. In 1976, for example, the Comptroller and Auditor General's Department attempted to obtain access to certain Programme Analysis and Review reports. This led to a Treasury instruction that Programme Analysis and Review reports were 'not to be made available to the Comptroller and Auditor General or his Department even on a confidential basis'. The Treasury memorandum went on to say that, quite apart from the substance:

It will be necessary to protect the confidentiality of the PAR identification. If in any approach the PAR reference is used ... it will be necessary to frame any response as to avoid confirming or denying this status. This can be done by explaining that PAR titles are confidential ... but saying that there are of course many reviews conducted in many different ways, and then going on to say if there is or is not a policy review on this subject completed or in progress before dealing with the substance of what can be offered.

Social planning

Strong social planning is vital if socialist policy is to be successfully implemented. And this requires the introduction of several new mechanisms within the policy process. These will be necessary to ensure comprehensive planning across Whitehall, a clear specification of policy objectives and the encouragement of public and Parliamentary debate about these objectives.

Joint approach to social policy

First, a future government must develop an effective joint approach to social policy. This idea was tried in the mid 1970s, quickly ran out of steam during the life-time of the last Labour government and was effectively buried by the Thatcher administration. In their 1975 report, *A Joint Framework for Social Policies*, the Central Policy Review Staff argued the case for 'improved co-ordination between services as they affect the individual' and for 'better analysis of, and policy prescriptions for, complex problems – especially when they are the concern of more than one department'.[28]

Currently, as was argued in Chapter 3, fragmentation and overlap derive from *ad hoc* developments emanating from two or more government departments which produce results that are clearly not in the best interests of the individuals and families which they are designed to help. Examples abound in many fields: income maintenance, provision for the under-5s, the care of old people, etc.

A Joint Approach to Social Policy unit, staffed by administrative Civil Servants, professionals and outside political advisers, should be set up in the Cabinet Office. It should report to a Cabinet committee chaired by the prime minister. Only with this lead can a joint approach to social policy develop authority within Whitehall and become an important instrument for developing and monitoring the social strategy.[29]

Social impact statements

A second means of instituting effective social planning would be through social impact statements. This derives from the American idea of 'family impact statements' which were a feature of the Carter–Mondale election campaign in 1976. They were also once supported by Mr Patrick Jenkin, while Shadow Spokesman on Social Services. Despite this interest shown in opposition on both sides of the Atlantic, neither Carter's nor Thatcher's administration introduced them. This is hardly surprising, perhaps, for as one Tory politician remarked 'what would you say about the family impact of the Immigration Bill?'.

The case for family impact statements has been developing within Britain. Indeed, James Callaghan, while prime minister, noted that 'I don't believe that the Government has done enough, hardly started to consider as a whole, the impact of its policies on the family when we take our decisions in Cabinet and in government.'[30] A particularly important feature of family impact statements is that they would focus attention, not only on inequalities between income groups, but also on those which exist between families with different responsibilities for children and other dependent relatives. Frank Field has argued that 'such statements accompanying major budget pronouncements, social security changes, housing and education reforms, could begin to change the framework in which politicians think'.[31]

While the impact on families (of different kinds) should be a key focus of any new impact statement, they would need to go wider than this and should become a key means of monitoring the implementation of the social strategy. Indeed, for a Labour government, they would be a major means of relating individual pieces of legislation – and other policy items – to the overall objectives of the social strategy. Social impact statements would be attached to new Parliamentary Bills and other policy measures and would spell out, in some detail, the intended effects of the policy on different families and individuals. The statements should include analysis under a number of headings among which the following would feature:

1. The impact on families, households and individuals of different kinds.
2 Inequality – the effect on class, income, sex, race and other forms of inequality.
3. The association between the new policy and existing, related policies from different departments.
4. The impact on unemployment and poverty.
5. Implementation; how the policy would be administered, issues of complexity, etc.

A social policy development council

The third social planning initiative should be the creation of a social policy development council.[32] It would act as a complementary body to the National Economic Development Council and like that body would include representatives of both sides of industry, but also voluntary bodies, academics, consumer groups and those from local government and health authorities. A social policy development council would consider not only the impact of policy on service areas, but also the combined effects of policy decisions on individuals, families and communities. The council should have a strong, independent chairperson, and have the right to call for evidence from government departments. A major function would be the forecasting of future trends and needs, and hence policy initiatives. It would be a means of focusing also on those issues which, because of longer timescales, are often neglected in the hurly-burly of week-to-week politics.

The council would include among its functions the initiation of research. Currently, there is no organization or research institute in Britain which has as its task the monitoring and evaluation of social trends and policies or the forecasting of future needs and problems. The council would take on this role. It would undertake its own research and publish regular reports, including an annual social policy review. It would focus, perhaps, particularly on those issues that do not fall neatly into one department's orbit. Its staff would come from local and central government, the academic world, and from voluntary organizations and pressure groups.

Departmental policy planning

In recent years there has been a move towards establishing policy, planning and resources units within government departments. However, the evidence suggests that these are relatively weak within their departments and are not, as yet, making much impact. There is a need to establish and develop strong units of these kinds to be staffed not only by mainstream Civil Servants and Civil Service professionals, but also by outside advisers. The Left in Britain has been too slow to argue the need for effective control over resources within social policy. As argued in Chapter 10, it has been a crucial error to leave it to the Right in British politics to argue the need for effective financial monitoring and evaluation of resource distribution. Given the many pressing needs that will be on policy agendas in the future, it is even more important that a reforming government ensures that resources are being spent effectively and that increases in public expenditure make significant and immediate impacts on the welfare of citizens, rather than merely contributing to the growth of spending levels *per se* and the development of high-salaried bureaucracies. Policy, planning and resources units within departments will enable ministers to take more effective control of their departments and thus to report properly to Parliament on questions of planning and resources. As the House of Commons All Party Committee on Public Accounts has argued, 'The present position is that a Minister often does not have the information he reasonably needs in order to control the public expenditure for which he is responsible.' Moreover, the Committee suggested that 'the form of public expenditure is often not sufficiently tested to see whether the same results could be obtained for less money or indeed better results for the same money'.[33]

Departmental reorganization

Existing patterns of departmental organization should also be looked at critically to see whether any reform could aid the implementation of the social strategy. An obvious candidate for critical examination is the DHSS. The case for the amalgamation of social security, health and personal social services in one department has never been made out convincingly. The existing department is far too large and in practice there are few signs of co-operation between, say, social security and personal social services. (During the 1983/4 DHSS Social Work Service initiative on informal care, which has clear implications for

242 SOCIAL POLICIES FOR THE FUTURE

social security, not one official from the social security side of DHSS took part in a series of national and regional meetings: 'We did ask one but he couldn't make it.')

The link between health and personal social services should be preserved and these areas should be the basis for a new Department of Health and Community Welfare. Social security should be linked with the Inland Revenue into a new Department of Income and Social Security. This would make particular sense if an integrated tax–benefit scheme was introduced. Even without this reform, the new department is necessary to oversee all policies that bear on the distribution of income.

While ideas for a social policy development council and other new mechanisms might be seen as mere extensions of existing Whitehall bureaucracy – and will certainly be so criticized by opponents – they are in truth means of countering excessive bureaucracy, testing out means against ends and rationalizing both policy-making systems and methods of implementation. They are, among other things, aids both to efficiency and policy effectiveness and would thus aid the elimination of unnecessary expenditures.

In order to ensure that the goals of the social strategy were being implemented, one idea would be to publish on an annual basis an overall, comprehensive social strategy statement which would relate existing policies, performances and practices to the strategy and might incorporate much of the material currently published in the annual Public Expenditure White Papers.

Conclusion

12 A New Commitment to Welfare

There are wrongs that must be righted – bitter woes that seek redress,
   We can hear our sisters calling in their weakness and distress;
We need the power to lift them from their sad and evil plight,
   'Tis for this we want the Franchise – and we claim it as our right.

Anon[1]

Aneurin Bevan once observed a great and simple truth, that 'there is no test for progress other than its impact on the individual'.[2] For me, one particular individual comes to mind.

In November 1970 I visited an old lady of 84 years of age, as part of a research project on hypothermia and the effects of cold conditions on elderly people. I wanted to gain some first-hand experience of the problems. Mrs Brown (not her real name) lived in Westminster – not exactly a stone's throw, but not far, from the Houses of Parliament and Whitehall.

Her situation remains vivid in my mind and I often recall her problems – I made several subsequent visits. An extract from the notes made after the first visit summarizes her circumstances:

The flat consists of one large bed-sitting room, a kitchen, a bathroom and a hall. The hall, in fact, serves as her living room, and it would appear that she spends a lot of her time in this hall. The reason for this is simply that the bed-sitting room is too cold. This room has a high ceiling and a very large window. It would obviously be very difficult to keep warm. An electric two-bar fire in the wall is not used, but instead she uses her own two-bar electric fire. She claims that the Council one is too expensive.

Mrs Brown spends 56–57s a week on fuel and light and her rent is £3 9s. 4d. So this leaves her with about £3 2s. for her other necessities. This financial situation leaves her very short of food ... After lunch all that she seemed to have was some coffee, with some sterilised milk in the evening. 'I get so hungry, I keep on eating bread and butter all the time.' One payment she keeps up is her insurance; three shillings a week. This is to pay for her funeral. But she is worried that this policy is only worth £50 and 'that won't bury me'.

Despite her excessive expenditure on heating Mrs Brown was often cold. When it got really cold she wore two jumpers and sometimes a coat, but of course, she could not use the electric fire all the time. She did not have the fire on during the course of the interview and yet it was chilly in the flat. She complained that her hands and arms were often cold. At night she must have been a good deal colder. She used one hot water bottle and would have liked another but '... they're 10s. aren't they?'

Mrs Brown was 'very grateful' for the money she received from 'the Assistance', it was a 'great help'. Her own mother had not received any such help in her time and she had had six children to bring up on her own. Her attitude to the Council about housing, however, was different. She claims that when she visited this flat with an official from the Housing Department, she only saw it from the front door, as the workmen were in. If she had seen the big window in the main room, she would never have taken it. She now wanted to move to a smaller and warmer flat. She had asked the Council, ... but all to no avail. Her local doctor had written to the Council on her behalf, she said, but he had not been hopeful; 'they screw it up and throw it in the bin'.

Today there remain large numbers of elderly people like Mrs Brown – indeed many more given rising fuel costs and the greater proportion of elderly people in their late 70s, 80s and 90s. However, there are other groups too in desperate circumstances: the young unemployed – Britain's rejected generation; poor families struggling to bring up their children, black people who are denied a fair opportunity simply because of their skin colour; many women, simply because of their gender; disabled people, and the older unemployed, thrown on a human scrap heap in middle age with little chance of decent jobs in the future. Yet, while the need to provide urgent and proper help to these groups remains the most pressing reason for Britain to preserve and develop its Welfare State, the argument for adequate social policies is a wider and more fundamental one, for the Welfare State is a key institution within British society: its development will be a major force for good, while its demise has serious repercussions not only for the poor, but for all citizens.

At the last general election there was a sense in which the Labour Party had become the victim of its own propaganda. Probably at every election since the war, a leading Labour politician has warned the electorate that if returned to power, the Tories would 'destroy' the Welfare State. In retrospect, this can be seen as only a little more than mere propaganda, for while the advent of Conservative administrations has not augured well for the Welfare State, postwar administrations under Churchill, Eden, Macmillan, Douglas-Home and Heath have not involved the destruction of social services and benefits. Labour Oppositions have rightly criticized governments for spending too little on these services and for presiding over a growing gap between public squalor and private affluence, but the fact remains that the Welfare State survived. Indeed, public spending on social services and benefits has often increased in real terms under Conservative administrations. This is, in part, because wiser Conservatives than those who are now in power saw the necessity of a Welfare State to give credence to its 'One Nation' politics and because they realized that, carefully developed, the Welfare State need not offer any serious threat to a concentration of power in the hands of a small privileged minority, nor to the unequal distribution of resources within society.

The threat

That situation has now radically changed. The advent of Mrs Thatcher and the election of the Conservative Party in 1979 heralded a new era in British Tory politics. From the Conservative point of view it was an era that was urgently required, given the desperate condition of the economy. Capitalism was in crisis and a way out of that crisis involved an attack on working-class conditions. For the first time since the war, Conservatives turned their backs on a belief – even the pretence – that they should govern in the interests of the whole community. To reduce taxation and public expenditure, the Conservatives set about the dismantling of our Welfare State. And yet, was this happening when all, including the rich, had to make sacrifices? Far from it, for as a deliberate act of government policy, the rich were growing richer.

Benefit cuts and restrictions on spending for services such as home helps and meals on wheels have been matched by substantial tax cuts for the rich. This administration's first budget in 1979, awarded 34 per cent (a total of £1.56 billion) to the top 7 per cent of taxpayers. By contrast the 10 per cent of low income taxpayers received only 2.2 per cent of all tax cuts. The Chancellor awarded a married man on £400 a week a cut in his *weekly* tax bill of £42.55, slightly higher than the *annual* tax cut for a man on £50 a week.[3] This fiscal bias against the poor, and towards the rich, has been substantial over the whole period, as shown in Chapter 3. Moreover, while Conservative economic policies were insuring that more people were unsuccessful, not least in terms of obtaining jobs, Conservative social policies made them poorer by such means as drastically reducing their opportunities for obtaining council housing, by increasing the charges for school meals and medicines, and by holding down the real value of social security payments.

The Tory appeal to sacrifice for the common good is nothing less than an organized hypocrisy, for while many have suffered as a result of Conservative policies, their major supporters, the rich and the powerful, have done well. This is no idle rhetoric, but rather an accurate and reasonable evaluation. Thus, while the NHS has suffered, the private sectors to which many Cabinet ministers, including the prime minister, subscribe, flourishes.

Many of the poorest children are denied decent school meals, yet the children and grandchildren of ministers eat well in private schools; and while the elderly relatives of the powerful are cared for, many of those in other classes are neglected. The Establishment classes continue to receive good salaries (and disproportionately high pay awards), often from more than one job, at a time when 4 million citizens pay the full sacrifice by not having a job at all. 'To him that hath shall be given. To him that hath not shall be taken away even that which he hath' has become the driving force behind the actions of those who already have the best health, education, incomes, housing and other provisions.

Tory social policies are extending and deepening inequalities in Britain, and the refashioning of the Welfare State plays a crucial role in this process. The aim is to create a Welfare State reserved for the working class, the poor and the weak, while encouraging the 'successful' to purchase their own health, education and other services, with fiscal and other inducements. In brief, Conservative social policy involves the legitimization and institutionalization of 'Two Nations' or, as Mrs Thatcher might put it, a move back towards 'Victorian values'. It is creating a society increasingly characterized by growing inequality, not only in terms of class and income, but also geography, sex, race, family responsibilities and age.

It is not, however, only the private market that is boosted, for in the important and expensive area of health and personal social services, voluntary bodies, the 'community' and the family are all being urged to take on greater burdens, not least in terms of care of the frail elderly: this means greater pressures on women in particular.

The Conservative Welfare State of the future would be one predominantly for the poor, the unsuccessful, and for disproportionate numbers of the elderly, black people and one parent families, with more recipients in the north than in the south. It would be characterized by an increasing use of the means test, more rigorous policing of benefit entitlements and poor quality, for as Richard Titmuss noted 'poor people's services are invariably poor services'.[4]

Because of the anxieties of Tory 'wets' and concern from other groups, some of the policies dear to the heart of the Tory Right wing have not yet been implemented. However, given the pathetic performance to date of those who are wet, both in name and in deed, can there be any doubt that this Conservative government headed by a strong, confident and courageous leader – and with all the lessons behind it of some seven years of Whitehall experience – could not embark on policies the like of which we have not yet experienced? We may have seen nothing yet, and Tory social policies for the rest of the 1980s could well see the virtual end of council housing as we know it today, further encouragement for private schools, radical changes affecting the administration and delivery of welfare services to encourage private provisions, the end of the present means of financing the NHS with the introduction of private insurance or other schemes to aid private medicine; and within social security, the de-indexation of national insurance pensions – a crucial change for Treasury hardliners, the substantial reduction of child benefit levels, and continued pressure on the level of unemployment, supplementary and other benefits.

Those who attempt to laugh off such an extreme prediction include many who, in 1979, would have sneered at suggestions that, under the Conservatives, council-house building would be reduced to a third of its former level, that the school meals service would be devastated, that the statutory pensions link with wages would be ended and the State Earnings Related Pension Scheme fundamentally reduced; that prescription charges would be increased seven times and that numbers of university places would actually contract.

If the arguments against the social policies of the New Right are to win public support, it is necessary to consider the impact of government decisions, not just at the level of individual benefits and specific services, but more broadly – and fundamentally – in terms of wider social and moral consequences.

Two nations

What kind of society is emerging under the impact of Conservative social policy? While a decade of extreme Conservative rule throughout the 1980s would undermine Britain's economic and social structure, this would be associated also with a moral decline. The move away from collective provision, combined with a rampant individualism, far from allowing more choice and liberty, would be associated with increasing greed, disregard for human suffering and social division. As Mr Prentice, while a Tory minister, explained: 'If you believe economic salvation can only be achieved by rewarding success and the national income is not increasing, then you have no alternative but to make the unsuccessful poor.'[5] But it would not only be the poor who would suffer, for the wider social costs of institutionalizing, encouraging and subsidizing through tax cuts the ability to walk by on the other side of the road would be menacing.

In evaluating the future of social policy, therefore, it is important to assess not only the most obvious gainers and losers (who does best and worst out of different policy decisions) but also other longer-term – less tangible and quantifiable, but more fundamental and crucial – consequences. For, while some clearly are gaining from the politics of Thatcherism – as their bank balances would readily show – even they may yet have to face the effects of the policies they voted for.

The effect of Tory social policies must be judged against their impact on the overall moral health of our society. The logical outcome of Tory social policies is a more divided, more conflict-ridden, less caring, less tolerant, more vicious, and more violent society. Already there are signs of this: seven years after the start of a Tory administration that has sought to replace the ethics of the Welfare State with the cruel rule of the jungle, it is perhaps hardly surprising that some people are acting accordingly. Urban riots were the most obvious indication, but so too are increasing crime, prostitution, drug addiction (an epidemic now in some neighbourhoods), suicides among the unemployed, and family violence.

The State today spends more on the police, and proclaims the importance of 'law and order', while respect for the law declines and order deteriorates. The result of Tory 'social' policy, if left unchecked to do its worst throughout the 1980s, would be to create a bizarre and frightening society where the rich enjoy their riches, but increasingly turn a frightened eye towards the powerless: a society where we sell more videos but also more burglar alarms, more yachts and more karate classes, and where service industries to provide leisure and entertainment for the well-to-do grow in parallel with those services designed to protect them. (Burglar alarms and other forms of protection gadgetry are already a growing feature of British advertising. Self-defence instruction is also on the increase.)

The 1980s could, therefore, be a decade not only of increasing poverty and inequalities and the rapid growth of Two Nations in education, health, housing and work, but also a period of unprecedented division and conflict affecting not just the poor but also the suburban majority and better-off. It could become a society increasingly characterized by urban violence, by racial discord and conflict, by despair and apathy among some, but by political extremism by others. It will be a testing and difficult time for our democracy, with more violent conflict between police and the protesters, who demonstrate their grievances in the manner the dispossessed have always done – for want of any real alternative.

Tory Britain will also be a society divided in its judgement about the cause of social malaise. The well-to-do, many of those with jobs and those more likely to be nearer the south coast than the north-east, will complain about the excessive burden on the public purse of those out of work who, it would be widely assumed, had only to pedal a little further to find jobs – Norman Tebbit's mass army of cyclists seeking vainly the reality behind the monetarist rhetoric.

Many scapegoats will be found – black people, one parent families, trade unionists, agitators in general, and lax parents – to explain the manifold problems resulting from economic and social recession. Remedies will flow from the lips of those who seek to blame the victims. The manifestations of social evil would be under the public and mass media spotlight – their causes neglected. Those with position, property and power would abhor violence in righteous indignation and yet many of them, by their own actions and votes, would have encouraged that same violence. Indeed, our society would do well to heed the words of Robert Kennedy in 1968, on hearing of the assassination of Martin Luther King:

For there is another kind of violence, slower but just as deadly, destructive as the shot or the bomb in the night. This is the violence of institutions; indifference and inaction and slow decay. This is the violence that afflicts the poor, that poisons relations between men because their skin has different colors. This is a slow destruction of a child by hunger, and schools without books and homes without heat in the winter.[6]

Faced with violence, division and conflict, the Conservative response under present leadership is not an about-turn on policy, but an expansion of an increasingly armoured police force, where the chilling sound of the electronic siren signals a growing alienation between police and community. It was, appropriately enough, in 1984 that talk of a drift towards a police state – in the wake of striking miners being turned back or arrested on their way to picket, and other incidents – seemed more like fair description, rather than oratorical, Orwellian flight of fancy. Britain could be a society where more and more no-go areas blight the urban landscape; and where the young with no future are increasingly conscripted into schemes for the unemployed, a reserve army with depressed minds who serve to depress wage rates.

The challenge

In earlier chapters a radical approach to social policy in the 1980s and beyond was discussed. These reviewed some major policy areas and discussed some key themes and general principles, rather than attempted to develop a detailed programme. That job needs to be done, and is being done to some extent.[7]

This book has been written in the belief that Britain needs a Welfare State, not only for the very important reasons of giving help to the poor, the weak, the sick, the disabled, elderly people and other groups, but also for the sake of the community as a whole.

Democratic socialism is concerned with *all* the people, not just the few at the top – the rich and powerful. Indeed, it is the bitterest irony that the Conservative Party has taken upon itself the claim to be the party of Britain, the patriotic party – yet it embraces a philosophy that holds the majority of people in contempt and wishes to provide them with only minimal services, facilities and opportunities. They are not concerned at the threat to liberties posed by mass unemployment, poverty and underspending on education and health. To the privileged, issues of liberty in social policy boil down to nothing more than their demand for private education and medicine. Such usage is not merely inaccurate or too narrow – it is an obscenity.

For socialism, social policy represents the way to build, step-by-step, and policy-by-policy, the just society. But the development of *policy* needs to be placed in a wider context. Indeed, it is important for the Labour Party to act on two levels. The first is at the level of legislation, policy and action, when Labour in power is able to exercise a popular mandate. The second, equally important in the longer term, is at the level of persuasion and education. This recognizes that most of the people (and most Labour Party supporters) are *not* socialists, although they do subscribe to many socialist policies. Equality, social justice and respect for fellow citizens can in part be legislated for, but essentially involves a battle for hearts and minds. It is a battle not easily won in a society where many seek to seduce with greed and self-interest. There is, therefore, a dilemma as to whether to proceed with legislation when there is clear evidence of public opposition to some social policies. Of course, this is no dilemma for authoritarians, but it is a live one for democratic socialists who wish to promote equality as a means of obtaining greater freedom and liberty. For democratic socialists, the ends do *not* justify the means, but rather the means themselves help to determine both the possibility of obtaining ends, and the nature of the end-results.

To make this point is not to show any wavering of support for socialism – far from it. It is simply to say that socialism is not about constructing some wonderful blueprint for Utopia – an exquisite poem, merely to be recited by an activist élite – but rather that it involves building, step-by-step, policy-by-policy, a living society for the benefit of all people.

At the heart of the challenge that faces democratic socialists is the role and function of the State in helping to build a democratic, free and equal society. But the last fifteen years or so have witnessed a growing disillusion with State services and their capacity to deliver efficient and humane provisions and benefits. And yet, alongside this critique, the Left has failed to develop a coherent and workable strategy to build an alternative approach. There has been a flowering of new ideas and perspectives – feminist, environmentalist, democratic – but no agreed constructive programme has emerged. Moreover, this failure has allowed the Right to construct a fanciful and incredible – but to some electors, believable – argument that in place of State services, the private market can provide education, health, pensions and other services that are necessary.

The challenge for democratic socialists is therefore to take stock of the radical critique that first emerged in the 1960s and that has been tested, to some extent, in the 1970s, to see what of value can be utilized in the 1980s and beyond. And with this knowledge we need to construct a *Welfare Community* which will involve developing a new radical consensus in favour of collective action. If we fail to build this new alliance, we will not see a new Labour government and there will be a diminishing role for the State in human welfare during the 1980s with potentially disastrous results. For, as Tawney wisely observed: 'It is still constantly assumed by privileged classes that, when the State holds its hand, what remains, as a result of its inaction, is liberty. In reality, as far as the mass of mankind is concerned, what commonly remains is, not liberty, but tyranny.'[8]

Social policy seems to many – politicians included – a dull, if worthy, area of government. It is about benefit regulations and service delivery, and other mundane matters. It is thought to be altogether less important than other areas of policy – the economy, defence and foreign policy. Yet most people are more affected by social policy than other areas over which government has influence. More importantly it is through social policy – in its broadest sense – that men and women, both those in power and all citizens, can make moral judgements and decisions. Titmuss, for example, argued that in regard to Britain's blood donor system:

... detailed, concrete programmes of political change – undramatic and untheatrical as they may often appear to be – can facilitate the expression of man's moral sense. Thus, it serves as an illustration of how social policy, in one of its potential roles, can help to actualize the social and moral potentialities of all citizens.[9]

More than four decades on from the Beveridge Report, a future government must act with the authority and moral purpose of Britain's first majority Labour administration that implemented the greater part of the Beveridge Plan and much else besides. That will require courage and determination, commodities in scarce supply during the 1960s and 1970s. A future Labour administration must never forget that its purpose is not to manage the existing order of society more efficiently than its political rivals, but rather to transform that society into something altogether more fair and just. This will require taking effective power, not just the seal of office, and to beware what Tawney termed the 'exaggerated discretion' which was the 'characteristic failing of Labour governments'.[10] In this respect, Mrs Thatcher has done Labour a considerable favour, for she has shown that it is possible to take power and to exercise authority.

Labour in the 1980s needs to keep in balance a clear vision of, and commitment to, the ideals of democratic socialism – and therefore have in mind the overall direction in which policy should go – and yet have a respect for the immediate needs and problems of people and their willingness to support radical and socialist policies. If the former is not present, one becomes party to a mere liberalism of capitalism, whereas without the latter, power in the first place cannot be achieved and maintained.

In the past, Labour won power when its overall socialist commitment was related closely to current needs, problems and aspirations. Socialism must not – cannot – be communicated in ways which only a middle-class party membership can comprehend. Rather, we must explain why it *is* possible to build a community which will not tolerate preventable infant mortality, a society which can so organize its resources that its older members do not have to die in winter simply because they are too cold to live; and why it is possible to create a nation which has the confidence in its future to provide for its children, regardless of their origins, the best schools and health service that can be mustered. Social policy is the means of restoring confidence in the British people so that together we can build one society and a future for all.

The choice

The next election will therefore involve a choice, not only between two contrasting sets of social policy but, more generally, between the abandonment or the development of the Welfare State. Moreover, this involves an important decision about the future of British society, as to whether it should be motivated primarily by individual gain or by the common good. The Conservatives clearly are inspired by the spirit of Samuel Smiles – an emphasis on self-reliance – nothing less and nothing more than a 'pulling yourself up by your bootstraps' mentality.

During these recent Tory years the lights of a civilized society have started to flicker and dim, and we are at the dawn of a new dark age of greed, insensitivity to need and intolerance, where our social policies are ones dictated by the criteria of a private market, and administered by those who know the price of everything – even health – and the value of nothing.

A future for all

In this book, I have used often the words, spoken or written, of others, radicals and socialists, who down the years have managed to express – in a passage or a phrase – the idealism and the hopes of ordinary men and women. Yet it is the hopes of those ordinary people themselves, their struggles and their work over the generations, that are the true inspiration. In the past, some died for their beliefs, others were persecuted and many more strove (their work often unrecognized), sometimes in vain and sometimes with concrete results.

During this century Britain developed a 'Welfare State' and, while often imperfect (and certainly representing just the first tottering steps), it was based on principles simple and clear that people understand and respect: that all men and women are equal and should be free; that all have rights and responsibilities that should be recognized; that among these are rights to food and warmth, shelter, good health and education, recreation, equal treatment before the law and personal safety – regardless of sex, race, income, class or creed.

These decent principles are now threatened by the Tory onslaught on the Welfare State. It is therefore these principles that must be fired anew to not only save our social policy, but also to end the Two Nations that is Conservative Britain, and to build instead *one* society – equal, tolerant and free.

References

1 Introduction

1 Margaret Thatcher, *Let Our Children Grow Tall: Selected Speeches, 1975–1977*, Centre for Policy Studies, 1977.
2 'Reform of Social Security' (Green Paper), Cmnd 9517, HMSO, 1985; 'Reform of Social Security' (White Paper), Cmnd 9691, HMSO, 1986.
3 Thatcher, *Let Our Children Grow Tall*.

2 From Consensus to 'Crisis'

1 Sir William Beveridge, *Pillars of Security*, George Allen & Unwin, 1943, p. 42.
2 Sir William Beveridge, *Social Insurance and Allied Services*, Cmd 6404, HMSO, 1942.
3 Derek Fraser, *The Evolution of the British Welfare State*, Macmillan, 1973, p. 145.
4 *Social Insurance and Allied Services*, para. 300.
5 *Employment Policy*, Cmd 6527, HMSO, 1944.
6 Rudolf Klein (ed.), *Inflation and Priorities*, Centre for Studies in Social Policy, 1975, Table 1.3.
7 Harold Macmillan, *The Middle Way*, Macmillan, 1938.
8 See Andrew Gamble, *The Conservative Nation*, Routledge & Kegan Paul, 1974.

9 *Freedom in the Welfare State*, Fabian Society, 1964, p. 3.

10 T. H. Marshall, *Social Policy*, Hutchinson, 1965, p. 97.

11 Anthony Crosland, *The Future of Socialism*, Jonathan Cape, 1956, p. 59.

12 Labour Party Conference, Scarborough, 1 October 1963.

13 *Royal Commission on Local Government in England, 1966–1969*, Cmnd 4040, HMSO, 1969.

14 National Health Service, *The Administrative Structure of the Medical and Related Services in England and Wales*, HMSO, 1968.

15 *Royal Commission on the Constitution, 1969–1973*, Cmnd 5460, HMSO, 1973.

16 *The Civil Service: Report of the Committee*, Cmnd 3638, HMSO, 1968.

17 *Report of the Committee on Housing in Greater London*, Cmnd 2605, HMSO, 1965.

18 *Report of the Committee on the Rent Acts*, Cmnd 4609, HMSO, 1971.

19 *Public Schools Commission: First Report*, HMSO, 1968.

20 Central Advisory Council for Education, *Children and their Primary Schools*, HMSO, 1966.

21 *Report of the Committee on Local Authority and Allied Personal Social Services*, Cmnd 3703, HMSO, 1968.

22 A. H. Halsey, *Educational Priority*, Vol. 1, EPA Problems and Priorities, HMSO, 1972.

23 J. Higgins, N. Deakin, J. Edwards and M. Wicks, *Government and Urban Poverty: Inside the Policy-making Process*, Basil Blackwell, 1983.

24 Centre for Urban and Regional Research and Department of Social and Economic Research, *Cities in Trouble*, Discussion Paper No. 39, University of Glasgow, 1981.

25 *The National Plan*, Cmnd 2764, HMSO, 1965.

26 Christopher Booker, *The Seventies: Portrait of a Decade*, Allen Lane, 1980.

27 *The Labour Government 1964–1970*, Pelican Books, 1974, p. 57.

28 *The Government's Expenditure Plans 1980–81 to 1983–84*, Cmnd 7841, HMSO, 1980, Table 1.2.

29 *Social Insurance and Allied Services*, para. 270.

30 Organization for Economic Co-operation and Development, *The Welfare State in Crisis*, OECD, Paris, 1981, p. 5.

31 R. Bacon and W. A. Eltis, *Britain's Economic Problem: Too Few Producers*, Macmillan, 1978.

32 Richard Rose and Guy Peters, *Can Government Go Bankrupt?*, Macmillan, 1978.

33 James O'Connor, *The Fiscal Crisis of the State*, St Martin's Press, New York, 1973.

34 H. Glennerster, 'Public Spending and the Social Services: The End of an Era?', in M. Brown and S. Baldwin (eds), *The Year Book of Social Policy in Britain*, Routledge & Kegan Paul, 1980, p. 15.

35 Paul Ormerod, 'The Economic Record', in N. Bosanquet and P. Townsend (eds), *Labour and Equality*, Heinemann Educational Books, 1980, p. 52.

36 ibid., pp. 53–4.

37 Frank Field, *Inequality in Britain: Freedom, Welfare and the State*, Fontana, 1981, p. 102.

38 ibid., p. 106.

39 D. E. Butler and Richard Rose, *The British General Election of 1959*, Macmillan, 1960, p. 55.

40 B. S. Rowntree and S. R. Lavers, *Poverty and the Welfare State*, Longmans Green, 1951.

41 Quoted in K. Coates and R. Silburn, *Poverty: The Forgotten Englishmen*, Penguin, 1970, p. 14.

42 Labour Party, *Let's Go with Labour for the New Britain*, 1964.

43 See David Bull (ed.), *Family Poverty*, Duckworth, 1971, Chapter 1.

44 Brian Abel-Smith and Peter Townsend, *The Poor and the Poorest*, Bell, 1965, p. 30.

45 'An Incomes Policy for Families', 1970, reprinted in, Frank Field, *Poverty and Politics*, Heinemann Educational Books, 1982, Chapter 7.

46 Supplementary Benefits Commission, *Evidence to the Royal Commission on the Distribution of Income and Wealth*, Report No. 6, *Lower Incomes*, Cmnd 7175, HMSO, 1978, p. 28.

47 See Adrian Sinfield, *What Unemployment Means*, Martin Robertson, 1981.

48 See Lesley Rimmer and Jennie Popay, 'Employment Trends and the Family', Study Commission on the Family, 1982, p. 25; and *Social Trends*, 15, Central Statistical Office, HMSO, 1985, Table 4.18.

49 Sinfield, *What Unemployment Means*, pp. 11–15.

50 *Royal Commission on the Distribution of Income and Wealth*, Report No. 1, Cmnd 6171, HMSO, 1975.

51 *Half Our Future*, a Report of the Central Advisory Council for Education (England), HMSO, 1963; *Children and their Primary Schools*, HMSO, 1967.

52 David Butler and Anne Sloman, *British Political Facts, 1900–1979*, Macmillan, 1980, p. 303.

53 *Report of the Committee on Housing in Greater London*, Cmnd 2605, HMSO, 1965.

54 *Old Houses into New Homes*, Cmnd 3602, HMSO 1968, Appendix.

55 John Greve, Dilys Page and Stella Greve, *Homelessness in London*, Scottish Academic Press, 1971; Bryan Glastonbury, *Homeless Near a Thousand Homes*, George Allen & Unwin, 1971.

56 Barbara Wootton, in Philip Bean and Stewart MacPherson (eds), *Approaches to Welfare*, Routledge & Kegan Paul, 1983, p. 286.

57 For an analysis, see Alan Deacon and Jonathan Bradshaw, *Reserved for the Poor: The Means-Test in British Social Policy*, Basil Blackwell/Martin Robertson, 1983.

58 ibid., Table 2, p. 131.

59 Jonathan Bradshaw, *Equity and Family Incomes, an analysis of current tax and benefit policy*, Study Commission on the Family, 1980, p. 20.

60 See Deacon and Bradshaw, *Reserved for the Poor*.

61 David Donnison, *The Politics of Poverty*, Martin Robertson, 1981, p. 185.

62 Supplementary Benefits Commission, *Annual Report 1976*, Cmnd 6910, HMSO, 1977, Table 12.3.

63 Wootton, *Approaches to Welfare*, p. 286.

64 Douglas Jay, *The Socialist Case*, Penguin, 1947, p. 258.

65 National Health Service, *The Administrative Structure*; Royal Commission on Local Government.

66 *Guardian*, 8 April 1980.

67 A. Richardson, 'The Politics of Participation: a study of schemes for tenant participation in council housing management', Ph.D. thesis, London School of Economics, 1977; National Consumer Council, *Soonest Mended*, 1979.

68 *A New Partnership for Our Schools*, HMSO, 1977, p. 43.

69 Central Policy Review Staff: *A Joint Framework for Social Policies*, HMSO, 1975.

70 See, for example, *People and their Families*, HMSO, 1980.

71 *Policy for the Inner Cities*, Cmnd 6845, HMSO, 1977, paras. 71 and 33.

72 Malcolm Wicks, 'Social Policy for the Inner Cities', in M. Brown and S. Baldwin (eds), *The Year Book of Social Policy in Britain*, 1977, Routledge & Kegan Paul, 1978.

73 Donnison, *The Politics of Poverty*.

74 Trog, shown in Butler and Rose, *The British General Election*, p. 201.

75 Mark Abrams and Richard Rose, *Must Labour Lose?*, Penguin, 1960, p. 19.

76 David Butler and Donald Stokes, *Political Change in Britain*, Penguin, 1971, p. 414.

77 ibid., p. 415.

78 ibid., p. 417.

79 ibid.

80 David Butler and Dennis Kavanagh, *The British Election of October 1974*, Macmillan, 1975, p. 273.

81 Dick Leonard, in David Lipsey and Dick Leonard (eds), *The Socialist Agenda: Crosland's Legacy*, Jonathan Cape, 1981, p. 48.

82 Peter Taylor-Gooby, *Public Opinion, Ideology and State Welfare*, Routledge & Kegan Paul, 1985.

83 Peter Golding and Sue Middleton, *Images of Welfare*, Martin Robertson, 1982.

84 ibid., p. 62.

85 ibid., p. 63.

86 ibid., p. 90.

87 ibid., p. 77.

88 Crosland, *The Future of Socialism*, p. 357.

89 'Social Policy since Titmuss', *Journal of Social Policy*, April 1979, 152.

90 Anthony Crosland, *Socialism Now*, Jonathan Cape, 1975, p. 26.

91 At a civic luncheon in Manchester Town Hall, 9 May 1975.

3 Counter-Revolution: The Tory Attack

1 Gospel According to St Luke, 10:31.

2 Anthony Crosland, *The Future of Socialism*, Jonathan Cape, 1964, p. 27.

3 ibid., pp. 27–8.

4 ibid., p. 28.

5 See *Deserting the Middle Ground: Tory Social Policies*, Fabian Society, 1978.

6 Andrew Gamble, *The Conservative Nation*, Routledge & Kegan Paul, 1974.

7 Sir Keith Joseph, *Reversing the Trend: A Critical Reappraisal*, Centre for

Policy Studies, 1975; Sir Keith Joseph, *Stranded on the Middle Ground*, Centre for Policy Studies, 1976.

8 Harold Macmillan, *The Middle Way*, Macmillan, 1938.

9 Joseph, *Stranded on the Middle Ground*.

10 ibid.

11 Margaret Thatcher, *Let Our Children Grow Tall: Selected Speeches, 1975–1977*, Centre for Policy Studies, 1977.

12 *The Right Approach*, Conservative Party, 1976.

13 Quoted by Dick Leonard, in David Lipsey and Dick Leonard (eds), *The Socialist Agenda: Crosland's legacy*, Jonathan Cape, 1981, p. 49.

14 R. M. Titmuss, *Social Policy: An Introduction*, George Allen & Unwin, 1974, p. 30–31.

15 Hansard, Written Answers, 21 March 1984, cols. 479–86; 30 March 1983, cols. 177–84; 17 February 1982, cols. 151–4; 3 December 1981, cols. 187–92; 26 March 1986, col. 530.

16 Conservative Central Office, *The Conservative Manifesto*, Conservative Party, 1979.

17 *The Government's Expenditure Plans 1980–81 to 1983–84*, Cmnd 7841, HMSO, 1980, para 2.

18 ibid.

19 *The Government's Expenditure Plans 1981–82 to 1983–84*, Cmnd 8175, Vol. I, HMSO, 1981, para. 2.

20 *The Government's Expenditure Plans 1982–83 to 1984–85*, Cmnd 8494, Vol. I, HMSO, 1982, p. 2.

21 Memorandum by Terry Ward, Appendix 1, Third Report from the Treasury and Civil Service Select Committee, Session 1983/84, *The Government's Expenditure Plans 1984–85 to 1986–87*, Cmnd 9134, HMSO, 1984.

22 *Expenditure Plans 1984–85*, Vol. II, Table 2.1.

23 *The Government's Expenditure Plans 1985–86 to 1987–88*, Cmnd 9428, Vol. I, HMSO, 1985, Table 1.6.

24 Fifth Report from the Treasury and Civil Service Committee, Session 1981/82; *Expenditure Plans 1982–83*, para. 9.

25 Note by Mr Christopher Johnson, Appendix II, Third Report from the Treasury and Civil Service Committee.

26 Third Report, Treasury and Civil Service Committee, para. 23.

27 ibid., Table 1.

28 For a useful analysis see Ray Robinson: 'Restructuring the welfare state: an analysis of public expenditure 1979/80–1984/5', *Journal of Social Policy*, Vol. 15, Part I, January 1986.

29 *Expenditure Plans 1985–86*, Vol. II, Table 2.12.5.

30 ibid., Table 3.4.

31 ibid., p. 32.

32 *Expenditure Plans 1986–7*, Vol. I, Chart 1.2.

33 Expenditure figures for specific programmes in this section are drawn on *Expenditure Plans 1985–86*, Vol. II, Table 3.7.

34 *Housing and Construction Statistics 1973–1983*, HMSO, 1984, Table 6.1.

35 Conservative Central Office, *The Conservative Manifesto*.

36 *Social Trends*, 14, Central Statistical Office, HMSO, 1983, 120.

37 *Expenditure Plans 1984–85*, Vol. II, p. 51.

38 *Social Trends*, 14, 120.

39 *Social Trends*, 15, Table 8.14.

40 ibid., p. 132.

41 Hansard, 4 July 1985, cols. 202–7.

42 Hansard, 13 March 1985, col. 149.

43 David Donnison, *The Politics of Poverty*, Martin Robertson, 1982, Chapter 7.

44 Department of Health and Social Security, *Report by the Comptroller and Auditor General*, National Audit Office; *Housing Benefit Scheme*, HMSO, 1984.

45 Labour Party, *Thatcher's Britain 1984*, the Labour Party and *New Socialist*, 1984, p. 43.

46 Association of Metropolitan Authorities, *Defects in Housing*, Part 3, March 1985.

47 *Social Trends*, 14, 123.

48 *Expenditure Plans 1985–86*, Vol. II, Table 3.11.2.

49 *Expenditure Plans 1982–83*, Vol. II, p. 45.

50 *Second Report from the Social Services Committee*, Session 1981–82, House of Commons Paper 306, 1982.

51 *Financial Times*, 9 August 1983.

52 *Expenditure Plans 1984–85*, Vol. II, p. 76.

53 *The Times*, 2 August 1983.

54 *Guardian*, 31 August 1983.

55 *Sunday Times*, 24 July 1983.

56 *The Times*, 10 November 1983.

57 *The Times*, 3 November 1983.
58 *The Times*, Letters, 21 March 1984.
59 *NHS Dental Treatment: What it Costs and How the Cost has Risen*, British Dental Association, 1983.
60 *Expenditure Plans 1984–85*, Vol. II, p. 77.
61 *Expenditure Plans 1986–87*, Vol. II, Table 3.14.
62 *Social Trends*, 16, 127–8.
63 *The Times*, 11 October 1982.
64 *The Times*, 23 June 1980.
65 Labour Party, *Thatcher's Britain*, p. 33.
66 At the Conservative Party Conference, Brighton, 1982.
67 *Expenditure Plans 1985–86*, Vol. II, Table 3.11.2.
68 *Expenditure Plans 1980–81*, Vol. II, p. 107.
69 *Expenditure Plans 1981–82*, Vol. II.
70 Adrian Webb and Gerald Wistow, 'Public Administration and Policy Implementation: the Case of Community Care', *Public Administration*, vol. 61, spring 1983, 21–44.
71 ibid.
72 Association of Directors of Social Services, *Report of the Second Survey of the Extent of Cuts/Savings in Expenditure on the Personal Social Services*, 1980, p. 33.
73 Adrian Webb and Gerald Wistow, *Whither State Welfare? Policy and Implementation in the Personal Social Services, 1979–1980*, Royal Institute of Public Administration, 1982, p. 53.
74 ibid., Table 4. Figures updated by the Family Policy Studies Centre from CIPFA social service actuals.
75 Valerie Macleod, *Whose Child? The Family in Child Care Legislation and Social Work Practice*, Study Commission on the Family, 1982, p. 58.
76 London Borough of Bexley and Bexley Health District, *Report of the Panel of Inquiry into the Lucy Gates Family Inquiry*, November 1982, Vol. 1, chairman's report.
77 Colin Hughes, 'Drifters in an uncaring world', *The Times*, 26 March 1984.
78 Colin Hughes, 'Doctor protests over cost of hospital cash cuts', *The Times*, 28 March 1984.
79 *Expenditure Plans 1986–87*, Vol. II, Tables 3.12.5 and 3.16.10.
80 *Expenditure Plans 1985–86*, Tables 3.10.3, 3.15.7 and 3.16.9.
81 Department of Education and Science, form R.O.1, Local Education Authority Returns, 1985.

82 *Sunday Times*, 29 June 1980.

83 Hansard, Vol. 976, 18 December 1979, col. 260.

84 Department of Education and Science, *Report by Her Majesty's Inspectors on the Effects of Local Authority Expenditure Policies on the Education Service in England – 1981*, HMSO, 1982.

85 *Expenditure Plans 1985–86*, Vol. II, p. 149.

86 D. Bull and P. Wilding (eds), *Thatcherism and the Poor*, Child Poverty Action Group, 1983, Chapter 9.

87 Department of Education and Science, School Meals Census, Form 214M, 1984.

88 *Expenditure Plans 1982–83*, Vol. II, p. 40.

89 *Expenditure Plans 1986–87*, Vol. II, Table 3.12.16.

90 *The Times*, 'Redundant dons to be paid up to £55,000', 21 January 1982.

91 *Expenditure Plans 1982–83*, Vol. II, p. 40.

92 For a full discussion, see Maurice Kogan and David Kogan, *The Attack on Higher Education*, Kogan Page, 1983.

93 Hansard, Written Answers, 10 March 1986, cols. 387–8.

94 Bull and Wilding, *Thatcherism and the Poor*.

95 ibid.

96 *Expenditure Plans 1986–87*, Vol. II, Table 3.15.6.

97 Bull and Wilding, *Thatcherism and the Poor*.

98 *The Times*, 8 February 1985.

99 *Expenditure Plans 1985–86*, Vol. II, Table 3.12.4.

100 ibid., Table 3.12.4.

101 *Low Income Families Tables, 1983*, DHSS, 1986.

102 Hansard, Written Answers, 25 June 1985 and 8 April 1986.

103 See Peter Taylor-Gooby, *Public Opinion, Ideology and State Welfare*, Routledge & Kegan Paul, 1985, Chapter 4; R. Klein and M. O'Higgins (eds), *The Future of Welfare*, Basil Blackwell, 1985.

104 Titmuss, *Social Policy*, pp. 30–31.

105 Prime minister's speech at the Women's Royal Voluntary Service National Conference 'Facing the New Challenge', 19 January 1981.

106 Conservative Party Conference, Blackpool, 1977.

107 Figures supplied by Gallup.

108 Speech, 22 September 1982, Conservative Central Office, 591/82.

109 'Thatcher's think-tank takes aim at the Welfare State', *Economist*, 18 September 1982, 25–6.

110 Speech, 10 May 1982, Treasury Press Office, 86/82.

111 'Mountains out of molehills?', *Economist*, 9 October 1982, 22.

112 Malcolm Dean, 'Ministers rethink Welfare State', *Guardian*, 17 February 1983.

113 *New York Times*, January 1984.

114 *Reform of Social Security*, Cmnd 9517, HMSO, 1985.

115 ibid. p. 32.

116 ibid.

117 ibid., p. 28.

118 Melanie Henwood and Malcolm Wicks, *Benefit or Burden?: The Objectives and Impact of Child Support*, Family Policy Studies Centre, 1986.

4 Inequality

1 R. H. Tawney, 'Poverty as an industrial problem', reproduced in *Memorandum on the Problem of Poverty*, William Morris Press, 1913.

2 Clement Attlee, *As It Happened*, Heinemann, 1954, p. 166.

3 Anthony Crosland, *The Future of Socialism*, Jonathan Cape, 1956, p. 25.

4 *Royal Commission on the Distribution of Income and Wealth*, Report No. 7, Cmnd 7595, HMSO, 1979, p. 17.

5 C. Playford and C. Pond, in Frank Field, *The Wealth Report* (2), Routledge & Kegan Paul, 1983, p. 37.

6 *Royal Commission on the Distribution of Income and Wealth*, Report No. 1, *Initial Report on the Standing Reference*, Cmnd 6171, HMSO, 1975, p. 168.

7 Frank Field, *Inequality in Britain: freedom, welfare and the state*, Fontana, 1981, p. 157.

8 Treasury and Civil Service Committee, *The structure of personal income taxation and income support*, HMSO, 1983, p. xi.

9 David Piachaud, 'Prices and the Distribution of Incomes', London School of Economics, mimeograph, 1976.

10 Playford and Pond, *The Wealth Report* (2), pp. 46–7.

11 See A. B. Atkinson and A. J. Harrison, *Distribution of Personal Wealth in Britain*, Cambridge University Press, 1978; Frank Field (ed.), *The Wealth Report* (1), Routledge & Kegan Paul, 1979; Frank Field (ed.), *The Wealth Report* (2), Routledge & Kegan Paul, 1983.

12 Atkinson and Harrison, *Distribution of Personal Wealth*.

13 A. B. Atkinson, *Unequal Shares: Wealth in Britain*, Allen Lane, 1972, p. 22.

14 'Let Us Work Together: Labour's Way Out of the Crisis', Labour Party Manifesto, 1974.

15 C. Pond, 'Wealth and the Two Nations', in *The Wealth Report* (2), p. 14.

16 Peter Townsend, *Poverty in the United Kingdom*, Penguin, 1979, p. 38.

17 *The Government's Expenditure Plans 1986–87 to 1988–89*, Cmnd 9702, Vol. II, HMSO, 1986, Table 3.15.6.

18 David Piachaud, *The Cost of a Child*, Child Poverty Action Group, 1979, p. 4.

19 Supplementary Benefits Commission, *Low Incomes*, Evidence to the Royal Commission on the Distribution of Income and Wealth, 1978, p. 28.

20 Low Pay Unit, *Low Pay Review*, No. 16, 1983.

21 *Sunday Times*, Business News, 3 June 1984; *New Earnings Survey 1983*, HMSO.

22 Aneurin Bevan, *In Place of Fear*, MacGibbon & Kee, 1961.

23 *Social Trends*, 15, 1985, Table 7.1.

24 Central Statistical Office, Annual Abstract of Statistics, HMSO, 1982, Tables 2.31 and 2.32; *Social Trends*, 15, Central Statistical Office, HMSO, 1985, Table 7.2.

25 Department of Health and Social Security, 'Inequalities in Health: report of a research working group', 1980; also available as *Inequalities in Health: the Black Report*, Peter Townsend and Nick Davidson (eds), Penguin, 1982.

26 Department of Health, 'Inequalities in Health', Table 2.1, p. 24.

27 Hansard, Written Answers, 15 May 1984, cols 143–44.

28 Department of Health, 'Inequalities in Health', p. 174.

29 Hansard, 15 May 1984, cols 143–4.

30 Department of Health, 'Inequalities in Health'.

31 ibid., p. 33.

32 *General Household Survey 1982*, HMSO, 1984, Table 8.4.

33 Sir John Brotherston, Galton Lecture, 1976.

34 Department of Health, 'Inequalities in Health', p. 3.

35 G. D. H. Cole, *Plan for Democratic Britain*, Odhams, 1939, p. 89.

36 A. H. Halsey (ed.), *Trends in British Society since 1900*, Macmillan, 1972.

37 *Social Trends*, 16, Table 3.1.

38 ibid., Table 3.7.

39 ibid., p. 51.

40 ibid., Table 3.22.

41 A. H. Halsey, A. F. Heath and J. M. Ridge, *Origins and Destinations: Family, Class and Education in Modern Britain*, Clarendon Press, 1980.

42 ibid.

43 ibid.

44 J. Le Grand, *The Strategy of Equality: Redistribution and the Social Services*, George Allen & Unwin, 1982, p. 58.

45 H. Glennerster, in P. Townsend and N. Bosanquet (eds), *Labour and Inequality*, Fabian Society, 1972, p. 101.

46 Halsey, Heath and Ridge, *Origins and Destinations*, p. 210.

47 ibid.

48 Halsey (ed.), *Trends in British Society*, Table 10.4; *General Household Survey 1982*, Table 3.2.

49 Halsey, *Trends in British Society*, Table 10.7, and Central Statistical Office, *Annual Abstract of Statistics*, HMSO, 1982, Table 3.66.

50 *Social Trends*, 7, Table 8.7.

51 Office of Population Censuses and Surveys, Monitor Reference GHS 84/1, 10 July 1984, Tables 9 and 10.

52 *Housing Policy: A Consultative Document*, Cmnd 6851, HMSO, 1977, para. 2.04.

53 *Social Trends*, 12, p. 152.

54 Malcolm Wicks, in T. Harris and J. Bradshaw (eds), *Energy and Social Policy*, Routledge & Kegan Paul, 1983, Chapter 6.

55 *General Household Survey 1982*, Table 5.28.

56 ibid.

57 ibid.

58 *General Household Survey 1977*, HMSO, 1979, Table 3.31.

59 ibid., Table 3.25.

60 P. Wedge and H. Prosser, *Born to Fail?*, Arrow Books, 1973, p. 26.

61 *Labour Weekly*, 28 May 1982, p. 17.

62 Ralph Miliband, *The State in Capitalist Society*, Quartet Books, 1969.

63 Ian Gough, *The Political Economy of Welfare*, Macmillan, 1979, p. 14.

5 Critical Perspectives

1 L. J. Hobhouse, *Liberalism*, 1911, Chapter 4, quoted in Robert Stewart (ed.), *Penguin Dictionary of Political Quotations*, Penguin, 1986.

2 Nicholas Bosanquet, *After the New Right*, Heinemann Educational Books, 1983, p. 2.

3 ibid., p. 1.

4 ibid, pp. 8–12.

5 F. Hayek, *Law, Legislation and Liberty*, Vol. 3, Routledge & Kegan Paul, 1979, p. 139.

6 Ralph Harris and Arthur Seldon, *Over-ruled on Welfare*, Institute of Economic Affairs, 1979, p. 183.

7 Milton and Rose Friedman, *Free to Choose*, Secker & Warburg, 1980, p. 127.

8 D. S. Lees, 'Health through choice' (first published 1961), reprinted in Ralph Harris (ed.), *Freedom or Free-for-All?*, Institute of Economic Affairs, 1965, p. 39.

9 ibid., p. 76.

10 ibid., p. 77.

11 ibid., p. 76.

12 ibid.

13 R. Harris and A. Seldon, *Over-ruled on Welfare*, p. 186.

14 ibid., p. 188.

15 ibid., p. 198.

16 ibid., p. 190.

17 R. M. Titmuss, *Commitment to Welfare*, George Allen & Unwin, 1968, p. 259.

18 Bosanquet, *After the New Right*, p. 152.

19 Organization for Economic Co-operation and Development, *Public Expenditure on Health*, Paris, OECD, 1977, quoted in Bosanquet, *After the New Right*, p. 156.

20 Aneurin Bevan, *In Place of Fear*, MacGibbon and Kee, 1961, p. 23.

21 For illustrations of the critique, see Roger Hadley and Stephen Hatch, *Social Welfare and the Failure of the State*, George Allen & Unwin, 1981; Evan Luard, *Socialism without the State*, Macmillan, 1979.

22 D. Donnison, *Urban Policies: A New Approach*, Fabian Society, 1983, p. 12.

23 E. Wilson, 'According to our needs', *New Statesman*, 10 September 1982.

24 A. H. Halsey, *Change in British Society*, Oxford University Press, 1978, p. 85.

25 R. M. Titmuss, *Essays on the Welfare State*, George Allen & Unwin, 1958, p. 34.

26 T. H. Marshall, *Social Policy*, Hutchinson, 1965, pp. 87–8.

27 See, for example, Ian Gough, *The Political Economy of Welfare*, Macmillan, 1979.

28 R. Grunberger, *A Social History of the Third Reich*, Penguin, 1974, Chapter 16.

29 Ramesh Mishra, *Society and Social Policy*, Macmillan, 1977.

30 F. Piven and R. Cloward, *Regulating the Poor: The Functions of Public Welfare*, Tavistock Publications, 1972, p. 3.

31 Derek Fraser, *The Evolution of the British Welfare State*, Macmillan, 1973, p. 28.

32 *Report of the Inter-departmental Committee on Physical Deterioration*, Cd 2175, Vol. I, 1904.

33 R. M. Titmuss, *Essays on the Welfare State*, p. 78.

34 D. Donnison, *The Politics of Poverty*, Martin Robertson, 1982, p. 24.

35 Vic George, *Social Security and Society*, Routledge & Kegan Paul, 1973, p. 1.

36 Fraser, *Evolution of the British Welfare State*, p. 152.

37 Quoted in D. Judd, 'Radical Joe Chamberlain', *New Society*, 28 October 1982.

38 Ralph Miliband, *The State in Capitalist Society*, Weidenfeld & Nicolson, 1969, p. 78.

39 Fraser, *Evolution of the British Welfare State*, p. 129.

40 Bevan, *In Place of Fear*, p. 24.

41 Frederick Engels, Introduction to the English Edition of *The Condition of the Working Class in England*, in K. Marx, *Engels on Britain*, Foreign Languages Publishing House, Moscow, 1962.

42 W. R. Scott and J. Cunnison, *The Injustices of the Clyde Valley During the War*, HMSO, 1924, Chapter 9.

43 R. K. Middlemas, *The Clydesiders*, Hutchinson, 1965, p. 60.

44 Engels, in Marx, *Engels on Britain*, p. 26.

45 Bevan, *In Place of Fear*, p. 99.

46 Anthony Crosland, *The Future of Socialism*, Jonathan Cape, 1956, p. 28.

47 Bentley B. Gilbert, *British Society, 1914–1939*, Batsford, 1970, p. 305.

48 Gilbert, *British Society*, p. 305.

49 Engels, in Marx, *Engels on Britain*, p. 51.

50 K. Marx and F. Engels, *The Communist Manifesto*, Progress Publishers, Moscow, 1848.

51 Ian Gough, *The Political Economy of Welfare*, p. 14.

52 For a critique see the two Fabian Society volumes: P. Townsend and N. Bosanquet (eds), *Labour and Inequality*, Fabian Society, 1972; P. Townsend and N. Bosanquet (eds), *Labour and Equality*, Heinemann Educational Books, 1980.

6 Social Changes towards the Year 2000: Population, Family and Work Patterns

1 Study Commission on the Family, *Families in the Future: A Policy Agenda for the '80s*, 1983, p. 7.

2 A. H. Halsey, in *Welfare State in Crisis*, OECD, 1981.

3 See Lesley Rimmer and Malcolm Wicks, 'The Challenge of Change: Demographic Trends, the Family and Social Policy', in Howard Glennerster (ed.), *The Future of the Welfare State*, Heinemann Educational Books, 1983.

4 *Social Trends*, 15, Central Statistical Office, HMSO, 1984, Table 3.2.

5 ibid., p. 46.

6 ibid., Table 3.2.

7 For a thorough analysis, see J. E. Ermisch, *The Political Economy of Demographic Change*, Heinemann Educational Books, 1983.

8 For a discussion, see Edward Craven, Lesley Rimmer and Malcolm Wicks, *Family Issues and Public Policy*, Study Commission on the Family, 1982; see also Study Commission on the Family, *Families in the Future*.

9 Quoted in D. Fraser, *The Evolution of the British Welfare State*, Macmillan, 1973, p. 155.

10 Sir William Beveridge, *Social Insurance and Allied Services*, Cmd 6404, HMSO, 1942, para. 108.

11 B. Abel-Smith, 'Marriage, Parenthood and Social Policy', lecture, Liverpool University, 1982.

12 British Society for Population Studies, *The Family*, Occasional Paper 31, Office of Population Censuses and Surveys, HMSO, 1983. Table 1.

13 ibid., p. 18.

14 *Report of the Committee on One Parent Families*, Cmnd 5629, Vol. I, HMSO, 1974, p. 31.

15 Lesley Rimmer, *Families in Focus*, Study Commission on the Family, 1981; see also Family Policy Studies Centre, *The Family Today: Continuity and Change*, Fact Sheet, 1984.

16 *Report of the Committee on One Parent Families*, p. 6.

17 Study Commission on the Family, *Families in the Future*, p. 11.

18 Family Policy Studies Centre, *Bulletin No. 2*, Summer, 1986.

19 *Social Trends*, 16, Table 2.15, HMSO, 1986.

20 Lesley Rimmer, *Conciliation: The Wider Context*, Study Commission on the Family, 1982.

21 Family Policy Studies Centre, *Divorce: 1983 Matrimonial and Family Proceedings Bill*, briefing paper, 1984, Section 1.

22 *Social Trends*, 16, Table 2.13.

23 Rimmer, *Families in Focus*, p. 44.

24 Jennie Popay, Lesley Rimmer and Chris Rossiter, *One Parent Families*, Study Commission on the Family, 1983, Table 1 and p. 9.

25 Family Policy Studies Centre, *One Parent Families*, Fact Sheet, 1984.

26 *General Household Survey 1982*, HMSO, 1984, Table 4.31.

27 Family Policy Studies Centre, *An Ageing Population*, Fact Sheet, 1984.

28 Mark Abrams, *Beyond Three-Score Years and Ten*, Age Concern, 1980.

29 Family Policy Studies Centre, *An Ageing Population*.

30 *General Household Survey 1982*, Table 5.20.

31 *The Government's Expenditure Plans 1986–87 to 1988–89*, Vol. II, Cmnd 9702–II, HMSO, 1986, Table 3.15.12.

32 R. M. Titmuss, *Essays on the Welfare State*, George Allen & Unwin, 1963, p. 56.

33 Lesley Rimmer and Jennie Popay, *Employment Trends and the Family*, Study Commission on the Family, 1982, Table 1; *Social Trends*, 14, Table 4.7.

34 Rimmer and Popay, *Employment Trends and the Family*, p. 14.

35 ibid., p. 15.

36 Family Policy Studies Centre, *Family Finances*, Fact Sheet, 1984, Table 2.

37 D. Manley and P. Sawbridge, 'Women at Work', *Lloyds Bank Review*, No. 135, 1980, p. 31.

38 Jean Martin and Ceridwen Roberts, *Women and Employment Survey*, Office of Population Censuses and Surveys, HMSO, 1984.

39 ibid., Table 2.5.

40 ibid.

41 ibid., Table 2.6.

42 Rimmer and Popay, *Employment Trends and the Family* pp. 50–51.

43 A. Hunt, *The Elderly at Home*, Office of Population Censuses and Surveys, HMSO, 1978, p. 63.

7 Principles for Social Policy: Equality and Liberty

1   R. H. Tawney, *The Radical Tradition*, Penguin, 1966, pp. 147–8.

2   Quoted by Tony Benn, in *Arguments for Socialism*, Jonathan Cape, 1979, p. 37.

3   Benn, *Arguments for Socialism*, p. 23.

4   Anthony Crosland, *The Future of Socialism*, Jonathan Cape, 1956, p. 51.

5   ibid., p. 67.

6   William Morris, 'Justice', reprinted in Asa Briggs (ed.), *William Morris: selected writings and designs*, Penguin, 1962, pp. 33–4.

7   Tawney, *The Radical Tradition*, p. 187.

8   ibid., p. 187.

9   Clement Attlee, *As It Happened*, Heinemann Educational Books, 1954, p. 142.

10 Tawney, *The Radical Tradition*, p. 166.

11 European Value Systems Study Group, *Beliefs in Britain Today*, Gallup survey in ten European countries, March–June, 1981.

12 John Rawls, *A Theory of Justice*, Oxford University Press, 1972, pp. 14–15.

13 R. Jowell and C. Airey (eds), *British Social Attitudes: The 1984 Report*, Gower, p. 63.

14 J. Mack and S. Lansley, *Poor Britain*, George Allen & Unwin, 1985, p. 259.

15 ibid., p. 284.

16 Jonathan Bradshaw, 'A Taxonomy of Need', *New Society*, No. 496, 30 March 1972, 640–43.

8 Social Strategy

1 Aneurin Bevan, Labour Party Annual Conference, June 1949.
2 See, for example, Conference of Socialist Economists London Working Group, 'The Alternative Economic Strategy', Conference of Socialist Economists Books and Labour Co-ordinating Committee, 1980; Michael Meacher, *Socialism with a Human Face*, George Allen & Unwin, 1982.
3 Quoted by Michael Foot, *Aneurin Bevan, 1945–1960*, Paladin, 1975, p. 76.
4 David Blake and Paul Ormerod (eds), *The Economics of Prosperity*, Grant McIntyre, 1980, p. 31.
5 Sir William Beveridge, *The Pillars of Security*, George Allen & Unwin, 1942, p. 43.
6 'The Rain that Kills', *Marxism Today*, November 1983, 2.
7 Home Office, *Statistics of Experiments on Living Animals*, 1984, Cmnd 9574.
8 World Health Organization, *Progress in Primary Health Care: A Situation Report*, 1983.
9 *Economist*, 24 December 1983, 54.

9 Social Policy

1 R. M. Titmuss, *Commitment to Welfare*, George Allen & Unwin, 1968, p. 116.
2 T. H. Marshall, *Social Policy*, Hutchinson, 1965, p. 7.
3 R. M. Titmuss, in *Essays on 'The Welfare State'*, George Allen & Unwin, 1963.
4 Iain MacLeod and Angus Maude (eds), *One Nation*, Conservative Political Centre, 1950, p. 18.
5 Titmuss, *Essays on 'The Welfare State'*, p. 44.
6 ibid., p. 45.
7 ibid.
8 *The Government's Expenditure Plans 1986–87 to 1988–89*, Cmnd 9702, Vol. II, HMSO, 1986, Table 2.24.
9 *The Government's Expenditure Plans 1979–80 to 1982–83*, Cmnd 7439, HMSO, 1979, Table 16; *Expenditure Plans 1986–87*, Vol. II, ibid.
10 Nick Morris and Peter Lambert, 'Rich pickings for south-east home buyers', *Guardian*, 13 August 1985.

11 Frank Field, *Inequality in Britain: Freedom, Welfare and the State*, Fontana, 1981, p. 136.

12 Titmuss, *Essays on 'The Welfare State'*, p. 53.

13 *Social Trends*, 13, Central Statistical Office, HMSO, 1980, Table 2.4.

14 *General Household Survey 1980*, HMSO, 1982, Table 10.35.

15 David Donnison, 'The Development of Social Administration', inaugural lecture, London School of Economics, 1962.

16 Malcolm Wicks, *Old and Cold: Hypothermia and Social Policy*, Heinemann Educational Books, 1978; Jonathan Bradshaw and Toby Harris, *Energy and Social Policy*, Routledge & Kegan Paul, 1983.

17 David Downes, *Law and Order: Theft of an Issue*, Fabian Society, 1983.

18 *Expenditure Plans 1986–87*, Vol. II, Table 2.11.

19 Lady T. Rhys Williams, *Something to Look Forward To*, Macdonald, 1943.

20 *Proposals for a Tax Credit System*, Cmnd 5416, HMSO, 1972.

21 A. W. Dilnot, J. A. Kay and C. N. Morris, *The Reform of Social Security*, Clarendon Press, 1984.

22 Lesley Rimmer, *The Changing Family: The Unit of Assessment in the Tax and Benefits System*, National Consumer Council, 1984.

23 Low Pay Unit, *Low Pay Review*, No. 13, 1983.

24 David Griffiths and Chris Holmes, 'To Buy or not to Buy ... Is that the Question?', *Marxism Today*, May 1984.

25 L. J. Hobhouse, 'Evolution of Property', in Charles Gore (ed.), *Property: Its Duties and Rights*, Macmillan, 1913, p. 10.

26 Labour Housing Group, *Right to a Home*, 1984.

27 *Social Trends*, 15, Table 2.5.

28 *General Household Survey 1977*, 1979, Table 3.31.

29 A. Butler, C. Oldman and J. Greve, *Sheltered Housing for the Elderly: Policy, Practice and the Consumer*, George Allen & Unwin, 1983; Anthea Tinker, *Staying at Home: Helping Elderly People*, HMSO, 1984; Rose Wheeler, *Don't Move, We've Got You Covered* (a study of the Anchor Housing Trust Staying Put Scheme), London, Institute of Housing, 1985.

30 Malcolm Wicks, *Rented Housing and Social Ownership*, Fabian Society, 1973.

31 A. Richardson, 'The Politics of Participation: A Study of Schemes for Tenant Participation in Council Housing Management', Ph.D. thesis, London School of Economics, 1977.

32 Griffiths and Holmes, 'To Buy or not to Buy?'

33 Department of Health and Social Security, 'Care in the Community: A Consultative Document on Moving Resources for Care in England', 1981, p. 2.
34 Titmuss, *Commitment to Welfare*, p. 104.
35 For a discussion see Melanie Henwood and Malcolm Wicks, *The Forgotten Army: Family Care and Elderly People*, Family Policy Studies Centre, 1984, p. 13.
36 *Expenditure Plans 1985–86*, Table 3.11.2.
37 Updated figures based on Chris Rossiter and Malcolm Wicks, *Crisis or Challenge? Family Care, Elderly People and Social Policy*, Study Commission on the Family, 1982, p. 83.
38 Henwood and Wicks, *The Forgotten Army*, Table 5.
39 Mark Abrams, *Beyond Three Score Years and Ten*, Age Concern, 1980.

10 Redistributing Resources and Raising the Revenue

1 David Donnison, *The Politics of Poverty*, Martin Robertson, 1982, p. 230.
2 Tessa Blackstone in Howard Glennerster (ed.), *The Future of the Welfare State*, Heinemann Educational Books, 1983, pp. 200–201.
3 ibid., p. 200.
4 *Social Trends*, 15, Central Statistical Office, HMSO, 1984 Table 6.2.
5 Gavyn Davies and David Piachaud, in Glennerster (ed.), *The Future of the Welfare State*, Chapter 4.
6 ibid., Table 4.8.
7 ibid., pp. 56–7.
8 K. J. Newman, International Comparisons of Taxes and Social Security Contributions in 20 OECD Countries, 1972–1982, *Economic Trends*, Central Statistical Office, February 1983, Table B, p. 83.
9 Hansard, Written Answers, 22 November 1983, col. 88.
10 Michael Meacher, 'A way out of the poverty trap', *The Times*, 18 March 1985.
11 *Wealth Tax*, Cmnd 5704, HMSO, 1974.
12 Frank Field, *Inequality in Britain: Freedom, Welfare and the State*, Fontana, 1981, p. 102.
13 *Statements on the Defence Estimates, 1984*, Cmnd 9227, Vol. I, HMSO, 1984, Fig. 4.

14 Labour Party, *The New Hope for Britain*, Labour Party Manifesto, 1983.
15 Jack Straw, Speech to Chartered Institute of Public Finance and Accountancy Annual Conference, 5 June 1984, p. 6.

11 Democratic Social Planning

1 G. D. H. Cole, *A History of Socialist Thought*, Vol 5, Macmillan, 1960.
2 Quoted by Anthony Wright, John Stewart and Nicholas Deakin, in *Socialism and Decentralisation*, Fabian Society, 1984, p. 4.
3 ibid.
4 Nicholas Deakin, in Wright, Stewart and Deakin (eds), *Socialism and Decentralisation*, p. 18.
5 For discussion see Deakin, ibid.
6 P. M. Barclay, *Social Workers: Their Role and Tasks* (The Barclay Report), 1982, Bedford Square Press.
7 Roger Hadley and Stephen Hatch, *Social Welfare and the Failure of the State*, George Allen & Unwin, 1981.
8 David Donnison, 'Take the heavy hand out of the Welfare State', *The Times*, 4 March 1983.
9 Bob Connell, in B. O'Meagher (ed.), *The Socialist Objective*, Hale and Iremonger, Sydney, 1983.
10 Richard Crossman, *The Diaries of a Cabinet Minister*, Vols 1, 2 and 3, Hamish Hamilton/Jonathan Cape, 1975, 1976 and 1977; Barbara Castle, *The Castle Diaries*, 1974, 1976, Weidenfeld & Nicolson, 1980.
11 For Tony Benn's own proposals see Chris Mullin (ed.), *Arguments for Democracy*, Penguin, 1982.
12 Michael Meacher, 'The men who block the corridors of power', *Guardian*, 4 June 1979.
13 Lord Armstrong, quoted by Meacher in 'The men who block the corridors of power'.
14 Meacher, 'The men who block the corridors of power'.
15 Richard Crossman, *Inside View*, Jonathan Cape, 1972, p. 73.
16 Meacher, 'The men who block the corridors of power'.
17 David Lipsey (ed.), *Making Government Work*, Fabian Society, 1982, p. 8.
18 See *First Report from the Select Committee on Procedure (Finance)*, Vol. 1, Report and Minutes of Proceedings, HMSO, 1983.

19 Joan Higgins, Nicholas Deakin, John Edwards and Malcolm Wicks, *Government and Urban Poverty: Inside the Policy-making Process*, Basil Blackwell, 1983, Chapter 4.

20 British Medical Association, 'Accidental Hypothermia in the Elderly', *British Medical Journal*, Vol. 2, 1964, p. 1,255.

21 Royal College of Physicians, *Report of the Committee on Accidental Hypothermia*, Royal College of Physicians, 1966.

22 Malcolm Wicks, *Old and Cold: Hypothermia and Social Policy*, Heinemann Educational Books, 1978.

23 For Michael Meacher's own account see 'Dying to Keep Warm: The Politics of Hypothermia', in *Cold Conditions*, National Fuel Poverty Forum, 1980; see also Malcolm Wicks, 'Cold Conditions, Hypothermia and Health', in *Energy and Social Policy*, Routledge & Kegan Paul, 1983.

24 'Purse or wallet? How the Cabinet did a switch-sell', *Sunday Times*, 20 June 1976.

25 'Killing a Commitment: the Cabinet *v*. the children', *New Society*, 17 June 1976.

26 For his own account of the saga, see Frank Field, *Poverty and Politics*, Heinemann Educational Books, 1982.

27 David Donnison, *The Politics of Poverty*, Martin Robertson, 1982, p. 149.

28 Central Policy Review Staff, *A Joint Framework for Social Policies*, HMSO, 1975.

29 See also report of the Economic and Social Research Council financed Joint Approach to Social Policy research project, University of Bath, University of Loughborough, and Royal Institute of Public Administration (forthcoming, Cambridge University Press).

30 James Callaghan, speech at the Women's Labour Conference, Southport, 14 May 1978.

31 Frank Field, *Fair Shares for Families*, Study Commission on the Family, 1980, p. 21.

32 As advocated by Peter Townsend – see *Community Care*, 31 March 1983.

33 House of Commons, *The Role of the Comptroller and Auditor General*, First special report from the Commission of Public Accounts, Session 1980/81, Vol. I, HMSO, 1981, p. 8.

12 A New Commitment to Welfare

1 Anon., 'What the Women Want' (c. 1900), distributed as a suffrage handbill, reproduced in Tony Benn (ed.), *Writings on the Wall: A Radical and Socialist Anthology, 1215–1984*, Faber & Faber, 1984, pp. 201–202.

2 Aneurin Bevan, *In Place of Fear*, MacGibbon & Kee, 1961, p. 20.

3 Ruth Lister and Louie Burghes, 'The unequal opportunities Budget', in *Poverty*, Child Poverty Action Group, August 1979, 11–12.

4 R. M. Titmuss, *Unequal Rights*, Child Poverty Action Group and the London Co-operative Society, 1968, p. 8.

5 Reginald Prentice, quoted by David Donnison, *New Society*, 22 January 1981, p. 153.

6 Robert Kennedy, 5 April 1968, while campaigning in Cleveland, Ohio.

7 See, for example, *Homes for the Future*, Labour Party, 1985.

8 R. H. Tawney, *The Radical Tradition*, Penguin, 1966, p. 168.

9 R. M. Titmuss, *The Gift Relationship*, George Allen & Unwin, 1970, p. 238.

10 R. H. Tawney, *Equality*, George Allen & Unwin, 1964, p. 204.

Index

MORE ABOUT PENGUINS, PELICANS, PEREGRINES AND PUFFINS

For further information about books available from Penguins please write to Dept EP, Penguin Books Ltd, Harmondsworth, Middlesex UB7 0DA.

In the U.S.A.: For a complete list of books available from Penguins in the United States write to Dept DG, Penguin Books, 299 Murray Hill Parkway, East Rutherford, New Jersey 07073.

In Canada: For a complete list of books available from Penguins in Canada write to Penguin Books Canada Limited, 2801 John Street, Markham, Ontario L3R 1B4.

In Australia: For a complete list of books available from Penguins in Australia write to the Marketing Department, Penguin Books Australia Ltd, P.O. Box 257, Ringwood, Victoria 3134.

In New Zealand: For a complete list of books available from Penguins in New Zealand write to the Marketing Department, Penguin Books (N.Z.) Ltd, Private Bag, Takapuna, Auckland 9.

In India: For a complete list of books available from Penguins in India write to Penguin Overseas Ltd, 706 Eros Apartments, 56 Nehru Place, New Delhi 110019.